ecpr PRESS

Constitutional Deliberative Democracy in Europe

Edited by Min Reuchamps
and Jane Suiter

ecprPRESS

First published by the ECPR Press in 2016

The ECPR Press is the publishing imprint of the European Consortium for Political Research (ECPR), a scholarly association, which supports and encourages the training, research and cross-national co-operation of political scientists in institutions throughout Europe and beyond.

ECPR Press
Harbour House
Hythe Quay
Colchester
CO2 8JF
United Kingdom

Typeset by Lapiz Digital Services

Printed and bound by Lightning Source

British Library Cataloguing in Publication Data

A catalogue record for this book is available from the British Library

HARDBACK ISBN: 978-1-785521-45-4
PAPERBACK ISBN: 978-1-785522-58-1
PDF ISBN: 978-1-785522-02-4
EPUB ISBN: 978-1-785522-03-1
KINDLE ISBN: 978-1-785522-04-8

www.ecpr.eu/ecprpress

ECPR Press Series Editors:
Peter Kennealy (European University Institute)
Ian O'Flynn (Newcastle University)
Alexandra Segerberg (Stockholm University)
Laura Sudulich (University of Kent)

More from the ECPR Press Studies in Political Science series:

Global Tax Governance
ISBN: 9781785521263
Peter Dietsch and Thomas Rixen
'Tax specialists may think they have little to learn from a book on global tax governance, especially one that concludes that the best solution is to create a new International Tax Organisation (ITO). They would be wrong. Anyone concerned with international taxation will benefit from this excellent collection of essays about the nature and possible resolutions of the conflicts within and between states about fiscal sovereignty, tax competition, and domestic and international equity that underlie the international tax discussion. The authors do not always agree with each other and few readers are likely to agree with all of them. But this book makes clear what is really at issue in this discussion and shows why even the recent prodigious efforts of the OECD-G20 BEPS group are most unlikely to produce any lasting solutions. For nation-states and economic globalisation to coexist, something like an ITO may indeed prove necessary.'
Richard Bird, University of Toronto

Decision-Making under Ambiguity and Time Constraints
ISBN: 9781785521256
Reimut Zohlnhöfer and Friedbert W. Rüb
'Associated with the work of US political scientist John W. Kingdon, for more than three decades, the Multiple-Streams Framework has informed the work of numerous policy scholars from all over the world. Featuring an excellent line-up comprised of well-known and more junior contributors, this edited volume offers a timely overview of key comparative, empirical-methodological, and theoretical issues raised by the Multiple-Streams Framework. This coherent book will interest the many policy scholars who draw on this now classic Framework.'
Daniel Béland, Johnson-Shoyama Graduate School of Public Policy, University of Saskatchewan

New Perspectives on Negative Campaigning
ISBN: 9781785521287
Alessandro Nai and Annemarie Walter
'The study of negative campaigning has mostly been about American elections.
Refreshingly, the essays in this book look at what happens in other countries. By
so doing, they truly offer new perspectives and thus advance our understanding
of attack politics. Recommended to anyone interested in elections and
campaigns.' **John G Geer, Vanderbilt University**

**Please visit www.ecpr.eu/ecprpress for up-to-date information about new
and forthcoming publications.**

Table of Contents

List of Figures and Tables

Contributors

The authors of this book are researchers who have strong records of academic publications on deliberative democracy but also have all been closely involved in the organisation of deliberative initiatives dealing with constitutional reforms.

Eirikur Bergmann is Professor of Politics and Director of the Centre for European Studies at Bifrost University in Iceland. He was also a member of Iceland's Constitutional Council, which delivered a bill to Parliament for a new constitution. His research interests within the field of international politics can be positioned in the intersection of European integration politics and international political economy. In that context, he also focuses on nationalism and identity politics. A further interest is within the field of constitutional politics. He has recently published *Iceland and the International Financial Crisis: Boom, bust & recovery* (London, UK: Palgrave Macmillan, 2014).

Didier Caluwaerts is a professor of political science at the Vrije Universiteit Brussel. His book *Confrontation and Communication: Deliberative democracy in divided Belgium* (Peter Lang, 2012) won the 2013 ECPR Jean Blondel award. He has published in *Acta Politica, Ethnopolitics, Politics, Res Publica, European Political Science Review, Government & Opposition, Journal of Elections, Public Opinion & Parties, Religion, State & Society, Journal of Public Deliberation* and *West European Politics*.

David Farrell holds the Chair of Politics at University College Dublin. A specialist in parties, electoral systems and representation, Professor Farrell's most recent book was the award-winning *Political Parties and Democratic Linkage*, published by Oxford University Press in 2011. He was the research director of the Irish Constitutional Convention.

Brigitte Geissel, Goethe University Frankfurt a.M., is Professor of Political Science and Political Sociology, Head of the Research Unit Democratic Innovations and Speaker of the ECPR Standing Group Democratic Innovations. She held fellowships, research and teaching positions at various universities and institutes, such as Harvard Kennedy School (USA); Social Science Research Centre, Berlin; Centre of Excellence on Democracy at Åbo Akademi (Finland); the Universities of Muenster, Berlin, and Illinois (USA) as well as the Vietnamese German University, Saigon (Vietnam). Her research interests include democratic innovations, new forms of governance (European Union, national, subnational), political actors (new social movements, associations, civil society, parties, political elites, citizens) and her recent publications have appeared in *Comparative Sociology, West European Politics* and *European Journal of Political Research*.

Sergiu Gherghina, Goethe University Frankfurt a.M., is post-doctoral research fellow and lecturer in Political Science, and a member of the Research Unit Democratic Innovations. He has held fellowships, research and teaching positions at various universities and institutes such as the Central European University,

Budapest; Queen Mary University of London; University of Siena and the Institute for East and Southeast European Studies in Regensburg. His research interests include political institutions (parties, governments, or legislatures), legislative and voting behaviour, democratisation processes, direct democracy in Central and Eastern Europe and deliberative democratic practices in constitutional change. He has recently published in *American Journal of Political Science, Comparative European Politics, East European Politics, European Union Politics, European Political Science, International Political Science Review* and *Party Politics*.

Kimmo Grönlund, Professor of Political Science at Åbo Akademi and Director of the Social Science Research Institute (Samforsk). His main research interests are participatory democracy, deliberative democracy, political knowledge, political behaviour, public opinion and elections.

Clodagh Harris is a senior lecturer in the Department of Government, University College Cork. Her research interests include: democratic theory and practice (particularly deliberative and participatory democracy); democratic innovations and citizen engagement and community education. She has published in leading international journals such as *Representation, European Political Science, Policy and Internet* and *Journal of Political Science Education*. She was a member of the Irish Constitutional Convention's Academic and Legal Advisory Group (2012–14).

Vincent Jacquet is PhD Student in political science at the Université catholique de Louvain (UCL) and recipient of a fellowship FRESH of the F.R.S.-FNRS and Member of the Institut de sciences politiques Louvain-Europe (ISPOLE). His research interests are participatory and deliberative democracy; political participation; local politics and democratic theory. He has published several works on democratic innovations and he is currently the co-coordinator of the G1000 citizens' iniative in Belgium.

Jonathan Moskovic holds a Master in political science from the Université libre de Bruxelles, Belgium, where he conducted research on the G1000 and the Irish Constitutional Convention. His research interests are political participation and deliberative democracy. He is currently the co-coordinator of the G1000 citizens' iniative in Belgium.

John Parkinson is Professor of Politics at Griffith University, Brisbane. He specialises in the conceptual analysis of policy, political relationships and institutions, covering things like deliberative democracy and democratic innovation; public participation in policy-making; and the narrative, performative aspects of policy and politics. He has published on deliberative experiments in the UK National Health Service, referendums around the world and symbolic representation in capital cities. He has recently published with Jane Mansbridge *Deliberative Systems: Deliberative democracy at the large scale* (Cambridge, UK: Cambridge University Press, 2012).

Min Reuchamps is a professor of political science at the Université catholique de Louvain and co-ordinator of the methodology for the G1000 in Belgium. He graduated from the Université de Liège and Boston University. His teaching and research interests are federalism and multi-level governance as well as participatory and deliberative methods. He has published over ten books and edited volumes on these issues. He has also recently co-edited the special issue The Future of Belgian Federalism with Kris Deschouwer for *Regional and Federal Studies* and his latest edited volume is *Minority Nations in Multinational Federations: A comparative study of Quebec and Wallonia* (London, UK: Routledge, 2015). He is the president of the French-speaking Belgian Association for Political Science (ABSP).

Stefan Rummens holds the position of Professor of Moral Philosophy at the Institute of Philosophy of the University of Leuven, Belgium. His main work is concerned with the theory of democracy generally. More specific research topics include deliberative democracy, populism, extremism, free speech, religion in the public sphere, representation and transnational democracy. Additionally, Stefan Rummens has an interest in meta-ethics. Here, more specific topics include the relevance of Wittgenstein for ethics, compatibilism and discourse ethics.

Jane Suiter is a senior lecturer at Dublin City University and deputy research director of the Irish Constitutional Convention. Her research is centred on deliberative and participatory democracy. She is a member of the ECPR standing group on Democratic Innovations. She is also co-convener of the PSAI specialist group Voters, Parties and Elections and is working on an IRC-funded project on the use of referendums in Europe. She was a member of the academic team for We the Citizens, an Atlantic philanthropy-funded experiment on deliberation chaired by Professor David Farrell and was also a member of the Irish Constitutional Convention's Academic and Legal Advisory Group (2012–14).

Julien Talpin is a research fellow at the French National Scientific Research Centre (CNRS) and Professor of Politics at the University of Lille 2. His research deals with the study of deliberative democracy from below, aiming at understanding how participatory experiences are lived by actors and shape their political and personal careers. He is currently investigating the conditions of inclusion of poor people and minorities in participatory processes in Europe and the US. He is co-editor of the French-language journal *Participations*. He has recently published *Schools of Democracy. How ordinary citizens (sometimes) become competent in participatory budgeting institutions* (ECPR Press, 2011); 'What can ethnography bring to the study of deliberative democracy? Evidence from the study on the impact of participation on actors', *Revista International de Sociologia* 70(2), 2012; 'When deliberation happens. Evaluating discursive interactions among ordinary citizens', in Geissel, B., and Joas, M. (eds) *Participatory Democratic Innovations in Europe. Improving the quality of democracy?* (Berlin, DE and Toronto, ON: Burdeish Publishers, 2013).

Preface

In Europe, deliberative democracy seems to have recently taken a constitutional turn. Iceland and Ireland have turned to deliberative democracy to reform their own constitutions. Estonia, Luxembourg and Romania have also experienced constitutional processes in a deliberative mode. In Belgium, the G1000, a citizens-led initiative of deliberative democracy, has fostered a wider societal debate about the role and place of citizens in Belgian democracy. At the same time, the European institutions have sought to introduce different forms of deliberative democracy (notably, but not only, the European Citizens' Initiatives) as a way to connect with citizens better. The aim of this book is to critically assess these developments, bringing together academics who have been involved in the designing of these new forms of constitutional deliberative democracy and the theorists who developed the ideas.

The project originated in a series of papers presented at a meeting of the Participatory and Deliberative Democracy (PDDG) – a new specialist group of the Political Studies Association of Ireland, under the auspices of the ECPR Standing Group on Democratic Innovations – which met over two intensive days in the fall of 2012 at the Royal Irish Academy in Dublin. This conference and workshop organised by Professor David Farrell (University College Dublin) was designed to coincide with the establishment of the Irish government's constitutional convention. PDDG draws its members from across the main Irish universities, North and South, thus comprising one of the largest pool of experts in this field on those islands. The participants also included some of the world's leading experts in the field who had been involved themselves in designing actual deliberative democracy: André Bächtiger (Universität Luzern); Eirikur Bergmann (Bifrost University); Didier Caluwaerts (Vrije Universiteit Brussels); Gemma Carney (National University of Ireland); Ken Carty (University of British Columbia); Patrick Fournier (Université de Montréal); Clodagh Harris (University College Cork); Kaisa Herne (Turku University); Min Reuchamps (Université catholique de Louvain); Gerry Stoker (Southampton University); Jane Suiter (Dublin City University); Henk van der Kolk (University of Twente); and Peter Vermeersch (KU Leuven).

The project made progress a few weeks later at a meeting organised by the G1000 and hosted by the KU Leuven and the Belgian Senate in Brussels on 19 December 2012. This meeting included the same group of scholars and some additional academics who had been at the forefront of organising constitutional deliberative settings, as well as speakers from civil-society organisations, in order to achieve a good mixture of the practical and the theoretical: Benoît Derenne (Foundation for Future Generations); Kimmo Grönlund (Åbo Akademi University); Seong Jae Min (Pace University); Josien Pieterse (Netwerk Democratie); Gerrit Rauws

(King Baudouin Foundation); Stef Steyaert (Levuur); Juan Ugarriza (El Rosario University); and Martin Wilhelm (Citizens for Europe).

From all this very rich material, this book came about. It includes chapters from some of the contributors to these events as well as some new contributors, in order to give the project more theoretical heft and make it a coherent whole. With the support of the French-speaking Belgian Political Science Association (ABSP) and its working group Démocratie, a third workshop was held at the Université catholique de Louvain on 23–4 October 2014, to bring together the contributors to the book as well as external discussants in order to thoroughly discuss and develop each chapter. This book is thus the result of these discussions and we would like to thank all the people who joined us in these reflections. This book owes much to every participant to this ongoing deliberative party. We hope this volume will help continue the conversation.

Min Reuchamps and Jane Suiter

Chapter One

A Constitutional Turn for Deliberative Democracy in Europe?

Jane Suiter and Min Reuchamps

Deliberative democracy and its constitutional turn

In recent years, public authorities and civil-society organisations, driven by increasing public disengagement and a growing sense of distrust between the public and their representatives, have been instituting exercises in public deliberation, often using 'mini-publics', that is relatively small groups of citizens, selected according to various criteria and representing different viewpoints, brought together to deliberate on a particular issue. From small-scale experiments, mini-publics have recently taken a constitutional turn, at least in Europe. Iceland and Ireland have turned to deliberative democracy to reform their constitutions. Estonia, Luxembourg and Romania have also experienced constitutional processes in a deliberative mode. In Belgium, the G1000, a citizen-led initiative of deliberative democracy, has fostered a wider public debate about the place and role of citizens in the country's democracy. At the same time, the European Union institutions have introduced different forms of deliberative democracy as a way to reconnect with citizens. These empirical cases are indicative of a possible 'constitutional turn' in deliberative democracy in Europe. These examples of constitution-making happened in a particular time and place but they may also serve as models for other events.

The purpose of this book is, first, to critically assess these developments, bringing together academics who have been involved in designing these new forms of constitutional deliberative democracy with theorists practised in evaluating normative standards. This combination of contributors allows us the opportunity to speak across the praxis divide, bringing empiricists and those involved in the design and implementation of these processes, together with more normatively engaged theorists. Second, we hope to be able to offer answers or, at least, clues to possible pathways to generalisation as to which kinds of participatory processes work best for constitutional change and under what conditions.

In essence, deliberative democracy is concerned with building and engaging with authentic and reasoned debate in order to decide on a course of action. In other words, if it is deliberative, it is inclusive and consequential (Dryzek 2009). Deliberation can take place in mini-publics and parliaments and among the masses and there are many high-profile real-world examples of innovation in deliberative democracy, notably the participatory budgeting practices that originated in Brazil

(Souza 2001); the deliberative polling exercises that have been applied widely (Fishkin 2009; Suiter, Farrell and O'Malley 2014); and the long tradition in Scandinavia of citizen-deliberation about complex issues at the intersection between science and society (Rose and Sæbø 2010), to name but a few. All share some features: they are based on some form of deliberation among samples of citizens; they aim to foster positive and constructive thinking about solutions (they are not simply protest movements); they seek genuine debate about policy content; they seek solutions beyond adversarial politics; and they seek to identify common ground. What's more, there is cross-fertilisation of existing models and techniques and a rising number of experiments that combine traditional modes of political participation with some elements of deliberation. The field of deliberative democracy is kicking and striving.

But why should deliberative democracy be an appropriate mode for constitution-making? Modern constitution-making started in the late eighteenth century. Elster (1995) describes seven waves of constitution-making, across Europe and North America as well as in their former colonies throughout the world. The first wave came before the end of the eighteenth century, with the novel constitutions that followed the American and French revolutions. The second wave swept through Europe following the revolutions of 1848, when around fifty new constitutions were introduced, including those in the many small German and Italian states. In the third wave, many of the states newly created after World War I, for example, Poland and Czechoslovakia, wrote their constitutions. Under pressure from the victorious allied forces, in the fourth wave, the defeated states of World War II, Germany, Italy and Japan, wrote new constitutions introducing democracy. The fifth wave came with the breakup of the British and French colonial empires, starting in India and Pakistan in the 1940s, gradually gaining momentum and then running through Africa in the 1960s. The sixth wave washed through southern Europe in the mid 1970s, with the end of dictatorships in Greece, Portugal and Spain. The seventh wave broke in Eastern Europe in the 1990s, with the collapse of communism and the end of the cold war leading to the introduction of many new and progressive constitutions; this was also the case in Finland, where the constitution of 2000 is a product of the mini banking crisis in Scandinavia in the 1990s.

Many of these cases of constitutional revision have three characteristics in common. First, they were instigated in response to crises or exceptional circumstances. They each happened at what Ackerman (1998) refers to as a 'constitutional moment', which mobilised social forces for fundamental change. Elster (1995) counts only two instances in which new constitutions were drawn up under non-crisis circumstances: Sweden in 1974 and Canada in 1982. All the others were responses to economic crisis, regime-change or revolution. Second, all involved, though to varying extents, the deliberation of elites. Third, many of the recent bouts of constitution-making have not resulted in long-lived documents (Kellermann, de Zwaan and Czuczai 2001; Albi 2005; Ginsburg and Dixon 2011).

The cases discussed in this book (*see* Bergmann 2016; Suiter, Farrell and Harris 2016; and Jacquet, Moskovic, Caluwaerts and Reuchamps 2016,

Chapters Two, Three and Four of this volume) were also products of crisis, particularly of the global financial crisis of 2008, and of the diminishing trust in institutions among European publics in general. Indeed, both Ireland and Iceland suffered large drops in GDP as a result of the banking crisis. Yet, given the importance of constitution-making, should it not preferably be undertaken at a time when rational reflection and consideration is possible (Elster 1995)? It is possible that the deliberative mode of this recent wave has, at least to some extent, been an attempt to overcome citizens' diminishing trust in institutions and that they can be distinguished from all previous waves in terms of who was deliberating and how they were doing so. This is an issue to which we shall return to in greater depth in the relevant country chapters.

Given the characteristics of the current political context and also of deliberative democracy, is this mode likely to be appropriate for constitution-making? Previous rounds of constitution-making involved the deliberation of elites – principally, constitutional lawyers, senior politicians and so on – who constituted the deliberative component of such assemblies as the framers of the US Constitution and the Constitutional Assembly in post-revolutionary France. In most, decisions were reached by a qualified majority of the delegates, although a few aimed at something close to consensus, for example, during the making of the 1949 German Constitution and the 1978 Spanish Constitution (Elster 1995). In several instances, however, citizens also had a role in constitution-making as well as elites (Fishkin 2011; Mendez and Wheatley 2013).

What is crucial in terms of constitutional deliberative democracy is that, in all cases, the central principle is an attempt to involve the public in deliberation. In this perspective, a version of the deliberative model involving a mini-public was the chosen route for the assemblies to deliberate. In addition, in terms of the how (or the throughput) of deliberation, Elster also noted that in many previous episodes of constitution-making, self-serving arguments tended to dress themselves in the garb of public interest. While there is no guarantee that a deliberative mini-public would not operate in a similar fashion, if it is functioning in conformity with deliberative criteria such as inclusiveness, equality transparency and publicity, it would not.

So why should a deliberative mini-public function in this normatively desirable fashion? Constitutions, as the supreme norms that shape legitimate law-making, must be normatively legitimate if citizens are to be considered under an obligation to obey the laws of their polity (Dworkin 1995). There is agreement in the literature that deliberative democracy is primarily focused on producing legitimate political outcomes (Manin 1987; Cohen 1998). Thus, introducing elements of deliberative democracy to constitution-making ought to make constitutional changes more legitimate. The link between the mini- and the maxi-public (that is, the whole of the people) will also be crucial here and that is an issue we shall return to later. In addition, as Elster (1995) notes, creating a constitution involves making collective choices under constraints, that is, constitutions are works produced by constituent assemblies rather than by individuals. Thus, in general, the goals of individual constitution-makers and the mechanisms by which these are aggregated into collective choices are vital. In theory, utilising the principles of deliberation should result in a process that functions so as to ground constitution-making in the thought-through will of the people.

In addition, the intrinsic importance of constitution-making requires that procedures be based on rational and logical argument: and the deliberative model is ideally suited to such tasks. Rawls (1999), for example, argued that deliberation should be central to a conception of public reason. Thus we might expect that constitution-making in a deliberative mini-public would result in policies and priorities being adopted that are better solutions than those that can emerge when framers are incentivised more towards horse-trading and log-rolling (Elster 1995). In other words, as Caluwaerts and Reuchamps (2015) argued, discussions that take place in the public sphere should have the capacity to translate the deliberation of the public into normatively valuable public outcomes. Thus, we would expect deliberative democracy to be appropriate for constitution-making, in that it will both give the process greater legitimacy and produce outcomes based on rational and logical argument.

However, there is still the issue of content. Constitutional deliberative democracy deals with issues that might, potentially, lead to a transformation of the polity; these deliberations also, potentially, need to include more abstract issues of principle and theory than some of the political issues traditionally associated with mini-publics. Many of the earlier mentioned examples of mini-publics are rooted in the practical, or the ordinary experiences of the public, focused on local spending, the environment and so on. However, the new wave of large-scale initiatives aimed at changing constitutions either directly or indirectly are, by their very nature, more abstract, less tied to the day-to-day realities of life, for the deliberating public. Yet there is no reason why some of these constitutional issues – from electoral systems, to marriage-equality, to producing new constitutions – should be beyond the competence of ordinary members of a mini-public to decide. The evidence from the wave of citizens'-assemblies in Canada and the Netherlands (Fournier *et al.* 2011) is that citizens embraced the technical elements of the proposals and many became experts. In other, more general mini-publics, such as Ireland's We the Citizens experiment (Farrell, O'Malley and Suiter 2013; Suiter, Farrell and O'Malley 2014), members deliberated on both political reform and redistribution to produce more informed and nuanced opinions.

As a result of this widening of the parameters of what is deemed possible within deliberation, other forms of constitutional deliberative democracy have emerged, especially in Europe. In Iceland, the output of a deliberative process has been presented in a referendum that confirmed the will of the population to change the constitution. In Ireland, the Convention on the Constitution is now done with its first deliberations and two referendums have been held, including one introducing same-sex marriage. These can be seen as examples of deliberative constitutional reform. In Belgium, even though the G1000 was not designed to affect the constitution of the country, it is currently widely replicated in different settings, in Belgium and elsewhere, and it has fostered a wider debate in society about the role and place of citizens in Belgian democracy (Caluwaerts and Reuchamps 2015). Last but not least, notably with the introduction of European Citizens' Initiatives, the European Union has paved the way for the introduction of new forms of democracy (Auer 2005). These developments also represent a number of forms and practices, including deliberative constitutional reforms (that is, constitutional reforms initiated via deliberative democracy procedures and not only by representative and/or direct-democratic ones); constitutional mini-publics (which are organised to deliberate about – some articles of – the constitution); and also deliberative events on issues that are not directly related to constitutional change but concerned with the nature of democracy in a polity (for instance, whether it should become more participatory and/or deliberative).

To sum up, the first two experiences discussed in the volume – Iceland and Ireland – are true examples of constitutional deliberative reform, while the latter – the G1000 in Belgium – is a *sui generis* form of deliberative democracy with a potential for political and constitutional transformation. We argue that, together, these can be envisaged as constitutional deliberative democracy and that there is now a need for a serious and systematic inquiry into these developments, which go to the heart of democracy. The choice of cases in this volume (Iceland, Ireland and Belgium) makes sense because all these cases were large-scale experiments and were similar from a methodological perspective. They call for a combined research endeavour, bringing together theoretical claims and empirical validations. Thus, this volume brings together not only theoretical and empirical researchers who have studied these cases but others who have been involved in the organisation of this constitutional turn in deliberative democracy.

In other words, we shall explore and reflect on innovations made in deliberative democracy as a result of its application to constitutional reform (Farrell 2014). This can be envisaged as a particular *form* of deliberative democracy – one that harnesses the democratic potential of mini-publics (Parkinson 2006; Pateman 2012) – or as instances of deliberative democracy in service of the masses (Niemeyer 2014). This is important, as the link between the mini- and the maxi-public is not yet fully conceptualised (Grönlund *et al.* 2014) and, in most cases, constitution-making is ratified by 'the people' at some point. Thus, while these constitutional deliberative processes are not themselves decision-making as proxies for mass-publics, they can be utilised for deliberation-making in mass publics. As Niemeyer (2014) argues, these mini-publics can distil, constrain and synthesise relevant discourse to be transmitted to the wider public. In at least two of our cases, in Iceland and in Ireland, this was the purpose of the mini-public: to act as a precursor to nationwide referendums on the same issues. In other words, to bring about a more discursive transmission of information rather than merely being information-providing (MacKenzie and Warren 2012). Importantly, these mini-publics can also act as capacity-builders; the media attention they generate and the open access they provide, at least potentially, means they can serve as deliberative exemplars, building and enhancing the reputation of deliberation more generally in society.

Assessing constitutional deliberative democracy

Starting from some emblematic cases of constitutional deliberative democracy, this book will address the constitutional turn in deliberative democracy across Europe and, more specifically, assess the – multi-faceted – legitimacy of this transformation. To this end, we propose a framework for assessing the legitimacy of constitutional reform in a deliberative setting that distinguishes between three kinds of legitimacy: input, throughput and output legitimacy. This approach builds on the seminal work of Easton (1965), who demonstrated the importance of understanding any political system in terms of its input and of its output as well as in terms of their interactions. These two normative criteria of systems' theory have often been discussed in terms of democratic legitimacy, starting with Scharpf in the context of the EU (1970). He divided democratic legitimation into *output*, that is the effectiveness of the EU's policy outcomes, and *input*, that is the responsiveness of the EU to citizen-participation. More recently, Schmidt has argued for the addition of a third normative criterion for evaluation: *throughput*, that is, to study the efficacy, accountability, openness and inclusiveness of the democratic processes under consideration (2013).

In the case of the European Union, moreover, scholars have been paying increasing attention to the mechanisms of 'throughput' legitimacy, which have long been among the central ways in which EU-level institutional players have sought to counter claims about the poverty of input legitimacy and to reinforce claims to output legitimacy (Schmidt 2013: 3).

Throughput legitimacy is thus the missing link between input and output. Interestingly, theories of deliberative democracy bring about the same concern for a focus on processes, in addition to the input and the output dimensions. Emphasising the procedural dimension of deliberative democracy, Cohen contends that 'outcomes are democratically legitimate if and only if they could be the object of free and reasoned argument among equals' (Cohen 1998: 74). This proceduralist approach to democracy, which is in line with other deliberative theorists (for example, Manin, Stein and Mansbridge 1987; Dryzek 2001), links inputs from equal citizens with outputs, understood as the outcome produced through deliberation. Scholars working empirically on deliberative democracy's legitimacy also stress the importance of this threefold model (Bekkers and Edwards 2007; Edwards 2007): democratic decision-making procedures have to be legitimate in the input, throughput and output phases. That is to say, such procedures have to make sure that the opinions and needs of ordinary citizens are translated, through deliberative procedures, into good political outcomes (Caluwaerts and Reuchamps 2015).

Such a threefold model of democratic legitimacy makes even more sense in an era of systemic approaches to deliberative democracy (Parkinson and Mansbridge 2013), where legitimacy does not rely on separate mini-publics but on close interactions between mini-publics and maxi-publics. Nonetheless, if such an approach is to be useful in assessing constitutional deliberative democracy, it should be theoretically qualified and, on this basis, empirically tested, as the remaining chapters of this book will do. Theoretically, we should define more precisely each of these three dimensions of deliberative legitimacy and how they could possibly be translated in practice. To this end, we adapt the analytical framework proposed by Caluwaerts and Reuchamps (2015) to the specificities of constitutional deliberative democracy.

Input legitimacy

It is often argued that a key dimension of deliberative democracy is the nature of the *representation* it allows. The question of *who* deliberates is crucial to understanding the input side. In this regard, lots of discussions have been about the principle of 'all-affected interests', which means that everyone affected by the issue at stake should be included in the deliberation; this raises the question of inclusion and democracy (Young 2000) and how inclusion can be operationalised in practice (Pedrini, Bächtiger and Steenbergen 2013).

Several answers can be given to the question of how deliberation should accommodate representation. It could call for socio-demographic representation; for discursive representation that would insist on a diversity of opinions and discourses rather than on a diversity of people; or a mixture of both. It could also be the case that the representation is biased, with self-selection and strong representation among all groups but, in particular, traditionally vulnerable groups. The technique used to delimit the *who* should also be under close scrutiny, as its consequences for representation can vary a lot depending on whether random selection, targeted selection or self-selection is in operation (Caluwaerts and Ugarriza 2012; Fung 2006).

Another key dimension of the input side is *agenda-setting*, that is, the *what* question. Fung has distinguished between 'hot' and 'cold' issues: the former might be of greater social and political interest but more productive of tension; the latter may provoke less tension but have less social resonance, within both the mini-public and the maxi-public (Fung 2007). Above all, how the agenda is decided is of crucial importance to understanding the dynamics of constitutional deliberative democracy. Several ways of agenda-setting, each fostering different consequences, can be found in practice. The process could have an open agenda: the entire population or all stakeholders are able/invited to set or vote on the agenda in an open-ended process. At the other hand of the spectrum, the agenda could be closed, decided on by formal institutions and with little room for introducing new issues. In-between options are also available. For instance, the agenda could be fixed but participants could also be allowed to introduce adjacent issues and question whether pre-chosen issues should be on the agenda at all.

A last dimension of the input side is the level of information of the people who deliberate, which can be referred to as 'epistemic completeness' (Mucciaroni and Quirk 2006). More specifically, it is not so much what deliberators know but how they can learn about the issues at stake. Ideally, participants have access to all relevant information and are – made – competent, with access to experts on the question, policy-makers and/or witnesses. In practice, however, efforts to inform deliberators may be limited to information booklets, with little room for extra learning and questioning. We can also see the interactions – and possibly the trade-offs – between the different dimensions of the input side. For instance, if the aim is to build constitutional deliberative democracy involving a large and diverse crowd of people, the question of information is even more important, to ensure sufficient epistemic completeness. Above all, while there are interactions *within* the input side, there are also interactions *between* input, throughput and output legitimacy, to which we turn now.

Throughput legitimacy

Deliberative democracy strongly emphasises the importance of the nature of the deliberation itself. In this regard, *representation* is not the only key question: the question of *participation* is also critical. To what extent are the participants given the chance to take part in deliberation? There might be substantively inclusive – not just formal – participation: every participant is given an equal voice in the discussion and efforts are made to create a genuine group feeling, in order to lower the threshold of participation. There might be a difference between 'real' and 'formal' inclusive participation, however: in the latter, participants would be given equal speaking time formally but no extra effort would be made to ensure that less at-ease participants benefit from the deliberation. Instead, the discussions might then be characterised by exclusion and patterns of discursive domination. Several factors might have an impact on the nature of participation: for instance, the role of the facilitators (Myers 2007); group-composition (Caluwaerts and Deschouwer 2013) and, more specifically, the gender balance among participants (Mendelberg, Karpowitz and Goedert 2014); and the use of multiple languages (Caluwaerts and Reuchamps 2014).

Another dimension of the throughput side is the question of how deliberation is translated into decision. This co-ordination can occur through transformation, that is, solution-finding through discussion. Yet because politics is more about conflict than consensus (Mouffe 2000), other options exist, such as a combination of discussion and voting or simply voting; and there is a place for voting in deliberative democracy (Saward 2008: 67–8). The question raised by the choice between these different options, however, is what are the possible consequences of the voting mode on the quality of deliberation itself? This is why attention should be paid to this dimension of throughput legitimacy. Above all, as Schmidt has argued for the throughput dimension within the EU (2013), the transparency of processes seems to be crucial to their legitimation.

In most instances, constitutional deliberative democracy will rely on a portion of its whole public, a mini-public. But the link between this mini-public and the maxi-public is a key dynamic that has an impact on both the throughput side and the output side. For the former, the question is the contextual dependence or independence of the mini-public. While there will always be connection between the mini-public and the maxi-public, deliberation could take place largely in a political and public vacuum; or it could be the case that some political actors and media aim to steer participants' decisions in a certain direction and thus undermine the legitimacy of the event. The contextual independence of the deliberation should therefore be taken into account when assessing the legitimacy of constitutional deliberative democracy.

Output legitimacy

With output legitimacy we come to the core of the relationship between the mini-public and the maxi-public. As Dryzek puts it: 'decisions still have to be justified to those who did not participate' (2001: 654). The question of political uptake is therefore crucial in assessing constitutional deliberative democracy; that is, how the society at large takes up the issues raised by the mini-public. It is also in close interaction with the nature of the representation and of agenda-setting on the input side. In the chosen conception of the input dimension, choices may already have been made that have an impact directly on the likely political uptake. For instance, it could have been decided from the very beginning that any recommendations from the constitutional deliberative forum would be put to the popular vote in a referendum. Feedback from the mini-public to the maxi-public could also be organised through more informal means, such as by televising the deliberations or through possible interactions between the maxi-public and the mini-public during the process itself – therefore having a beneficial effect on the throughput legitimacy. The question of what is politically or even, in this case, constitutionally, done with the results of deliberative democracy is a key dimension of its output legitimation.

The corollary is that there is a need for some sort of accountability from the formal constitutional actors, likely to be parliamentarians but also, possibly, the government, to the mini-public and to the maxi-public. In this regard, there could be regular feedback: government agents report on the decisions and progress made to participants and the general public. It could also be the case that feedback is provided only on demand by participants or simply that the maxi-public and participants are kept in the dark about the uptake of their proposals.

Last but not least, even though the focus should be on potential constitutional changes brought about through deliberative democracy, we should not put aside the potential social uptake of deliberative processes. The process of constitutional deliberative democracy could foster social changes as the decisions and/or the model of deliberation is taken up by other groups, to be reproduced on a smaller scale. Minimally, we could expect an increased awareness of the constitutional deliberative process and of its proposals among the public at large. Nonetheless, research on citizens' assemblies on electoral reform in Canada and in the Netherlands has shown that large portions of the society were not aware of the deliberative-democracy processes in motion (Fournier *et al.* 2011). The social – and not only political – uptake induced – or not – by constitutional deliberative democracy should therefore be assessed in any endeavour to gauge its legitimacy.

Analysing constitutional deliberative democracy

The chapters in this book use this three-fold legitimacy analytical framework to assess the legitimacy of constitutional deliberative democracy and reflect on the transformation of our current democracies it might make possible. The first three chapters apply the framework to the cases of Iceland – in Chapter Two by Eirikur Bergmann; Ireland – in Chapter Three by Jane Suiter, David Farrell and Clodagh Harris; and Belgium – in Chapter Four, by Vincent Jacquet, Jonathan Moskovic, Didier Caluwaerts and Min Reuchamps. These chapters bring together a very rich supply of empirical material and they form a comprehensive analysis that the remainder of the book's chapters will draw on for their analysis.

In Chapter Five, Brigitte Geissel and Sergiu Gherghina perform a comparison of these three country-cases in light of the literature on democratic innovations, which sheds light on input, throughput and output legitimacy dynamics in a comparative fashion. In the wake of this comparative assessment, in Chapter Six, Julien Talpin discusses the legitimacies, as he calls them, of constitutional deliberative democracy and highlights the difficult move from mini-publics to deliberation in the public sphere, raising the question of how constitutional reforms can be deliberative. Kimmo Grönlund, in Chapter Seven, brings in additional empirical material from five experiments organised in Finland that allows him to delve into the designing of mini-publics for constitutional deliberative democracy.

All this empirical material is taken further by Stefan Rummens in Chapter Eight, in which he develops six theses about the legitimacy of mini-publics in the democratic system. The closing Chapter Nine, by John Parkinson, offers a conceptual conclusion that connects the key themes of this volume with the emerging deliberative-systems approach, to ask both how deep these constitutional innovations run and how deep they can and should run. All in all, this book seeks to open up a deliberation about the constitutional deliberative democracy turn.

References

Ackerman, B. (1998) *We the People*, vol. 2, *Transformations*, Cambridge, MA: Harvard University Press.

Albi, A. (2005) *EU Enlargement and the Constitutions of Central and Eastern Europe*, Cambridge, UK: Cambridge University Press.

Auer, A. (2005) 'European Citizens' Initiative', *European Constitutional Law Review* 1(1): 79–86.

Bekkers, V., and Edwards, A. (2007) 'Legitimacy and democracy: a conceptual framework for assessing governance practices', in Bekkers, V., Dijkstra, G., Edwards, A. and Fenger, M. (eds) *Governance and the Democratic Deficit: Assessing the legitimacy of governance practices*, Aldershot, UK: Ashgate.

Cain, B. E., Dalton, R. J., and Scarrow, S. E. (eds) (2003) *Democracy Transformed? Expanding political opportunities in advanced industrial democracies*, Oxford, UK: Oxford University Press.

Caluwaerts, D., and Deschouwer, K. (2013) 'Building bridges across political divides: experiments on deliberative democracy in deeply divided Belgium', *European Political Science Review* 6(3): 427–50.

Caluwaerts, D., and Reuchamps, M. (2014) 'Does inter-group deliberation foster inter-group appreciation? Evidence from two experiments in Belgium', *Politics* 34(2): 101–15.

— (2015) 'Strengthening democracy through bottom-up deliberation: an assessment of the internal legitimacy of the G1000 project', *Acta Politica* 50(2): 151–70.

Caluwaerts, D., and Ugarriza, J. E. (2012) 'Favorable conditions to epistemic validity in deliberative experiments: a methodological assessment', *Journal of Public Deliberation* 8(1): 1–19.

Cohen, J. (1998) 'Deliberation and democratic legitimacy', in Bohman, J. and Regh, W. (eds) *Deliberative Democracy: Essays on reason and politics*, Oxford, UK: Blackwell.

Dalton, R. J., Cain, B. E., and Scarrow, S. E. (2003) 'Democratic publics and democratic institutions', in Cain, B. E., Dalton, R. J. and Scarrow, S. E. (eds) *Democracy Transformed? Expanding political opportunities in advanced industrial democracies*, Oxford, UK: Oxford University Press.

Dryzek, J. S. (2001) 'Legitimacy and economy in deliberative democracy', *Political Theory* 29(5): 651–69.

— (2009) 'Democratization as deliberative capacity building', *Comparative Political Studies* 42(11): 1379–1402.

Dworkin, R. (1995) 'Constitutionalism and democracy', *European Journal of Philosophy* 3(1): 2–11.

Easton, D. (1965) *A Systems Analysis of Political Life*, New York, NY: John Wiley & Sons.

Edwards, A. (2007) 'Embedding deliberative democracy: local environmental forums in the Netherlands', in Bekkers, V., Dijkstra, G., Edwards, A. and

Fenger, M. (eds) *Governance and the Democratic Deficit: Assessing the legitimacy of governance practices*, Aldershot, UK: Ashgate.

Elster, J. (1995) 'Forces and mechanisms in the constitution-making process', *Duke Law Journal* 45(2): 364–96.

Farrell, D. M. (2014) '"Stripped down" or reconfigured democracy', *West European Politics* 37(2): 439–55.

Farrell, D. M., O'Malley, E., and Suiter, J. (2013) 'Deliberative democracy in action Irish-style: the 2011 We the Citizens pilot citizens' assembly', *Irish Political Studies* 28(1): 99–113.

Fishkin, J. S. (2009) *When the People Speak: Deliberative democracy and public consultation*, Oxford, UK: Oxford University Press.

Fishkin, J. S. (2011) 'Deliberative democracy and constitutions', *Social Philosophy & Policy* 28(1): 242–60.

Fournier, P., van der Kolk, H., Carty, R. K., Blais, A., and Rose, J. (2011) *When Citizens Decide: Lessons from citizens' assemblies on electoral reform*, Oxford, UK: Oxford University Press.

Fung, A. (2006) 'Varieties of participation in complex governance', *Public Administration Review* 66(s1): 66–75.

— (2007) 'Minipublics: deliberative designs and their consequences', in Rosenberg, S. W. (ed.) *Deliberation, Participation and Democracy: Can the people govern?* Basingstoke, UK and New York: Palgrave Macmillan.

Ginsburg, T., and Dixon, R. (2011) *Comparative Constitutional Law*, Cheltenham, UK: Edward Elgar.

Grönlund, K., Bächtiger, A., and Setälä, M. (eds) (2014) *Deliberative Mini-Publics: Involving citizens in the democratic process*, Colchester, UK: ECPR Press.

Kellerman, A. E., de Zwaan, J. W., and Czuczai, J. (eds) (2001) *EU Enlargement: The constitutional impact at EU and national level*, The Hague, NL: Asser Press.

MacKenzie, M. K., and Warren, M. E. (2012) 'Two trust-based uses of minipublics in democratic systems', in Parkinson, J. and Mansbridge, J. (eds) *Deliberative Systems: Deliberative democracy at the large scale*, Cambridge, UK: Cambridge University Press.

Manin, B. (1987) 'On legitimacy and political deliberation', *Political Theory* 15(3): 338–68.

Mendelberg, T., Karpowitz, C. F., and Goedert, N. (2014) 'Does descriptive representation facilitate women's distinctive voice? How gender composition and decision rules affect deliberation', *American Journal of Political Science* 58(2): 291–306.

Mendez, J. and Wheatley, F. (eds) (2013) *Patterns of Constitutional Design: The role of citizens and elites in constitution-making*, Farnham, UK: Ashgate.

Mouffe, C. (2000) *Deliberative Democracy or Agonistic Pluralism?*, Vienna, Austria: Institute for Advanced Studies.

Mucciaroni, G., and Quirk, P. J. (2006) *Deliberative Choices: Debating public policy in congress*, Chicago, IL: University of Chicago Press.

Myers, G. (2007) 'Enabling talk: how the facilitator shapes a focus group', *Text and Talk – An interdisciplinary journal of language discourse & communication studies* 27(1): 79–105.

Niemeyer, S. (2014) 'Scaling up deliberation to mass publics: harnessing mini-publics in a deliberative system', in Grönlund, K., Bächtiger, A. and Setälä M. (eds) *Deliberative Mini-Publics: Involving citizens in the democratic process*, Colchester, UK: ECPR Press.

Parkinson, J. (2006) *Deliberating in the Real World: Problems of legitimacy in deliberative democracy*, Oxford, UK: Oxford University Press.

Parkinson, J., and Mansbridge, J. (eds) (2013) *Deliberative Systems: Deliberative democracy at the large scale*, Cambridge, UK: Cambridge University Press.

Pateman, C. (2012) 'Participatory democracy revisited', *Perspectives on Politics* 10(1): 7–19.

Pedrini, S., Bächtiger, A. and Steenbergen, M. R. (2013) 'Deliberative inclusion of minorities: patterns of reciprocity among linguistic groups in Switzerland', *European Political Science Review* 5(3): 483–512.

Rose, J., and Sæbø, Ø. (2010) 'Designing deliberation systems', *Information Society* 26(3): 228–40.

Saward, M. (2008) 'Democracy and citizenship: expanding domains', in Dryzek, J. S., Honig, B. and Phillips, A. (eds) *Oxford Handbook of Political Theory*, Oxford, UK: Oxford University Press.

Scharpf, F. W. (1970) *Demokratietheorie zwischen Utopie und Anpassung*, Konstanz, DE: Universitätsverlag.

Schmidt, V. A. (2013) 'Democracy and legitimacy in the European Union revisited: input, output and "throughput"', *Political Studies* 61(1): 2–22.

Souza, C. (2001) 'Participatory budgeting in Brazilian cities: limits and possibilities in building democratic institutions', *Environment & Urbanization* 13(1): 159–84.

Suiter, J., Farrell, D. M. and O'Malley, E. (2014) 'When do deliberative citizens change their opinions? Evidence from the Irish Citizens' Assembly', *International Political Science Review*, published online, doi: 10.1177/0192512114544068.

Young, I. M. (2000) *Inclusion and Democracy*, Oxford, UK: Oxford University Press.

Chapter Two

Participatory Constitutional Deliberation in the Wake of Crisis: The Case of Iceland

Eirikur Bergmann[1]

A crisis in democratic representation is increasingly evident in established democracies, manifest, for example, in escalating public protest as well as increased volatility between elections and in rising support for populist right-wing parties. One solution targeted at enhancing democratic legitimacy through increased public involvement in politics is the initiatives instigated to bring public decision-making to *ad hoc* citizens' panels – often referred to as 'mini-publics'. One of the most far-reaching of such initiatives is the constitutional-reform process initiated in Iceland in 2010, in the wake of the global financial crisis.

Indeed, initiatives for political reform are often instigated in wake of crisis (Elster 1995). Just as a crisis in capitalism can open up our imagination to alternative 'economic imaginaries' (Jessop 2004), constitutional revisions are usually only embarked upon in the aftermath of severe political or economic crisis (Elster 1995). This is what Ackerman (1998) refers to as a 'constitutional moment', when a catastrophe mobilises societal forces for fundamental change (Teubner 2011). This chapter will first briefly set out the context for this Icelandic constitutional moment in 2009 and then examine the reform process from the perspective of input, throughout and output legitimacy.

Effect of the financial crisis

The scale of the crisis in Iceland was unprecedented. The country's three international banks, amounting to 85 per cent of the country's financial system – which had grown ten times larger than the country's GDP in less than a decade – came tumbling down within a single week in early October 2008. The stock exchange and the equity market were virtually wiped out and the tiny currency, the ISK, tanked, spurring rampant inflation which, in the following weeks and months, ate up most people's savings. Property values dropped by more than a third and unemployment reached levels never seen before in the life of the young republic, 9 per cent in 2009. The ruined currency finally stabilised at below half its pre-crisis value, following the introduction of currency controls. In the wake of this scale of dislocation, Iceland's constitutional revision was one of many reform projects, albeit the most ambitious.

---

1.   The author was one of the twenty-five members of the Constitutional Assembly.

Indeed, in the wake of the crisis, Iceland came closer than most countries ever get to being able to start with a clean slate. Iceland's constitutional process, its constitutional moment, after the crash of 2008 is thus in line with this apparent pattern of constitution-making following crisis and could, perhaps amongst other such initiatives, mark the start of a new wave spreading out in the wake of the international credit crunch. Constitutional revision had already been instigated in deliberative mini-publics in Belgium, Ireland and Estonia, for example. Many initiatives were embarked upon; some were bids to resurrect the failed Icelandic political model but others attempted to implement more permanent changes to the political system. There was a clear popular call for political reform; a 'New Iceland' was to emerge from the ruins (for more, see Bergmann 2014). From the citizens' side, many non-governmental groups were founded and they promoted a variety of routes out of the crisis. Ordinary people not only took to the streets in protest but also engaged much more actively in public discussion – in the mainstream media as well as on blogs and through social media. Many called for the establishment of Iceland's Second Republic or, in data lingo, the updating of the system to 'Iceland 2.0'.

Calling for an extraordinary election for a Constitutional Assembly, which was to write a new constitution, was, however, the most ambitious of these efforts aimed at political reform.[2] However, even as economic recovery was taking root, most of these initiatives for significant political reform were caught in what can be described as a 'new critical order', characterised by the intense politicisation of reform issues by the parties defeated at the first post-crisis election in spring 2009, which took hold in post-crisis Iceland and, in effect, caused the reform process to founder.

The crisis also dealt a devastating blow to Icelandic politics. Key government institutions and the political class stood accused of having sponsored the rise of the failed neo-liberal model and being responsible for its subsequent collapse. As a result of a series of largely non-violent protests, branded the 'pots-and-pans revolution' (*búsáhaldabyltingin*), the centre-right government of the time, led by the hegemonic Independence Party (IP) (the largest party by some margin, 1944–2009) in coalition with the Social Democratic Alliance (SDA), was ousted in February 2009.[3] The new, fragile, left-wing caretaker government was led

---

2. It should be noted that Reykjavik City Council also embarked on its own participatory democracy initiative, though perhaps on a lower level. The initiative Better Reykjavík is an online consultation forum, in which citizens are given the chance to present their ideas on issues regarding the services and operations of the City of Reykjavík and, in some cases, to vote for options on projects. For more, see http://betrireykjavik.is (accessed 27 January 2016).

3. The Icelandic political party system traditionally consisted of four main parties: the Independence Party (IP), Icelands' old right-wing hegemonic power; the agrarian Progressive Party (PP), which is based on traditional national sentiments with roots in agriculture; the rather internationalist and left-of-centre Social Democratic Alliance (SDA); and the further-left-leaning, feminist and environmentalist Left Green Movement (LGM). Alongside the four main parties there had always been a fifth and sometimes a sixth *ad hoc* or shorter-lived party, often formed to campaign on a specific issue. The longest-standing of these was the Womens List, which was active during the 1980s and 1990s.

by the SDA, in coalition with the Left Green Movement (LGM). This minority government was backed by a new leadership within the Progressive Party (PP), which had, until 2007, served as junior partner in coalitions with the IP. A well known activist for social reform, Mrs Jóhanna Sigurðardóttir, who belonged to the far left of the SDA, became Iceland's first female Prime Minister.

Politicisation and the new critical order

The constitutional-revision process was to be an integral part of Iceland's recovery from the most profound crisis to hit the republic since its creation in 1944, as Prime Minister Jóhanna Sigurðardóttir, for example, said in her 2011 New Year's Eve address (Sigurðardóttir 2011). As a result of the internal political upheaval, the process was subsequently highly politicised within a political climate that could be called a 'new critical order', in which the defeated parties opposed most reform initiatives and contested understandings of what constituted 'recovery'. Fierce infighting over defining the crisis and recovery took place. While this was politically quite widespread, the strongest opposition was amongst IP representatives now in opposition.

Parliament appointed a Special Investigation Commission – a 'truth committee' – to analyse events leading up to the crash and investigate whether government ministers had been at fault. The government appointed a Special Prosecutor, who was to investigate criminal activity in the financial sector leading up to the crash. In order to regain access to international markets, the government agreed to guarantee the Icesave deposits – of the fallen Icelandic bank – in UK and the Netherlands and applied for EU membership, mainly to underpin its monetary policy by adopting the euro. Jointly, these moves were aimed at securing Iceland's economic framework for the future. The political-party system was also being challenged, not only by widespread leadership renewal within the established parties but also by a flood of new parties; for example, the Best Party took political control of the capital city and its leader, a well known comedian, became mayor of Reykjavik in 2010.

The constitutional process was thus but one of many reforms instigated to resurrect Iceland after the bank crash. Instantly, however, the process became highly politicised. The once hegemonic Independence Party (IP), recently ousted from government, fought fiercely against the constitutional process every step of the way, perhaps feeling that the whole exercise was an attack on their political heritage. The conservative agrarian Progressive Party (PP), were initially supportive of the process but later turned against it. Leading up to the spring 2009 election, the new leadership of the PP had focused their strategy for regaining trust on this proposal for a nationally elected Constitutional Assembly, which, they insisted, would help the healing process needed for reconstructing Iceland's 'social contract', which had been ripped apart in the crisis. It is indicative of just how polarised Icelandic politics were becoming that when the new left-wing government agreed to a Constitutional Assembly, many PP parliamentarians suddenly started to distance themselves from the process and gradually emerged as some of the project's most forceful critics. While the new Prime Minister, Jóhanna Sigurðardóttir, and many of her colleagues were eager supporters of the convention, there was also a good deal of opposition amongst prominent ministers within the government. Many coalition parliamentarians either remained silent or were suspected of only paying lip-service to the project while quietly plotting against it.

Furthermore, it was widely expected that any proposed new constitution would, with clear public approval, stipulate that natural resources were the collective property of the nation, as opinion polls have consistently and firmly indicated was the will of the electorate. This is key to understanding the harsh political debate over the constitutional-reform process and the politicisation of the whole project. The dispute over the Individually Transferable Quota system (ITQ) has indeed been branded 'the battle of Iceland'. Over more than three decades, control of Iceland's fishing quota had amounted to the greatest political dispute in the country. For years, there had been a clear majority in opinion polls for rolling back the fishing quota virtually given away in the 1980s. However, despite massive public support, an article acknowledging the public ownership of fish stocks had not previously been added to the constitution. The IP, which has close links with the Association of Fishing Vessel Owners (LÍU), had always stood against such an amendment. This might partly explain the IP's opposition to the draft constitution.

An unfinished project

It should also be noted that constitutional reform had been on the agenda of Icelandic politics ever since the republic was established in 1944, when the country finally emerged from Danish rule while Denmark was still under Nazi occupation. The independence celebrations were held in Parliamentary Fields (Þingvellir), the site of the medieval parliamentary court, which, in the more than 100-year-long independence struggle, had become the holy site of Iceland's national spirit (Hálfdanarson 2001). In order to show the world that Icelanders were united in announcing their independence, the 1944 Parliament agreed not to make other changes to the constitution of the Icelandic kingdom other than those directly stemming from the establishment of the republic – thus, only changing the articles on the role of the Danish king to include references to a nationally elected Icelandic president. As a result, 95 per cent of the electorate agreed to establish the republic on the basis of the temporary constitution that the king of Denmark had handed to Icelanders in 1874, on the thousandth anniversary of settlement. Until that point, the constitution been changed only slightly, to provide for home rule in 1904 and for sovereign status in 1918 (resulting in the 1920 Constitution of the Icelandic Kingdom). The Union Act of 1918 contained a sunset-clause, stipulating that either country could end the relationship after twenty-five years. The massive support for the 1944 constitution was thus due to the fact that a Yes vote was seen as the national duty of all Icelanders; but such a vote was not necessarily evidence of approval of the content of the constitution itself, though many political opponents of constitutional reform have used it as such when arguing against change.

At the foundation of the republic in 1944, the founding fathers (they were all men) had announced that complete constitutional revision would be instigated immediately (Jóhannesson 2011). However, mostly because of political infighting and the intense politicisation of the issue, Icelandic parliamentarians had been unable to agree on anything other than minor changes up to the period of the financial crisis. When the constitutional-reform process was jump-started in 2009, therefore, constitutional revision was, in many regards, very much an unfinished project – perhaps even a thorn in the side of the young republic, as parliamentarians were never able to agree on either the process of reform or the content of a new constitution. The crisis thus provided a context and a platform for the politicians to discover a way out of the trenches of traditional party politics, outsourcing the drafting of a new constitution to a nationally elected external body. The primary mover for that initiative was Prime Minister Jóhanna Sigurðardóttir, who had been one of very few long-standing supporters of the call for such an external constitutional assembly.

The constitutional process in Iceland thus mirrors in some ways similar initiatives that governments elsewhere in Europe have instigated to build citizen-participation into public decision-making in order to increase democratic legitimacy (for more, *see* Suiter and Reuchamps 2016, Chapter One of this volume). As in Iceland, many of these deliberative mini-publics were initiated in the wake of crisis, precisely in order to regain legitimacy in the eyes of the public. The Irish 2013 Constitutional Convention was also held in wake of the financial crisis (*see* Suiter, Farrell and Harris 2016, Chapter Three of this volume, for greater detail). Then there are grassroots civil-society initiatives, such as the G1000 in Belgium (for more, see Caluwaerts and Reuchamps 2015 and Jacquet, Moskovic, Caluwaerts and Reuchamps 2016, Chapter Four of this volume) and the People's Assembly (*Rahvakogu*) in Estonia in 2014 (Rahvakogu n.d.). Apart from the Irish case, none of these other mini-publics have yet been successful in pushing through real change, however.

A few similar exercises outside Europe can be mentioned. In 1998, the Australian Prime Minister called a Constitutional Convention, which, for example, discussed Australia's link with the British monarchy. The deliberative aspect of the work was, however, limited, as most decisions were taken by vote (for more, see Webb 2000). Further similarities are found in public participation in local-level budgeting in South America, most obviously the participatory budgeting process in Porto Alegre in Brazil (for more, see Wampler 2007).

Input legitimacy

In 2010, pressured by an angry public, the new left-wing government decided to start a constitutional-review process, which would draft a new constitution in three phases. First, a National Forum of a thousand people, randomly selected by stratified sampling, would gather for a one-day meeting to discuss the principles and values on which the new constitution should be based. Second, a seven-member, political-party-appointed Constitutional Committee would be created to gather information, analyse the core issues discussed by the National Forum and propose ideas for constitutional revision. Third, and most importantly, Parliament called for a national election of an independent, twenty-five-member Constitutional Assembly, which would revise Iceland's constitution or, possibly, draft a completely new one, on the basis of the work of the National Forum and the Constitutional Committee review. The Independence Party fought against the exercise in parliament but reluctantly accepted a compromise after having proposed the National Forum be added to the process.

Structure and process

In terms of input, this was a novel structure involving a three-phase engagement, that is, of randomly selected citizens, appointed experts and nationally elected individual representatives. This unique setup was effectively and quite simply a political compromise: on the left, many called for an elected Constitutional Assembly of non-party-political individuals working alongside the Icelandic parliament for an extensive period of time to have the mandate to draft the new constitution, which would be put to binding referendum; others, mainly on the right, simply wanted to consult citizens a little while keeping the drafting of any constitutional amendments within parliament. The latter group, led by the IP, was never committed to the process.

The National Forum in 2010 was based on the initiative of a grassroots civil-society movement, the Anthills (*Maurapúfan*), which, the year before, had held a similar event named National Assembly (*Þjóðfundur*) in order to map ideas for reform. The Anthills assembly was perhaps similar to 'We the Citizens' in Ireland and the G1000 citizens summit in Belgium. The crisis had spurred nationwide interest in political reform. The National Assembly tapped into this new interest, giving ordinary people the opportunity to express their frustrations and wishes. Some 900 participants were randomly selected by stratified sampling, in addition to 300 representatives of different civil-society associations and interest groups. The 2009 National Assembly of 1,200 participants was divided into small roundtable groups, each led by professional facilitator. At the end of the process, a handbook mapping the discussions and drawing conclusions was published. Many of the conclusions were bordering on the simplistic; many were reflective of the financial crisis, including, for example, an emphasis on honesty, equal rights, respect, justice, love, responsibility, freedom, sustainability and democracy (Fillmore-Patrick 2013).

The 2010 National Forum, based on the 2009 civil-society National Assembly, was, on the other hand, a government-initiated body. This time, 950 randomly selected Icelanders were brought together in Reykjavik on 6 November 2010. Perhaps indicative of already declining general interest in the project, the mobilisation rate dropped significantly, from more than half to 20 per cent, meaning that 5,000 people had to be invited to fill all the places. The Forum's task included identifying the main values on which the constitutional drafting should be based. The report produced by the National Forum was both wide-ranging and far-reaching. Among its main demands were better protection of human rights; the protection of Iceland's sovereignty and language; and guarantees that the nation's resources would remain in public ownership. The Forum also agreed that the weighted votes that give proportionally higher influence to rural constituencies should be abolished and each vote should have equal weight. It also called for representatives to be elected through preferential voting (National Forum 2010).

The parliament-appointed seven-member Constitutional Committee, consisting of constitutional experts with links to specific political parties and also non-specialist party trustees, represented the country's political parties. The Constitutional Committee had a dual task: first to administer the National Forum and draw conclusions from its deliberations and then to list potential changes to the constitution for the Constitutional Assembly to consider. Soon, though, the Committee was split in two camps, each proposing its own suggestions for change, which were listed in its report as propositions A and propositions B. This highlighted the high level to which the Committee's task had become politicised.

The third and final component of the three-phase process was a nationally elected Constitutional Assembly. On 27 November 2010, Icelanders were called to the polls to elect between twenty-five and thirty-one individuals, depending on gender distribution, who were trusted with the actual drafting of a new constitution. In its operations, the Constitutional Assembly – which later turned into the Constitutional Council – partly corresponds to the Citizens' Assembly in British Columbia, the Dutch BurgerForum and the Irish Constitutional Convention. Unlike these bodies, however, the Icelandic Constitutional Council was not randomly or self-selected but nationally elected; this was also partly the case of the Australian Citizens Assembly (Webb 2000).

As has been mentioned before and, indeed, similarly to some of the other cases, the process in Iceland was, right from the beginning, heavily politicised. Because of this, the opposition of the IP and the lukewarm support of many governmental MPs diminished the input legitimacy of the process.

Problems and participation

In all, 522 candidates stood for election to the Constitutional Assembly, marking an unprecedented political involvement of ordinary citizens in Icelandic politics. The electoral system was based on the Irish voting system of PR Single Transferable Vote (PR-STV). Each candidate collected signatures from more than thirty supporters, which meant that almost 5 per cent of the entire population signed to support for one of the candidates. The vast number of candidates overwhelmed the media, who were faced with the impossible task of covering the politics and preferences of each of the numerous candidates. This was a special extraordinary election and thus it was only to be expected that the level of media coverage proved to be only one quarter of the normal coverage of periodically fixed Icelandic elections (Kolbeins 2012). Still, the entire macro-public was very much aware of the elections.

Only 37 per cent of the electorate participated in this unique election. Perhaps because of the troubled political climate, the political parties did not field candidates and interest organisations refrained from putting up candidates and, instead, gave public support to various individuals. Days before the election, however, the IP secretariat distributed to its members a list of candidates considered 'favourable' to the party. This low turnout and lack of participation further diminished input legitimacy.

Twenty-five members[4] from a broad range of backgrounds were elected, including a few of those the IP secretariat had listed in its circular. Among the elected were lawyers, artists, priests, professors, political scientists, media people, former MPs, doctors, a company board-member, a farmer, a campaigner for the rights of handicapped people, a mathematician, a nurse and a labour-union leader. Thus, representation was relatively broad. However, soon after the results were announced, opponents of the process complained that only previously well known individuals had been elected, mostly from the ranks of the left-leaning Reykjavik elite. Though, most were not affiliated with any political party or party-political association, this criticism further undermined input legitimacy.

To deal with the complexity of the voting and the fact that voters would have to spend much more time in the ballot booths than in a parliamentary election, given the length of the ballot paper, the electoral authorities decided to change the set-up, mainly by increasing the number of election booths within polling stations. This proved to have grave consequences for input legitimacy when, in January 2011, the six justices appointed to rule on the election declared it null and void on purely technical grounds, concluding that, by adapting to the uniqueness of the election, the election authority had deviated too far from rules on Parliamentary elections, by which this extraordinary election was also to abide. There was never any hint of foul play (for more, see Meuwse 2012), however. The six-member court was split, four against two. Though all of the justices belonged to the Icelandic Supreme Court, this ruling was formally made by a special administrative ruling body, not the Supreme Court itself.

---

4. Þorvaldur Gylfason, professor of economics and newspaper columnsist; Salvör Nordal, Director of the Ethics Institute at Univeristy of Iceland; Ómar Ragnarsson, media presenter and nature-protection activist; Andrés Magnússon, physician; Pétur Gunnlaugsson, radio host; Þorkell Helgason, mathematics professor; Ari Teitsson, farmer; Illugi Jökulsson, writer and columnist; Freyja Haraldsdóttir, activist for rights of disabled people; Silja Bára Ómarsdóttir, lecturer in international politics; Örn Bárður Jónsson, pastor; Eiríkur Bergmann, associate professor of politics and newspaper columnist; Dögg Harðardóttir, manager and Christian religious activist; Vilhjálmur Þorsteinsson, investor; Þórhildur Þorleifsdóttir, theatre director and former MP for the Womens List; Pawel Bartoszek, mathematician and newspaper columnist; Arnfríður Guðmundsdóttir, professor of theology; Erlingur Sigurdarson, high-school teacher; Inga Lind Karlsdóttir, TV presenter; Katrín Oddsdóttir, lawyer and activist; Guðmundur Gunnarsson, trade union chairman; Katrín Fjelsted, physician and former MP for the IP; Ástrós Gunnlaugsdóttir, political science student; Gísli Tryggvason, consumer spokesperson; and Lýður Árnason, filmmaker and physician.

This was an extraordinary decision, which delivered an almost fatal blow to the whole process. The ruling was criticised for 'not only being poorly reasoned but ... also materially wrong' (Axelsson 2011). Professor Gylfason, one of the elected members, has indicated that the leading judge in the case, a 'staunch party man' of the IP, was suspected of having drafted one of the complaints, which, in his capacity as the judge leading the charge he then 'used as pretext for invalidating the election' (Gylfason 2012: 11). This, however, has not been proved.

Faced with this unique decision – the first general national election in modern times to be invalidated, not only in Iceland but in the whole Western world (Gylfason 2012: 11), and solely on trivial technical grounds – the governmental Parliament majority decided to simply appoint those individuals elected to the Constitutional Assembly to a Constitutional Council, which would perform more or less the same task. This, however, severely damaged the input legitimacy of the process. The IP argued against the appointment and one of the Assembly members-elect, Inga Lind Karsldóttir, who had a connection with the IP, refused the appointment. A substitute was brought in in her place.

Throughput legitimacy

The Constitutional Council thus started its work in April 2011 in a rather awkward situation. The economy had recently collapsed amid a financial crisis, the previous government had been ousted as a result of widespread popular protest and the Council's own mandate had been called into question by the invalidation of the constitutional election. The Council, working full time, was endowed with a 700-page report from the Constitutional Committee and an extensive 'value map' from the thousand-person National Forum. This extensive information-gathering and citizens' input helped to compensate for some of its lost legitimacy.

Despite the very different positions espoused by its members, the Council was able to unite on three main initial tasks: first, to update the human-rights chapter of the old constitution so that it incorporated social and civil rights and to add a chapter on nature-protection and the collective ownership of natural resources; second, to divide more clearly the branches of government; and third, to develop functional tools for increasing direct democracy, for example, with preferential voting in parliamentary elections and clear guidelines on how the people could call for referendums on vital issues. Council-members broke into three working-groups along these lines.

Opinion polls indicated that popular trust of Parliament was at an historic low, with less than one in ten feeling content with its work. Professor Jón Ólafsson claims that the Council made a point of distancing itself from Parliament, in fact, and that some of its members 'expressed openly their hostility to the "political elites"'. He claims that the members saw themselves as representing the general public rather than the privileged elite and that as a result of widespread anti-establishment rhetoric, the Council 'alienated itself from the Parliament' (Ólafsson 2012).

A 'crowd-sourced' constitution?

Contrary to the advice of many constitutional experts, such as Professor Jon Elster, who visited Iceland at the time, the Council decided to open up its work to the public as much as possible. This interactive engagement with the public was at the expense of the more typical distance at which professional politics takes place. The whole process had been heavily politicised in a harsh exchange between politicians. The Council believed that inviting all those interested in participating might help it regain legitimacy in the eyes of the public. This is similar to the practice of the Belgium G1000.

This opening-up was achieved through a variety of means. Through social-media outlets like Facebook and Twitter, the Council attracted several thousand submissions in addition to 370 formal proposals via more traditional correspondence. On Facebook alone, there were 3,600 posts. The Council also put its meetings and working documents online. Even foreigners who could overcome the language barrier were allowed to participate. Viewing it from a distance, the international media branded the Council's production as the world's first 'crowd-sourced' constitution, drafted by the interested public in clear view of the world. The drafting process was covered extensively not only by the Icelandic media but also by most major international news outlets. The Council welcomed this attention and used it to its advantage in domestic politics. 'Crowd-sourced' was, however, never a realistic description of the drafting process.

Despite open access and the existence of a robust secretariat staffed with many experts to assist the Council, the Council was not able to plough through all the extensive public input systematically, as it only had four months to complete its task. Some Council members never looked at any of it; it was entirely up to each member to navigate through the information and decide what to take in or consider. Furthermore, members never felt obligated to adopt inputs they did not agree with.

Many in the international media, including the *International Herald Tribune* (Morris 2012), nevertheless reported that enthusiasts for open government around the world were insisting that the Icelandic constitutional process should serve as model for how ordinary people could wrest power from the political elites that have monopolised political decision-making.

Iterative deliberation and voting

Professor Jón Ólafsson (2012) claims that, in effect, the Council worked without a clear methodological approach to the main principles of its work. However, rather than developing the document in a traditional linear fashion, the Council had decided to apply the 'agile' method of iteration (doing things in many rounds rather than in consecutive order, often used in software development), completing the document gradually in several rounds.

The three committees deliberated separately on articles within their particular segment. Each week, the committees presented their proposal to the Council plenary meetings, which were open to the public. Council debated each proposed article and agreed on relevant changes and amendments before they were posted on the Council website as provisional articles for perusal by the public. When comments and suggestions had been received from the public as well as from experts, the Council posted revised versions of the articles. In this manner, the document was gradually refined and the final version of the new constitution arrived at in several rounds of revision. In all, the Council published twelve separate drafts. In a final round, the Council voted on each article and any proposed amendments to them by show of hands. The decision-making process in the Council was thus a mixture of deliberation and open-ballot voting.

Despite wide initial differences in opinion and occasional vigorous open disputes, the Council adopted the new constitution unanimously. The emphasis on solidarity and unanimity grew stronger among the members as their work progressed, precisely because it was viewed as being vital in order for the Council to present a unified front against anticipated political resistance. In this way, the Council was focused on increasing its throughput legitimacy, having suffered in the input phase. In this it was relatively successful. Scholars in the Comparative Constitutions Project at Chicago University, who analysed the draft, claimed that this constitution-making process was tremendously innovative and participatory and concluded that it would be at 'the cutting edge of ensuring public participation in on-going governance' (Elkins, Ginsburg and Melton 2012).

Content

In the mandate issued to it by Parliament, the Constitutional Council was instructed to address a number of tasks: re-examining the foundation of Icelandic governance; the role of the legislature and the executive and their division of power; the role of the President of the Republic; the independence of the judiciary; the electoral system and constituencies; public participation, including use of referendums; the transfer of state powers to international organisations; and ownership of natural resources. In addition, the Parliamentary resolution stipulated that the Council could include other constitutional matters on its own initiative.

Amongst the main challenges facing the Council was that the mechanics of the existing constitution, which was based on the Danish nineteenth-century governmental model, no longer mirrored the democratic governmental system in Iceland. Since independence in 1944, comprehensive constitutional debate had been needed but mostly absent, fostering an ever-growing list of constitutional problems.

The 1944 Constitution, for example, attributed a range of governmental duties and powers to Iceland's largely ceremonial President – for example, to appoint ministers, suspend Parliament, negotiate international treaties and even exempt people from specific laws. After all these and many other powers were given to the President, however, they were then whisked back in two articles stating that the President transferred his power to government ministers and was not responsible for governmental decisions. This had left an ambiguity as to the proper role of the President and even as to the nature of the governmental system. Traditionally, the President had operated as a ceremonial head of state but not as head of the government. As in other parliamentary democracies, the Prime Minister was the head of the government. Iceland had therefore been classified as a parliamentary republic, like Germany, Greece, Ireland and Italy. However, in recent years, some scholars had been reinterpreting the constitution as describing a semi-presidential system (for example, Kristjánsson 2012). President Ólafur Ragnar Grímsson, first elected in 1996, had gradually been accepting that interpretation in his description of the role. In the 2012 presidential election, candidates could not even agree on the role of the President or the nature of the governmental system (Bergmann, 2012).

Despite the Constitution's stipulation that governmental power could not be transferred abroad, because of ambiguity in the nineteenth-century text, Iceland had been able to enter into the European Economic Area agreement, which had brought the country into the EU single market in exchange for its implementing all relevant EU laws. The 1944 Constitution was full of these sorts of misconceptions, which had resulted in ambiguous and often contradictory interpretations of the text. The Council understood that the greatest danger of the old Constitution was that the blurred lines between branches of government made it possible for strong leaders to gradually gain control of all three branches of government – the executive, the legislative and even the judiciary – through political appointments to the bench. The Council therefore came to the conclusion that it would be impossible for a twenty-first century republic to keep the old constitutional model; it would be like basing a new space-shuttle design on the architecture of a horse-drawn cart.

The 1944 Constitution had allowed the executive to assume power from the legislature and the courts. Through the decades, leaders of coalition governments had gained almost complete control of Parliament. This had been illustrated when the leaders of the IP and the PP (Prime Minister Davíð Oddsson and Foreign Minister Halldór Ásgrímsson) had decided, without consulting Parliament or any of their colleagues, to support the US by enlisting Iceland in the 'coalition of the willing' before the invasion of Iraq in 2003. Another example is found in the appointment of judges to the Supreme Court. The justice ministers of the same parties (IP and PP) had, throughout the decades, appointed the vast majority of all new judges. Under the proposed constitution, Parliament would be more independent from the government and the misleading articles on the purely formal power of the President were to be removed or moved to more appropriate sections.

Furthermore, as expected and discussed before, the proposed constitution explicitly stipulated that natural resources were the collective property of the nation. As has already been mentioned, this might partly explain the IP's opposition to the draft constitution.

Output legitimacy

By mid 2011, Council members had reached a consensus on a draft constitution in a process with relatively high throughput legitimacy. This came as a surprise to many, including Parliament, which had no set plan for how to proceed. One of the main reasons for the cool reception given to the draft in Parliament was clearly that the Council had refused to co-operate with Parliament or political parties on the drafting. Members of Parliament and others among the political elite therefore felt alienated from the draft. The experience of the Irish Constitutional Convention, on the contrary, indicates that involving politicians in the process helps to secure output legitimacy, as MPs became campaigners for the process within Parliament, which, in the end, has to implement a mini-public's recommendations.

No sooner had the Icelandic draft constitution been handed over than the traditional political quarrel started – perhaps not surprisingly as, throughout the process, the establishment of the IP had fought tooth and nail against the entire project (for more detail, see Gylfason 2012). Holding an extremely fragile and fluctuating majority (several MPs of both coalition and opposition sides changed parties during the term), the coalition government spent a full year navigating the draft through parliamentary procedures. Another hurdle emerged when President Ólafur Ragnar Grímsson voiced strong objections to the draft – arguing that the role of the President would have been significantly altered in the new governmental system (Bergmann 2012). This put a further dent in output legitimacy.

The referendum

Finally, Parliament settled on holding an advisory referendum on 20 October 2012. Six questions were on the ballot. The primary question was whether the draft should be the basis for a new constitution for Iceland. Five sub-questions dealt with the most debated articles in the draft: public ownership of natural resources; increased use of referendums; increased personal voting; equal weights of votes; and disestablishing the state church. Around half of the electorate turned out for the referendum, of which two-thirds accepted the draft as the basis of a new constitution, which Parliament was to complete (Niðurstöðum þjóðaratkvæðagreiðslunnar lýst 2012).

This overwhelming support for the proposal came as a surprise to many. The fate of the whole exercise was, however, still in the hands of Parliament. Running out of time leading up to the April 2013 election, the government reached an agreement to delegate the decision on the bill for a new constitution to the next Parliament. Further changes to the bill were required by the new Parliament, which appointed a new parliamentary constitutional committee to navigate through the complexities in which the process was entangled. In the meantime, the Venice Commission of the Council of Europe, which advises governments on constitutional changes, had praised the process and spirit of the draft while also recommending further analysis on the more radical changes (European Commission for Democracy Through Law (Venice Commission) 2013).

Similar to the fate of some previously mentioned initiatives, Iceland's participatory constitutional deliberative process also fell victim to traditional party-political infighting. Throughout the process, the government ran into difficulties in dragging the reform over all the hurdles of necessary democratic processes. In the post-crisis climate, it was the Icesave dispute, which Iceland had with the UK and the Netherlands over responsibility for the deposits of the fallen Landbanki in those countries, which was to dictate political developments. After winning a landslide victory in the 2009 election immediately after the crash, the two left-wing government parties were heavily punished in the 2013 election. Their support started to deteriorate when they pushed the first Icesave agreement with the UK and the Netherlands through Parliament in late 2009. The majority support for the draft constitution did not translate into support for pro-draft-constitution parties; rather, other issues like the Icesave dispute and concerns over household debt dominated the election campaign. Thus, though the referendum's positive result for the draft might have boosted output legitimacy in the short term, it proved insufficient to do so in the long term.

2013 parliamentary election

In the 2013 election, the SDA and LGM were punished heavily by the electorate. In fact, the SDA suffered the greatest loss of any party in the history of the republic. The volatility of Icelandic politics was perhaps best illustrated by the fact that two new parties were able to pass the 5 per cent threshold necessary to win seats in Parliament in the 2013 election. Bright Future, which was created out of representatives from the Best Party and splinters of the SDA, won six seats and the Icelandic version of the international Pirate Party won four seats. This was the first time a Pirate Party had won seats in any national parliamentary election. However, even though a record number of the electorate voted for non-traditional parties, the conventional party system withstood the challenges to it. With the Citizens' Movement dissolving in the 2013 election, the revolutionary forces from four years before were mostly gone.

The 2013 election marked a paradigm-shift away from post-crisis politics and, as a result, the constitutional reform process lost momentum, similarly to the fate of proposals out of the Dutch BurgerForum. After the election, the PP was able to lead a new right-of-centre coalition government with the IP (the IP was weakened after its leadership had decided to support the left-wing government's second Icesave agreement in late 2011). Subsequently the new government quietly abandoned the constitutional process and appointed its own constitutional committee, consisting of party-political appointees, including many of the country's most conservative constitutional lawyers. In September 2014, the chairman of the committee, Professor Emeritus Sigurður Líndal, resigned, saying there was neither interest nor reason to change the current constitution (Pétursson 2014). Interestingly, however, his successor, civil servant Páll Þórhallsson, said in a radio interview that the committee would base its work on the recent constitutional drafting process (Þórhallsson 2014). Furthermore, some of the opposition parties in Parliament have stated that they would attempt to ratify the proposed constitution if they were in government. The process might thus still be alive at the time of writing.

Conclusion

The Icelandic post-crisis constitutional process is an example of a political reform initiative instigated in the wake of crisis, in a bid to regain lost democratic legitimacy. Such constitutional mini-publics have been operated in Australia, Canada, Holland, Ireland and Belgium. Apart from Ireland, where the government agreed to put some of the Convention recommendations to referendum, these mini-publics have not yet resulted in much significant political change. The same is true for the Icelandic constitutional process, which was repeatedly hijacked by party-political infighting. Playing on Elster's (1995) count of the successive 'waves' of constitution-making, a new wave has thus not yet gathered much momentum.

The low turnout in the extraordinary election did not help in securing input legitimacy for the Icelandic process. The entire exercise was then almost killed off when the Supreme Court annulled the Constitutional Assembly election on technical grounds and Parliament appointed those elected to the Constitutional Council, trusted with the same tasks. From the outset, many criticised the whole exercise as a pet project of Prime Minister Sigurðardóttir, even an unwelcome distraction from dealing with serious economic reform, which was of much more vital interest to the public. This further undermined the input legitimacy of the exercise from the outset.

Lost legitimacy was somewhat won back in the throughput phase. Public participation was high and the deliberative process within the Council proved successful and was celebrated in media. All of the members actively participated throughout and, in the end, Council unilaterally approved the draft constitution. Thus, throughput legitimacy was high.

Furthermore, when the electorate approved the proposed constitution by two-thirds in a national referendum, much of the legitimacy that was lost with the Supreme Court ruling was won back in the early output phase. However, caught in a new critical order of Iceland's post-crisis politics, the constitutional process, like many other proposals for political reform, again ran into trouble in the implementation phase. The Constitutional Council had, furthermore, attracted powerful enemies, for example, much of Parliament, the President and the vastly influential fishing-industry lobby, who combined to undermine its operation and proposals. In the end, the project failed in terms of the draft being ratified as Iceland's new constitution.

Still, the process, perhaps somewhat paradoxically, served as a healing exercise for society after the crash. The exercise stimulated wide public discussion, in which ordinary citizens were able to contribute to the promise of a resurrected and reformed Iceland. The exercise has therefore contributed to the heightened expectation of greater public participation in public decision-making. Whether that is turned into permanent change is another story.

After the crash of 2008, many ambitious proposals and initiatives for widespread political reform were caught in what can be described as a new critical order that was taking hold in post-crisis Iceland, which was marked by political infighting. The post-crisis left-wing government failed in its quest to create a New

Iceland, from the ruins of the old. Though former Prime Minister Geir Haarde was, in a controversial move, found guilty of not holding enough government meetings leading up to the crash, politicians were not really held accountable for the devastating events. However, quite a few of the leading bankers found to be responsible for the crisis were investigated and some heavy sentences were handed down. Still, for the most part, those involved were able to embark upon new business ventures. Meanwhile, the government was not able to push the Icesave agreement through referendums and opposition to EU membership grew, ultimately bringing the accession negotiations to a halt. Likewise, the constitutional process was also caught in the political infighting characterising the new critical order in which most proposals for reform were discredited.

Interestingly, however, regardless of whether the process will ever lead to any significant change in Iceland, the exercise attracted substantial attention from abroad. Countless articles have been written about it in international media and the Icelandic case has been the subject of academic studies in many books, seminars and conferences around the world. Its lessons have been reported in relation to similar exercises elsewhere, for example, in discussions around the Irish Constitutional Convention and in debates in the UK on a possible British Constitutional Convention in the wake of the Scottish independence referendum in September 2014 (see, for example, Renwick 2014). Furthermore, to mention just one more example, the Icelandic process was reportedly partly used as a model in a constitutional-reform process in Mexico.[5] Thus, despite perhaps failing nationally, its spirit has spread widely abroad, which counts as significant output legitimacy.

---

5. Information reported in presentation by Mexican senator Mario Delgado Carillo at ITS RIO event, Democracy & Technology Expert Meeting, Rio de Janeiro, Brazil, 29 August 2014.

References

Ackerman, B. (1998) *We The People*, vol. 2, *Transformations*, Cambridge, MA: Harvard University Press.

Axelsson, R. (2011) 'Comments on the Decision of the Supreme Court to invalidate the election to the Constitutional Assembly', University of Iceland, available at: http://www.dv.is/blogg/tresmidja/2011/2/2/urskurdur-haestarettar-maladur-melinu-smaerra/ (accessed 17 March 2016).

Bergmann, E. (2012) Svarti Pétur – breytt staða forseta Íslands og frumvarp Stjórnlagaráðs, *Skírnir*, (spring) available at: http://www.academia.edu/6535298/Svarti_Pétur_-_Breytt_staða_forseta_Íslands_og_frumvarp_Stjórnlagaráðs (accessed 26 January 2016).

—   (2014) *Iceland and the International Financial Crisis: Boom, bust and recovery*, Basingstoke, UK and New York: Palgrave Macmillan.

Caluwaerts, D., and Reuchamps, M. (2015) 'Strengthening democracy through bottom-up deliberation: an assessment of the internal legitimacy of the G1000 project', *Acta Politica* 50(2): 151–170.

Elkins, Z., Ginsburg, T., and Melton, J. (2012) 'A review of Iceland's draft constitution', Comparative Constitutions Project, *Constitutional Review: Iceland 2012*, October 14, available at: http://comparativeconstitutionsproject.org/wp-content/uploads/CCP-Iceland-Report.pdf (accessed 26 January 2016).

Elster, J. (1995) 'Forces and mechanisms in the constitution-making process', *Duke Law Journal* 45(2): 364–96.

European Commission for Democracy Through Law (Venice Commission) (2013) *Draft Opinion on the Draft New Constitution of Iceland*, Strasbourg, available at: http://www.venice.coe.int/webforms/documents/?pdf=CDL-AD(2013)010-e (accessed 28 January 2016).

Fillmore-Patrick, H. (2013) *The Iceland Experiment (2009–2013): A participatory approach to constitutional reform*, Sarajevo: Democratization Policy Council, available at: http://dpc.djikic.com/uimages/pdf/dpc%20policy%20note%202_%20the%20iceland%20experiment.pdf (accessed 26 January 2016).

Gylfason, T. (2012) 'From collapse to constitution: the case of Iceland', available at: http://papers.ssrn.com/sol3/papers.cfm?abstract_id=2034241 (accessed 26 January 2016).

Hálfdanarson, G. (2001) *Íslenska þjóðríkið: uppruni og endimörk*, Reykjavík, IS: Hið íslenska bókmenntafélag.

Jessop, B. (2004) 'Critical semiotic analysis and cultural political economy', *Critical Discourse Studies* 1(2): 159–74.

Jóhannesson, G. T. (2011) 'Tjaldað til einnar nætur: uppruni bráðabirgðastjórnarskrárinnar', *Icelandic Review of Politics & Administration* 7(1) 61–72.

Kolbeins, G. H. (2012) 'The Icelandic media coverage of the constitutional assembly election', *Icelandic Review of Politics & Administration* 8(2): 367–88.

Kristjánsson, S. (2012) 'Frá nýsköpun lýðræðis til óhefts flokkavalds: Fjórir forsetar Íslands 1944–1996', *Skírnir*, (spring).

Meuwse, A. (2015) 'Popular constitution-making: the case of Iceland', in Galligan, D. and Versteeg, M. (eds) *The Social and Political Foundations of Constitutions*, Cambridge, UK: Cambridge University Press.

Morris, H. (2012) 'Crowdsourcing Iceland's Constitution', *International Herald Tribune*, 24 October, available at: http://rendezvous.blogs.nytimes.com/2012/10/24/crowdsourcing-icelands-constitution/?_r=0 (accessed 29 January 2016).

Niðurstöðum þjóðaratkvæðagreiðslunnar lýst (2012) [Official website of the National Electoral Commission of Iceland], available at: http://landskjor.is/landkjorstjorn/frettir-tilkynningar/nr/110 (accessed 26 January 2016).

Pétursson, H. H. (2014) 'Formaður stjórnarskrárnefndar hættir störfum', *Vísir*, 13 September, available at: http://www.visir.is/formadur-stjornarskrarnefndar-haettir-storfum/article/2014140919491 (accessed 17 March 2016).

Ólafsson, J. (2012) 'An experiment in Iceland: crowdsourcing a constitution', Bifrost University, working paper, incomplete draft, available at: http://www.yale.edu/polisci/conferences/epistemic_democracy/jOlafsson.pdf (accessed 29 January 2016).

Rahvakogu (n.d.) 'What is Rahvakogu?', available at: https://www.rahvakogu.ee/pages/what-is-rahvakogu (accessed 29 January 2016).

Renwick, A. (2014) *After the Referendum. Options for a constitutional convention*, London, UK: Constitution Society.

Sigurðardóttir, J. (2011) 'Áramótaávarp forsætisráðherra', [Prime Minister's New Year's Eve address], available at: http://www.forsaetisraduneyti.is/radherra/raedur_greinar_JS/nr/7023 (accessed 29 January 2016).

Teubner, G. (2011) 'A constitutional moment – the logics of "hit the bottom"', in Kjaer, P., Teubner, G. and Febbrajo, A. (eds) *The Financial Crisis In Constitutional Perspective: The dark side of functional differentiation*, Oxford, UK and Portland, OR: Hart Publishing.

Þjóðfundur (2010) 'The main conclusions from the National Forum 2010', available at: http://thjodfundur2010.is/frettir/lesa/item32858/ (accessed 29 January 2016).

Þórhallsson, P. (2014) 'Upp úr skotgröfunum', *Morgunútvarpið*, RÚV available at: http://www.ruv.is/frett/upp-ur-skotgrofunum (accessed 29 January 2016).

Wampler, B. (2007) *Participatory Budgeting in Brazil: Contestation, cooperation, and accountability*, University Park, PA: Pennsylvania State University Press.

Webb, M. (2000) 'When no means no: the failure of the Australian 1999 republican referendum and its root in the constitutional convention of 1988', Institute of Governmental Studies working paper, available at: http://escholarship.org/uc/item/4hp7z2qf.pdf (accessed 29 January 2016).

Chapter Three

The Irish Constitutional Convention: A Case of 'High Legitimacy'?

Jane Suiter, David M. Farrell and Clodagh Harris[1]

Internationally, the number of instances of citizen-involvement in issues of constitutional reform, whether through referendums, public initiatives or, in a small number of cases, through the creation of mini-publics that involve randomly selected citizens in public deliberation, has been growing. In December 2012, the Irish government joined this trend by establishing the Irish Constitutional Convention,[2] whose first working session was held on the weekend of 26–7 January 2013.

The unprecedented economic and financial crises that began in 2008 were a motivating factor in the creation of the Convention. Inside the euro area, Ireland was among the countries most affected by the crisis, due to its high dependence on international short-term funding (Lane 2012). The crises also prompted a reassessment of relations between the government and citizens (Farrell *et al.* 2012), with many questioning whether the existing political system was fit for purpose. There were some who argued that using a deliberative approach to reform the Irish Constitution would be valuable as it would directly involve citizens in decisions on constitutional reform, thereby enhancing diminished democratic legitimacy and potentially re-configuring democratic practice. It was this discussion that led to the decision to establish the Irish Constitutional Convention.

The Convention emerged out of a compromise between the two parties, Fine Gael and Labour, that came to power after the so-called 'electoral earthquake' of the 2011 general election. This election, which occurred in the midst of the economic crisis, saw the electoral wipe-out of Ireland's until-then-dominant Fianna Fáil party (Lutz 2003; also see Gallagher and Marsh 2011).

In the run-up to the February 2011 general election, all parties had included in their election manifestos or other policy documents proposals for establishing citizen-oriented deliberative forums (Suiter and Farrell 2011) to discuss possible constitutional reforms in a number of areas. Arguably, their decision to opt for citizen-led deliberative approaches was, at least partly, in response to public debates that questioned whether the Irish political system was fit for purpose,

---

1. The authors were members of the Academic and Legal Support Group that provided expert advice to the Convention.

2. See http://www.constitution.ie (accessed 8 February 2016); all reports, live stream archive, submissions, votes and so on are available on this site.

such as those led by the Political Studies Association of Ireland through its blog (available at: www.politicalreform.ie; accessed 12 February 2016).

The parties that formed the new coalition after the election had different ideas on such a body's composition and remit. In Fine Gael's case the proposal was specific: for a British-Columbia-style citizens' assembly (see Fournier *et al.* 2011) to consider electoral reform (which, given that the electoral system is embedded in the Constitution, amounts to a constitutional-reform issue). Labour's plan was more ambitious: it proposed the establishment of a constitutional convention (made up of equal proportions of politicians, experts and ordinary citizens) to consider a root-and branch-review of the Irish Constitution.

In designing the Convention, Irish policy-makers were strongly influenced by the citizens' assemblies on electoral reform in the Canadian provinces of British Columbia (2004) and Ontario (2007) and the Dutch citizens' forum (*BurgerForum*) of 2006. The Irish We the Citizens pilot citizens' assembly (2011), instituted by political scientists in Ireland to demonstrate to senior policy-makers and politicians that Irish citizens could be trusted to deliberate on complex matters (see Farrell *et al.* 2013 for a full description) was also influential.[3]

While following in the wake of previous deliberative forums, Ireland's Convention on the Constitution also followed new pathways in a number of areas, such as its composition, remit and outcomes. These, in turn, had an impact to varying degrees on its input, throughput and output legitimacy. This chapter examines the Convention across each of these dimensions of legitimacy, with reference to the criteria presented in the introduction to this volume, and highlights its innovations and the challenges it faced.

Input legitimacy

Representation

The most innovative aspect of the Convention when compared with other citizens' assemblies was the inclusion of political representatives. The Convention was made up of 100 members consisting of sixty-six citizens, thirty-three elected legislators and a chair, Tom Arnold (the former chief executive of a leading international charity). The citizen-members were selected at random by an independent market-research company, whose brief was to ensure that the membership was a reasonable reflection of the population in terms of gender, age, region, education and socio-economic status – a tall order with just sixty-six individuals but one that was broadly achieved (*see* Table 3.1). To allow for the possibility of members not being available for all meetings, a list of substitute members was drawn up

---

3. That initiative first travelled the country and culminated in a weekend-long citizen assembly made up of randomly selected members who debated on political reform and fiscal policy. It did not, however, have any politician-members: that innovation was unique to the Convention. Many of the academic team who founded that initiative went on to work on the Convention and its *modus operandi* was seen as a template for the running of the Convention.

Table 3.1: Citizen-members: age and social class

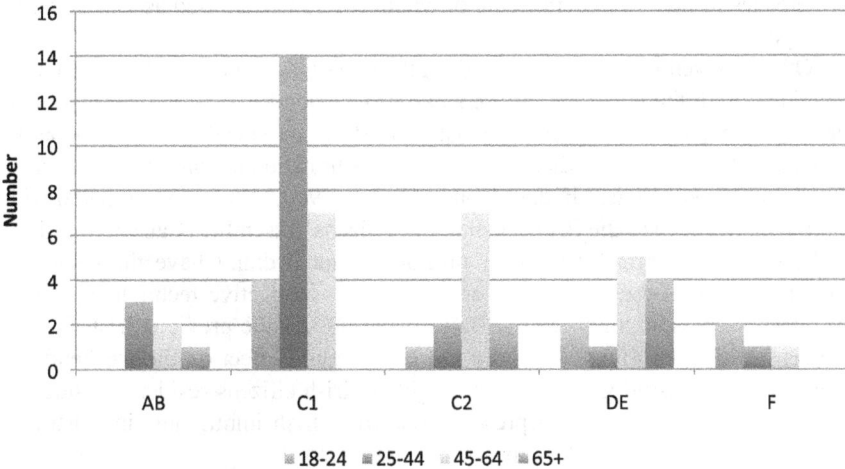

18-24 25-44 45-64 65+

at the same time. However, there were no homeless people, new Irish citizens or members of the travelling community on the Convention. This was due to a combination of factors: the recruiting techniques employed; the small sample size; and the lack of any specific effort to target these groups. Members were provided with travel expenses and with all accommodation and meals but no honorarium was paid; this was in large part influenced by the low budget for the process, discussed later in this chapter.

The political parties themselves determined how their members were selected: for example, Fine Gael asked for volunteers and the party whip selected the nominees, whereas the Labour Parliamentary Party voted on their nominees. All major political parties on the island of Ireland as well a group of independent representatives were invited to send members to the Convention. The inclusion of politicians from both sides of the border was novel: all the Northern Irish parties sent representatives, with the exception of the two Northern Irish Unionist parties (the DUP and the UUP), who declined. The parties' allocations were proportionate to their representation in parliament.

As was the case in other deliberative forums, concerted efforts were made to engage with those who had not been chosen to participate in the Convention – the 'maxi-public'. Broadcast, print and social media were used to invite public submissions. The volume of submissions received from citizens and interest-groups varied from topic to topic, with a few of the more controversial topics attracting very large numbers of submissions, discussed further later in this chapter. In all, the Convention received 2,500 submissions that ranged from single-line emails to lengthy and detailed proposals. Civil-society groups played a key role in bringing the work of the Convention to the attention of their members and the maxi-public, thereby enhancing its input legitimacy. They also had a crucial part to play in bringing to bear, through the submission-process and contributions to panels and regional meetings of the Convention (more on this later) the opinions and preferences of their members, some of whom could be classified as marginalised from politics.[4]

Other Convention efforts to include of the maxi-public included live-streaming meetings (with the exception of the small-group roundtable discussions); online posting of copies of the presentations; and setting up social-media accounts to engage with as wide an audience as possible, both nationally and internationally. The Convention's limited budget (approximately €900,000) when compared with similar bodies such as the British Columbia Citizens' Assembly (Can$ 5.5 million) and the Dutch BurgerForum (€5.1 million) meant it didn't have the resources to have a state-of-the-art website or to use truly interactive technology, which had been seen as strengths of the Belgian G1000 and the previous Irish We the Citizens initiatives. However, it did use ICT to good effect on the weekend the Convention discussed granting voting rights to Irish citizens resident outside the state. That weekend included presentations from Irish immigrants in Australia, North America, France and so on.

Remit: agenda-setting powers

The July 2012 resolution of the Houses of the Oireachtas (Irish houses of parliament) that established the Convention set out a specific remit, asking it to examine the following issues:

- Reduction of the presidential term of office to five years;
- Reduction of the voting age to 17;
- Review of the Dáil (lower house of parliament) electoral system;
- Irish citizens' right to vote at Irish Embassies in presidential elections;
- Provisions for same-sex marriage;
- Amendment to the existing clause in the Irish Constitution on the role of women in the home and encouraging greater participation of women in public life;
- Increasing the participation of women in politics; and
- Removal of the offence of blasphemy from the Constitution.
- '[F]ollowing the completion of the above reports, such other relevant constitutional amendments that may be recommended by it' (www. constitution.ie).

This somewhat eclectic mix of items, from the relatively 'cold' issue of the length of office of the Irish President (whose role is largely ceremonial) to the potentially 'hot' divisive issue of same-sex marriage, merely reflected the

---

4. Another feature of the Convention that set it aside from the citizens assemblies was the invitation given to advocacy groups to present their case to the convention members, thus allowing them a presence in the room.

decision of the inter-party negotiators of the parties that were forming a coalition government in 2011 to 'park' certain matters that were in their respective election manifestos and which couldn't be resolved easily during the febrile and intense negotiations that preceded the establishment of the coalition government.

Some initial criticisms of the Convention focused on its remit, which was criticised as too limited: for example Micheál Martin, leader of the main opposition party, Fianna Fail, described the agenda as unable to deliver any real political reform: 'At this moment of continued economic crisis and with lost public faith in the role of politics, proposing to give priority to discussing the President's term of office and the voting age is worse than ridiculous'.[5]

However, the Convention proved quite inventive in stretching its remit beyond the narrow confines set by the government, starting at its January 2013 weekend gathering – its first full meeting. There, the Convention considered two themes, namely, whether to reduce the voting age to seventeen and whether to reduce the President's term of office from seven years to five. Having read the briefing materials, heard from experts and advocacy groups and deliberated over the relevant arguments, the Convention members considered options that undoubtedly went beyond their brief. There was little dissent on this expansion of powers from the politician-members who belonged to the governing coalition that had initiated the Convention.[6] Specifically, the Convention voted in favour of:

- Reducing the voting age to sixteen (the age proposed by many of the advocacy groups promoting a reduced voting age), not seventeen (the age they were asked to consider);
- Reducing the age of candidacy for presidential candidates; and
- Giving citizens a direct role in the process of nominating presidential candidates. (The Convention voted against the proposal to reduce the presidential term.)

This willingness to extend the agenda beyond the specific question set by the government continued in all the remaining meetings. As Table 3.2 shows, this resulted in no fewer than forty specific recommendations by the Convention.

The Convention was also keen to make full use of the limited agenda-setting powers that permitted it to consider other possible areas for constitutional amendment. To determine which issues to discuss, the Convention actively encouraged submissions from the general public and civil society online and in writing. It also held nine regional meetings across the country to gather views on the issues that should be considered by the Convention. These were attended by almost 1000 people. In total, the Convention received over 800 public submissions

---

5.   'Constitution body reveals its members', 22 January 2013, available at: http://www.independent. ie/irish-news/constitution-body-reveals-its-members-28942991.html (accessed 8 February 2016).

6.   Privately, one politician-member noted that they were not at the Convention primarily as party representatives but as individual members; and thus they were not bound by the usual party discipline.

Table 3.2: Outcomes of Irish Constitutional Convention (as of 27 May 2015)

Topic	Convention's recommendations	% support[a]	Outcome
1. Reduction of presidential term of office to 5 years and align election date with local and European elections	No change to length of presidential term of office.	57	Government accepted.
	*Reduce minimum age of candidacy for presidential candidates.	50	Government accepted; referendum held 22 May 2015 (rejected).
	*Give citizens a say in the nomination process for presidential candidates.	94	Government rejected.
2. Reduction of voting age to 17	*Voting age should be reduced to 16.	52	Government accepted; then rescinded. Position now ambiguous.
3. Reform of clause on role of women in home and encouraging greater participation of women in public life	*Article 41.2 (on role of women) should be made gender-neutral to include other carers both 'in the home' and 'beyond the home'.	88	Government established task force; report awaited.
	Re: Art. 41.2.2 (state's support for carers), state should provide 'a reasonable level of support'.	b	Government established task force; report awaited.
4. Increasing participation of women in politics	* Constitution should be amended to include explicit provision on gender equality.	62	Government established task force; report awaited.
	Government action to encourage greater participation of women in politics.	97	Government established task force; report awaited.
	* Constitution should be amended to include 'gender-inclusive' language.	89	Government established task force; report awaited.
5. Provision for same-sex marriage	* Constitution should be amended to allow same-sex marriage.	79	Government accepted; referendum held 22 May 2015 (passed).
	State should enact laws incorporating necessary changed arrangements in regard to parentage, guardianship and upbringing of children.	81	Government accepted; legislation on adoption passed.
6. Review of Dáil electoral system	Electoral system should be amended to ensure smallest constituency size is 5-seater.	86	Government rejected.

Table 3.2 (continued)

Topic	Convention's recommendations	% support[a]	Outcome
	Electoral system should be amended to remove alphabetical order of candidates on ballot paper.	67	Electoral Commission should look into this.
	State should establish Electoral Commission.	97	Government accepted; public consultation in progress.
	Polling hours/days should be extended.	89	Electoral Commission should look into this.
	Better access to postal voting.	91	Government ignored.
	Improve accuracy of electoral register.	100	Government 'agreed' but committed to nothing new.
	Introduce measures to increase electoral turnout.	96	Government 'agreed' but committed to nothing new.
	Introduce political education programmes in schools.	95	Government 'agreed' but committed to nothing new.
	*There should be non-parliamentary ministers in government.	55	Government rejected.
	*Members of the Dáil should be required to resign their seats on being appointed to ministerial office.	59	Government rejected.
	*Citizen-initiatives should be introduced (for influencing parliamentary agenda and for calling referendums).	83	Government rejected.
7. Irish citizens' right to vote at Irish Embassies in Presidential elections	*Rights for citizens abroad and citizens in Northern Ireland to vote in presidential elections.	78	Government response expected imminently.
8. Removal of offence of blasphemy from Constitution	*Offence of blasphemy should be replaced by a new general provision to include criminalisation of incitement to religious hatred.	53	Government accepted; referendum promised but no date set.
	Sec. 36 of Defamation Act should be replaced by detailed legislative provisions to include religious hatred.	82	Government to give this 'more consideration'.

Table 3.2 (continued)

Topic	Convention's recommendations	% support[a]	Outcome
9. Dáil reform	*Constitutional reform to enhance status of office of Ceann Comhairle (Chair of the Dáil).	88	No response so far.
	*Constitutional reform to elect CC by secret ballot.	88	Government accepted.
	*Include references to Dáil committees in Constitution.	76	No response so far.
	*Amend Art. 17.2 re: government prior approval for expenditure proposals.	53	No response so far.
	Existing Dáil Reform Committee (DRC) should include external members and former TDs.	85	No response so far.
	DRC should bring forward proposals for genuine Dáil reform.	99	No response so far.
	Introduction of family-friendly hours.	63	No response so far.
	CC to chair a forum to set Dáil's agenda.	73	No response so far.
	Proportional allocation of committee chairs and secret ballot for their election.	84	Government accepted.
	More technical and professional resources for committees.	93	No response so far.
	Working Group of Committee Chairs should be given power to call Taoiseach.	70	No response so far.
	Introduce committee weeks.	89	No response so far.
	More 'free votes' on Dáil and committee business.	84	No response so far.
10. Economic, social and cultural rights	*Constitutional amendment to strengthen protection of ESC rights; that this be realised progressively, subject to maximum available resources and that this be justiciable.	85	No response so far.
	*In amending the Constitution, specific additional rights should be enumerated (housing, social security, etc.)	80–90	No response so far.

* Indicates those recommendations that should require a referendum to implement (18 by our estimation).
[a] The percentage support for a recommendation among ICC members. In some instances there were a series of votes on an item. The percentages reported here are the votes on the generic question. For more details, see the relevant ICC report. All available on www.constitution.ie.
[b] This option received plurality support out of a range of options.

on the 'any other amendment' item, covering thirty topics. These submissions were grouped into topic areas. Brief presentations on these areas were prepared by the Academic and Legal Support Group of the Convention, followed by a vote by the Convention members. The result was that the final two weekends were devoted to parliamentary reform and a proposal to include economic, social and cultural rights in the Constitution. Using an open, inclusive process to decide the two final topics added to the Convention's input legitimacy. However, the topics chosen were difficult to deal with: parliamentary reform because of the broad potential range of topics, the technicalities involved and the large gap in knowledge between politician- and citizen-members; economic, social and cultural rights due to the huge size of the issue.

Information

In support of epistemic completeness, an Academic and Legal Support Group, including four political scientists and a legal scholar, worked with the Convention in order to try to ensure full information was available to members. The group worked with the secretariat and suggested appropriate experts on both sides of each debate. It also supported the secretariat with the programme for each weekend. The Convention members had ultimate control over this process, as a steering-group comprising politicians and citizens could recommend changes to both the programme and the speakers for each weekend; although it was very rare for the steering group to do so. Indeed over 50 per cent of the members in a final survey rated the steering group as the 'least useful' aspect of the process. Whether this was a reflection of the preparatory work of the ALSG and the secretariat[7] or the tight management of the entire Convention process by the secretariat is difficult to tell.

The experts were then asked to liaise with one another to draw up accessible 'plain English' briefing documents on various aspects of each debate. These documents were emailed to all members in advance of the meeting, made available on the website and distributed in hard copy at the weekend meetings. In addition the experts – who included policy-makers, academics and interest-groups – made short presentations at the meetings and were available for both plenary and small-group question-and-answer discussions. In most areas, there were experts and interest-groups on both sides of the process; but in some areas, experts were asked to deliver a neutral assessment of both sides of the argument with interest-groups delivering opposing points of view. For example, on the issue of voting at age seventeen and reducing the presidential term, political scientists delivered the expertise on each side. On the issue of electoral reform, three political scientists spoke on the issues but not on directly opposing sides. In addition, there were

---

7.   The small secretariat consisted of three civil servants released from other duties throughout the process, supported by an intern. The members of the ALSG volunteered their time for free, as did all the experts who presented to the Convention.

advocates for both Yes and No arguing for their side. This was also the case on same-sex marriage, where legal and sociology experts talked on various issues, with advocates from same-sex-marriage groups and church groups providing opposing views. The Convention's small budget proved a limitation in this regard because its shortage of resources meant that, for the most part, the Convention was not in a position to fly in international experts. The final survey asked citizens which aspect of the process they found most useful in terms of making up their minds and some 79 per cent supported the expert plenary lectures. The final survey also asked a question on the impartiality of the experts. On the same-sex marriage and the electoral system weekends, 22 per cent of citizens felt there was some expert preference in both debates.

The Irish Convention contained a number of interesting features regarding inputs, in particular, how the Convention membership was comprised and the possibility to extend its brief. The inclusion of politicians was originally viewed with concern: it was feared that they would dominate the discussions and intimidate the citizen-members. The politician-members appeared to make every effort not to steal the limelight, however, particularly in the plenary discussions: as can be seen from the streamed video feed of these discussions. Indeed they could regularly be seen encouraging other members of their table to contribute. In addition there was little evidence of citizens being abusive towards politicians and, over time, their trust towards the politician-members increased: in our final survey, for instance, 75 per cent of citizen-members agreed or strongly agreed that their opinion of elected politicians had improved as a result of the Convention.

Throughput legitimacy

Participation

Convention meetings took place roughly once a month and lasted for most of a weekend (all day Saturday and all Sunday morning), with members voting at the end of the weekend on what recommendations to make. As mentioned at the outset, the mode of operation was 'deliberation', in which members were invited to engage in respectful discussions, asking questions of each other and the experts and citing reasons for their preferences. The process endeavoured to ensure substantially inclusive participation. What this meant was that the ninety-nine members (the chair being the hundredth) were arranged in circular tables of about eight (comprising a mixture of politician- and citizen-members). In general, there were either two or three politicians at each table, always from different parties, and table-composition differed from meeting to meeting.

At each table, there were also a trained facilitator and a note-taker. The role of the facilitator was to ensure that every member had an opportunity to speak; that discussions stayed on topic; and that members were respectful of other opinions. Note-takers noted each time a member spoke, to keep an eye to which members were contributing, with a view to flagging up potential problems if one or two individuals were dominating discussions at a table. Moreover, the feedback gathered by the Academic and Legal Support Group from the note-takers and facilitators at the end of each session ensured that the process and the work of the Convention was itself reflective and reflexive (brief feedback reports on preceding meetings were presented at subsequent meetings). The table allocations were rotated after each weekend so that members mixed with each other over the year.

Mindful of the gendered aspects of deliberation, the Convention endeavoured to make the process gender-inclusive by keeping a close eye on gender balance amongst those who presented to the Convention and the composition of the roundtables. Informed by the work of Karpowitz, Mendelberg and Shaker (2012), who found that women participate less than their equal share when in a minority and at equal rates when in a large majority (at least under majority rule), efforts were made to ensure that there was, at a bare minimum, gender-balance at each roundtable. In reality this proved difficult to achieve, as evidenced in Tables 3.3 and 3.4. From the outset, there were fewer female than male Convention members. This was in large part a consequence of low levels of female representation in the Irish parliament. The Convention's limited budget may also have had a negative impact here. Due to a shortage of resources, childcare facilities could not be offered, making it more difficult for women with young children to attend, thereby undermining the Convention's commitment to inclusion.

Table 3.3: Gender/member composition of the Convention

Male	Female	Citizens (male)	Citizens (female)	Politician (male)	Politician (female)
76	61	42	38	34	23

Table 3.4: Gender composition of roundtables

Weekend	Male majority	Equal	Female majority
1*	4(5)	7	2
2	4	5	4
3*	5(7)	5(7)	0(1)
4*	8(9)	4	0
5	7	6	0
6*	2(4)	5(8)	2
7	9	2	1
8	8	5	0
9	8	2	4
Total	55(61)	44(49)	13(14)

* Incomplete table-data for these weekends (not enough note-takers). For these weekends, the figures in parentheses refer to the table plan and the figures outside the parentheses are the confirmed figures from the available note-taker notes.

Achieving balance between information and small-group deliberation proved a challenge for the Convention. The tight timelines (ten topics over eight weekends) meant that very little time could be spent on a discussion of broader principles or values because a lot of essential and sometimes quite technical information needed to be covered. This was particularly true in the case of parliamentary reform, where the information gap between the politician- and citizen-members was too large to overcome in a single weekend. In this regard, the 'learning phase' included in the British Columbia and Ontario assemblies has much to commend it. However, feedback from politicians post-Convention revealed that 72 per cent of them thought that there was enough time to consider each issue and that it would have been too difficult to maintain interest over longer periods. Among citizens, 62 per cent felt that sufficient time had been devoted to each issue.

The roundtable deliberations were not recorded (apart, that is, from the notes provided by the note-takers). To have done so could have prevented members from freely expressing their views on the issues for discussion, particularly the more contentious ones. But without transcripts it is not possible to apply the Discourse Quality Index (DQI), an internationally regarded measurement of the quality of deliberation (see Steenbergen et al. 2003 and Steiner 2012 for a discussion of the DQI). Mindful of this limitation, instead, the research team included a number of Perceived Discourse Quality Index (PDQI) questions in the surveys distributed to members each weekend (for further information on the PDQI, see Caluwaerts and Reuchamps 2014). Questions asked included whether or not members changed their views as a result of the roundtable discussions and if they felt free to raise their views and ideas. For example, in the final survey, some 85 per cent disagreed or completely disagreed that 'I didn't always feel free to raise my views and ideas for fear of others' reactions'. On the whole, only 21 per cent disagreed or completely disagreed that they had changed their views.

Decision-making

The Convention made recommendations at the end of each meeting and sent a report to the Houses of the Oireachtas, to which government had committed to respond within four months. Decision-making in the Convention was through a mixture of deliberation and voting. A draft ballot paper was prepared during the course of the weekend's deliberations by the Academic and Legal Support Group and the Convention secretariat, with the assistance of the experts, and presented to the members for their approval on the Sunday morning. It is worth noting that every draft ballot paper generated discussion and required amendment, such was the level of members' engagement, interest and input.

The discussions endeavoured to meet the agreed deliberative democratic norms of inclusiveness, equality, 'reasonableness'/considered judgement and publicity (Smith 2009; Mansbridge et al. 2010) while the act of voting (in a secret ballot) gave all involved an equal say in the final decision. Ensuring the deliberations culminated in a vote also had the potential of delivering a clear verdict on the depth of feeling to the Government and media, necessary in particular when referendums to change the Constitution were being proposed.

The order of events for each weekend was generally as follows (depending on the topic, there was some variation):

- Short (15-minute) presentations by experts in the area (these varied for each topic), followed by questions and answers from the floor. The experts provided briefing documents several days in advance so that the members had an opportunity to inform themselves as well as possible. These 'plenary sessions' were televised and live-streamed (and are available on the website at www.constitution.ie).
- Small-group deliberation in closed session (no cameras).
- Plenary (open) session, to hear feedback from the deliberation.
- Presentations by a selection of advocacy groups.
- More deliberation, feedback and plenary discussions (possibly with more expert involvement).
- Agreement on the 'ballot paper' (to determine the Convention's recommendations on the topic).
- The vote on the recommendations. This was a simple majority vote of all members. All used the same ballot and it was a secret vote, so no breakdown of how politicians and citizens voted is possible.

Contextual independence

As a mini-public, the Convention was truly innovative in an Irish context, where, traditionally, participation tends to be associational and reflective of social-partnership processes that include business, trade unions, farming, and community and voluntary interests. A discussion of the merits and demerits of the consensual, collaborative nature of Ireland's neo-corporatist social-partnership model lies outside the scope of this chapter. However, it could be suggested that its collaborative, co-operative aspects were mirrored in the deliberations between the political and citizen-members and in the invitations to include various interest-groups in the panel discussions.

The Convention differed from other mini-publics as it included elected political representatives, including a member of the Irish government, from across a wide range of political parties on the island of Ireland. In this regard, it could be argued that it didn't operate in a political vacuum because the politician-members, as 'strategic actors', advanced the views and agenda of their political parties rather than deliberating in an open, non-strategic manner. However, the fact that the final recommendations were made using a secret ballot meant that political representatives were not bound by their party whip; also, it was clear from their plenary contributions that their deliberations were free and unconstrained. On the very few occasions when a political representative tried to push the Convention in a particular direction, the wider membership responded strongly in a negative manner.

The general tenor of debate in the media in advance of the Convention was negative. Journalists tended to focus on the lack of ambition of the topics to be covered and there was also controversy around the citizen-members' initial wish to remain anonymous. However, this is not to say that such coverage was extensive and, in the first sessions (on reducing the voting age and the presidential term of office), the members were largely deliberating in a public vacuum. At the other end of the scale, on the issue of same-sex marriage, there was a large amount of media attention and discussion in the weeks leading up the Convention meeting. In all cases, however, there were journalists present at the meetings, sitting at the back of the room, and reports in the media in the days following the deliberations. In addition, all plenary sessions were live-streamed and the Convention maintained a Twitter feed (@ConsConv) and hashtag (#ccven). Over the fourteen months of the Convention, there were over 15,000 uses of the hashtag, while the official account had 1,525 followers. For the most part, then, there was relatively weak contextual dependence.

By and large, the Convention fared well in terms of throughput legitimacy. The *modus operandi* that surrounds deliberative processes such as this, namely, the practice of having the members distributed in table-groups, each with a trained facilitator, meant that all members had opportunities to have their voices heard. Also, using a secret ballot to decide the recommendations ensured that all opinions were captured at the final decision-making stage.

Output legitimacy

We can begin to consider the output of the Irish Constitutional Convention under three separate headings: its impact on the Convention itself; on the general polity; and on society. As with its predecessors in Canada and the Netherlands, the initial indications are that the output in terms of the members themselves was positive. The final survey revealed that 100 per cent of the citizen-members, when asked if they regretted joining given the time and effort required, said 'no' and 79 per cent felt that good arguments were made.

Impact of the Convention

The terms of reference of the Convention stated that the Government would debate the contents of any report, on the floor of the parliament, within four months of the report being delivered. In terms of output, the Convention had an advantage in having politicians among the ranks of the members, in that this minimised the risk of a 'disconnect' between the Convention and the political class – a problem that was apparent in the cases of the Canadian and Dutch citizens' assemblies (Fournier *et al.* 2011). There, the political class quite deliberately stayed clear of the work of the citizens, making it difficult for these assemblies to gain much political purchase. Furthermore, what tended to occur – at least in the Dáil (the lower house) debates on the Convention's work to date – was that politician-members acted as 'cheerleaders' for the process. In all, some fifty political members have referred to the Convention during parliamentary debates to date. The following statement from a Sinn Féin non-Convention member, in reacting to the debate on same-sex marriage in the Dáil, is typical:

> I congratulate the Constitutional Convention on its excellent work to date. I had some reservations initially but I am pleased to see the Constitutional Convention take on a life of its own and begin to undertake the task of making some much-needed changes to [the Constitution]. When the Constitutional Convention met in April 2013, it was meeting to consider same-sex marriage. The Constitutional Convention voted a decisive majority in favour of changing the Constitution to allow civil marriage for same-sex couples. The Convention's strong endorsement of equal marriage rights in Ireland marks an historic step in the campaign for marriage-equality in Ireland and we are grateful to all members of the Convention who made this happen.

A number of the citizen-members publicly endorsed the process. At the first public regional meeting,[8] which took place in Cork in October 2013, five local citizen-members attended. Talking to a group of approximately 100 people, all spoke enthusiastically and positively about their work with the Convention. In particular, two members explained they had completely changed their views on issues as a result of Convention deliberations. One of them also stressed that he would never have agreed to speak in front of such a large group if it had not been for his experience of doing so at the Convention.

Another Convention-member (a private citizen rather than politician) regularly contributed after the Convention weekends to a prominent talk show (the Joe Duffy Show) on RTÉ Radio 1 (the national public-service broadcaster), where she championed the Convention process and its recommendations.

Media-coverage of the 2015 referendum on marriage-equality consistently referred to it as a Convention recommendation, thereby enhancing the visibility of the Convention's work and the legitimacy of the proposal, which was reflected in the outcome of the vote. Survey-analysis of vote-trends reveals that knowledge of the Convention was a significant factor in causing people to vote Yes in the referendum (Elkink *et al.* 2015).

Impact on polity and society

The Convention was mandated to make recommendations: that is, its role was advisory rather than declaratory. Its work resulted in forty separate recommendations for reform, of which it is estimated that eighteen would require a referendum to implement. Following each meeting, a Convention report was sent to the Houses of the Oireachtas for debate and for government consideration. The government gave a specific undertaking to respond, and in timely fashion, by way of a formal

---

8. In the final months of its operation, the Convention organised a road show of regional meetings around the country.

ministerial statement to the Parliament within four months of receipt of a report by the Convention.

Based on the government's response to the first three reports – which were all debated on schedule – there was some reason to expect that the government was taking this process seriously and that the output in terms of the polity was positive. These were the reports of the first three meetings that discussed: the voting age; the length of the presidential term of office (both of these items dealt with in Report No. 1); the role of women in the home and women in politics (both of these dealt with in Report No. 2); and same-sex marriage (Report No. 3; see www. constitution.ie for the reports). The reaction to these reports was as follows:

- The government agreed to hold three referendums (scheduled for early 2015) on: reducing the voting age to 16; reducing the minimum age for presidential candidates; and – of greatest significance – same-sex marriage. The government later reversed its decisions relating to the first of these referendums, which has been deferred indefinitely. The other two referendums occurred on the same day – 22 May 2015 – with the marriage-equality referendum passing by a safe margin (62 per cent in favour) and the presidential age referendum being roundly defeated. The latter outcome reflected the fact that the marriage-equality item completely overshadowed it.
- The other recommendations contained in these reports were referred either to the relevant Parliamentary committee or to a relevant government department taskforce for further consideration. This recommendation was made on the women in politics issue and the Government had already implemented some significant reform here, including the implementation of gender quotas.

While there has undoubtedly been some 'kicking into the long grass', the fact that the government held two referendums in spring 2015 is very significant. Subsequently, it was reported that the Government had signed off on a plan to hold a third referendum (to abolish the offence of blasphemy) possibly at a later date.[9] Nonetheless, at the time of writing, many of the subsequent reports have yet to be debated, although the report on Dáil reform was the subject of discussion by the Cabinet in January 2016, with several measures promised. In addition, as the Government's term drew to a close, the attention of members was likely directed more at the upcoming election. However, the government has indicated that, if re-elected, it will establish a second citizen-assembly specifically to consider abortion laws in Ireland, a very contentious subject and a constitutional one, given the current constitutional ban on abortion in Ireland.

The work of the Convention has generally been regarded very positively and both of the main opposition parties have asked that it be reconstituted. This view

9.   Referendum due on removing blasphemy from Constitution, 30 September 2014; see: http://www.irishtimes.com/news/politics/referendum-due-on-removing-blasphemy-from-constitution-1.1945835 (accessed 14 October 2014).

was shared by the Convention members, 100 per cent of whom agreed that the Government should establish another Convention when they were balloted on the matter on the final weekend. There was also agreement amongst them that this should happen in the lifetime of the next Dáil. In addition, in response to those groups disappointed that their proposals had not been chosen for deliberation as part of the 'any other amendments' item, the Convention once again considered the topics submitted under this item, as well as issues that had been raised in previous constitutional-review processes (the Constitution Review Group of 1995 and the All-Party Oireachtas Committee on Constitutional Reform of 1997), before recommending five issues that they believed should be prioritised for any future Convention. These five proposals included: the environment; Seanad (Senate) reform; local-government reform; the definition of the family; and the separation of church and state. The Convention model has also received a lot of international attention and has been proposed as a template for constitutional reform as far afield as Catalonia and the UK.

Finally, in terms of wider societal impact, it is envisaged that the Convention's website, which has archived the expert-briefing papers, submissions and expert and interest-group presentations, will serve as an important educational resource for the maxi-public during the referendum campaigns.

Conclusion

Despite initial criticisms from the media, some academics, and many in civil society of its limited remit and its composition, and concerns around governmental responsiveness, there is now broad agreement that, as a process, the Convention worked. For example, Dearbhail McDonald, legal editor of the *Irish Independent* newspaper, who was a self-professed 'huge Convention cynic', speaking on radio after the marriage-equality weekend, cited the Convention 'as a model for debating complex social issues' and queried whether such 'dispassionate, considered, mature debate would be replicated in a political context'.[10] Similar sentiments were expressed by academics and civil-society leaders who had also been critical of the process previously.

As with other such processes that form a potential part of the 'ecology' of democratic institutions, the Convention was, of course, not without its weaknesses. There was the challenge of achieving full inclusion and equality of voice and an overcrowded agenda that, on occasion, made it difficult to allocated sufficient time for information and deliberation. More recently, there has been the challenge of securing a response from the government to a number of Convention reports. As Table 3.2 indicates, these could result in yet more referendums in the near future. Thus, the output has yet to be fully tested in terms of citizens' responses to the referendum issues; but the positive outcome of the marriage-equality referendum

---

10. Available online at: http://www.rte.ie/radio1/drivetime/programmes/2013/0415/381555-drivetime-monday-15-april-2013/ (accessed 8 February 2016).

demonstrates the public-policy potential of the Convention approach to discussing areas of reform.

More generally, however, it could be argued that the success of the Convention does not rest solely on whether referendums recommended by it succeed. After all, under the Irish Constitution it is the wider citizenry that decides on constitutional change. So the very fact of Government agreement to hold referendums in response to Convention recommendations is in itself a measure of success. Another determinant of its success rests on its impact on the polity and wider society. This will depend on some or all of the following:

- citizens' responses to the referendums;
- the government's response to all of the Convention's recommendations, many of which will not require referendums;
- the establishment of a second Convention in the future;
- the use of the Convention as an information-resource in future referendum campaigns;
- the transferability of the process to other levels of government and issues nationally and to similar processes internationally; and
- how it adds to our understanding of deliberative processes in practice.

Ironically, it is in two of the areas that were initially a target of strong criticism – its composition and remit – that the Convention has been truly innovative in ways that contributed to its input, throughput and output legitimacy. The inclusion of politicians not only ensured greater parliamentary buy-in for the process and its recommendations (output legitimacy) but politician-members were an important source of information on institutional/technical issues, as recognised by citizen-member feedback expressed in the Convention's final report (www.constitution. ie) (input/throughput legitimacy). The remit, although originally quite tightly prescribed, was stretched by the Convention from the first weekend; this, plus the fact that it could consider other amendments and its decision to recommend items for future consideration, meant it had strong agenda-setting powers (input legitimacy). Finally the inclusion of civil-society organisations in the weekend presentations and in the process of deciding the 'any other amendments' brought context and the 'lived' experience to bear on the expert facts and analyses in ways that engaged Irish citizens nationally and internationally 'outside the room' (throughput legitimacy). They also, on occasion, were the means through which the interests of those who are traditionally marginalised from political processes were indirectly presented to the Convention (such as the views of homeless people during the discussion of economic social and cultural rights) (input legitimacy).

With the Convention, Ireland is keeping in step with the world's established democracies, where the trend in recent years has been towards engaging with citizens, increasing the scope for ordinary citizens to have a say in constitutional change. The Irish case provides one small step towards what might be conceived of as a 'deliberative turn' (Dryzek 2002) in praxis.

References

Caluwaerts, D. and Reuchamps, M. (2014) 'Does inter-group deliberation foster inter-group appreciation? Evidence from two experiments in Belgium', *Politics* 34(2): 101–15.

Dryzek, J. S. (2002) *Deliberative Democracy and Beyond: Liberals, critics, contestations*, Oxford, UK: Oxford University Press.

Elkink, J. A., Farrell, D. M., Reidy, T. and Suiter, J. 'Understanding the 2015 marriage referendum in Ireland: Constitutional Convention, campaign, and conservative Ireland', UCD Geary Institute for Public Policy Discussion Paper Series, WP2015/21, University College Dublin, Geary Institute.

Farrell, D. M., O'Malley, E. and Suiter, J. (2013) 'Deliberative democracy in action Irish-style: the 2011 We the Citizens pilot citizens' assembly', *Irish Political Studies* 28(1): 99–113.

Fournier, P, van der Kolk, H., Carty, R. K., Blais, A. and Rose, J. (2011) *When Citizens Decide: Lessons from citizen assemblies on electoral reform*, Oxford, UK: Oxford University Press.

Gallagher, M. and Marsh, M. (eds) (2011) *How Ireland Voted 2011: The full story of Ireland's earthquake election*, Basingstoke, UK: Palgrave Macmillan.

Karpowitz, C. F., Mendelberg, T., and Shaker, L. (2012) 'Gender inequality in deliberative participation', *American Political Science Review* 103(3): 533–47.

Lane, P. R. (2012) 'The European sovereign debt crisis', *Journal of Economic Perspectives* 26(3): 49–67.

Lutz, K. G. (2003) 'Irish party competition in the new millennium: change, or plus ça change?', *Irish Political Studies* 18(2): 40–59.

Mansbridge, J., Bohman, J., Chambers, S., Estlund, D., Føllesdal, A., Fung, A., Lafont, C., Manin, B., Martí, J. L. (2010) 'The place of self-interest and the role of power in deliberative democracy', *Journal of Political Philosophy* 18(1): 64–100.

Smith, G. (2009) *Democratic Innovations: Designing institutions for citizen participation*, Cambridge, UK: Cambridge University Press.

Steenbergen, M. R., Bächtiger, A., Spörndli, M. and Steiner, J. (2003) 'Measuring political deliberation: a discourse quality index', *Comparative European Politics* 1(1): 21–48.

Steiner, J. (2012) *The Foundations of Deliberative Democracy: Empirical research and normative implications*, Cambridge, UK: Cambridge University Press.

Suiter, J. and Farrell, D. (2011) 'The parties' manifestos', in Gallagher, M. and Marsh, M. (eds) (2011) *How Ireland Voted 2011: The full story of Ireland's earthquake election*, Basingstoke, UK: Palgrave Macmillan, pp. 29–46.

Chapter Four

The Macro Political Uptake of the G1000 in Belgium

Vincent Jacquet, Jonathan Moskovic, Didier Caluwaerts and Min Reuchamps[1]

After the election of 2010, Belgium attracted the interest of the international media because the kingdom went on to set the world record for a country without a government (541 days). More precisely, parties were unable to find an agreement on a potential reform of the federal architecture of the kingdom. In the context of the consociational nature of the political decision-making process in Belgium, a compromise is needed between the French-speaking and Dutch-speaking parties in order to form a government. However, since 2010, divergent opinions concerning state-reform between northern and southern areas had deprived the country of a fully functioning federal government for a prolonged period.[2]

In this context of a crisis of electoral institutions and government-formation, a group of citizens decided to 'do something'. After an appeal[3] by the writer David Van Reybrouck and the journalist Paul Hermant, a new team, composed of leaders of foundations, business-people and academics, implemented a large-scale deliberative process. The project did not seek to offer a radical alternative to representative democracy but rather to complement and breathe new life into it. It aimed to gather ordinary citizens in a setting that was conducive to open and non-coercive deliberation on possibly contentious social and political issues. The central idea was to facilitate citizens themselves experiencing the difficulty of building bridges and compromising over highly polarising issues. The deliberation was structured in three distinct phases: a phase of online public consultation; a citizen-summit (for a large-scale deliberation); and a citizen-panel (for an in-depth deliberation).

The G1000 in Belgium cannot be categorised as a form of constitutional deliberative democracy *per se*, in that it was never intended as a means to change the constitution. Its organisers explicitly sought to avoid any political and institutional ties and their focus was much more on guaranteeing best possible representativeness and a high quality of deliberation, rather than generating a strong political outcome (G1000 2012). So, while the G1000 did well in terms of representativeness and open agenda-setting (Caluwaerts and Reuchamps 2015), political uptake was very limited in the short term. However, the event put on

---

1. The authors were members of the Methodology and Research Unit of the G1000. They have been involved in the designing of the G1000.
2. The country was without a fully functioning government from 26 April 2010 to 5 December 2011.
3. The website http://g1000.org contains full information and the appeal can be read in English at http://g1000.org/en/manifesto.php.

the political agenda the issue of democratic innovation, both in the discourse of political actors and in the practices of citizen-participation.

The aim of this chapter is to analyse the potential impact of grassroots deliberative mechanisms such as the G1000. We first describe the deliberative design of the event and analyse its legitimacy by distinguishing the input, throughput and the output dimensions. We continue with an in-depth assessment of its political effect by looking at the uptake of its ideas in the media, the maxi-public as well as conventional political and social arenas.

The G1000

The G1000 aimed to offer a forum for large-scale deliberation in Belgium. In order to live up to its aspirations of inclusion and openness, the G1000 consisted of three phases. The first was an online public consultation, in which every volunteer was invited to propose an issue for discussion in the second phase, a citizen-summit, which consisted of a large, one-day deliberative 'mini-public', among 1,000 participants randomly selected from inhabitants of the country. The third phase was a more in-depth citizen-panel, to which thirty-two citizens were invited to deliberate and agree on precise proposals for public policies.

Phase 1: public consultation

The first phase consisted of a very open process of agenda-setting. The organisers did not determine the agenda of the citizen-summit, in contrast to the common practice in deliberative ventures (Kies and Nanz 2013). Rather, they were convinced of the importance of starting with an open agenda, which would be populated entirely by the public itself. They therefore launched a large-scale online 'idea-box', in which every citizen, no matter his or her opinion or background, could post the questions or problems that they believed should be deliberated at the G1000 citizen-summit. Moreover, they could also rate the ideas and proposals of others, allowing a more accurate reading of the salience of issues.

This process resulted in a total of over 2,000 ideas, dealing with all kinds of social, political and economic issues. In total, more than 6,000 people took part in this procedure. As most of the proposals appeared several times in the list, the ideas were subsequently clustered into twenty-five themes, based on the number of times they appeared and their individual rating. This list of twenty-five was placed online in October 2011 for a further round of public voting. In order to avoid a bias in the results, the twenty-five ideas appeared in a random order on the screen, so that the organisers had no influence on the final agenda. Through the media and via a large public campaign, citizens were invited to vote for their three preferred themes for the G1000, which turned out to be social security; welfare in a time of economic crisis; and immigration.[4] This large-scale public consultation

---

4. All the results are presented in the final report of the G1000, which is available on the website at: www.g1000.org (accessed 8 February 2016).

and the voting tool for the top twenty-five guaranteed that the agenda of the G1000 was open.[5]

Phase 2: citizen-summit

Following the public-consultation phase, the second part of the project consisted of a large-scale citizen-deliberation, the G1000 citizen-summit. Through a mixture of random selection and targeted recruitment (Caluwaerts and Reuchamps 2015), 1,000 citizens were invited to participate in a one-day deliberative event in Brussels, in order to reflect on and discuss their positions about the three issues that had been chosen during the public-consultation phase. Participants were randomly seated by roundtables of ten and experienced volunteers facilitated the discussion at each of the tables.

The G1000 event in Brussels was flanked by two side projects: G'Home and G'Offs. The former was a software application that served as a forum for online discussion while the latter provided local events for citizens to gather and discuss the same issues as in citizen-summit itself. The participant pool of the G'Homes and G'Offs was based entirely on self-selection. However, the chance to take part in local initiatives or even at home did lower the threshold for participation and allow a much larger group than those gathered in Brussels to discuss the same issues. To this end, there was a live stream of the event in Brussels, which was available online.

Phase 3: citizen-panel

The third phase of the G1000 project, also known as the G32, aimed at elaborating the ideas that came out the discussions at the citizen-summit. After all, the citizen-summit was a large event designed to facilitate the pooling and sharing of ideas. Given the fact that each round was relatively short and focused on exploring the diversity around the tables, the ideas and proposals made were, at that stage, still quite basic.

For three weekends, thirty-two participants gathered to work out policy proposals. These thirty-two citizens were randomly selected from a pool of 491 participants in the G1000, G'Offs and G'Home who agreed to be considered as potential G32 participants, which meant the significant time-commitment of participating in each of the three weekends. The stratified random selection of the thirty-two from the pool of the 491 participants was done with controls for diversity in terms of gender (sixteen women and sixteen men); language (eighteen Dutch-speaking, twelve French-speaking and two German-speaking); region (from each of the ten Belgian provinces and Brussels) and age (seven participants under thirty; nine between thirty and forty-five; nine between forty-five and sixty; and seven over sixty).

---

5. There was also an *ex post* IP check to prevent massive voting by a single individual or group.

The G32 took the format of a citizen-panel, which is used in policy processes throughout the world, such as in citizens' juries in the USA (Crosby and Nethercut 2005) or 'planning cells' in Germany (Garbe 1986). Such a deliberative design is much more intensive, since participants endeavour to propose specific policies and actions. A citizen-panel is also more open than a citizen-summit, since the participants have a much greater say in the process itself. In fact, citizens have the authority to decide what they wish to work on (the choice of the specific questions they want to tackle); how they want to work (the choice of the experts and stakeholders they wish to question); and, above all, on what they decide and then bring to the public debate (the choice of the outcomes they deliver).

Input, throughput and output legitimacy

In this chapter, mobilising the typology presented in Suiter and Reuchamps 2016, Chapter One of this volume, we analyse the legitimacy of the G1000 in three steps: the input, the throughput and the output, with a focus on the macro-uptake of its recommendations in the assessment of the output legitimacy.

Input legitimacy

The selection of participants is always a key question for the organisers of deliberative mini-publics. From an epistemic point of view, random selection is the best-suited selection technique (Caluwaerts and Ugarriza 2012). The organisers of G1000 wanted a large-scale deliberation with ordinary citizens and thus opted for random selection. The aim was to give to every inhabitant of the country the same probability to be selected for the G1000.

Practically, the participants were selected using Random Digit Dialling. As other authors have noticed, the use of random selection does not prevent the effect of self-selection (Smith 2009; Fung 2007). In order to mitigate this, the organisers also used quotas on gender, province and language in order to have a more appropriate representation of the Belgian population. In addition, and perhaps even more importantly, 10 per cent of the seats were reserved for a targeted recruitment of groups of people less likely to take up the opportunity to participate. For example, homeless people can be very difficult to attract with phone calls, and the G1000 therefore contacted local associations to help them to include this segment of the population. The idea behind all these efforts was to create the most inclusive process possible. As Caluwaerts and Reuchamps (2015) contend, the G1000's quality of representation requires a qualified assessment. The use of random selection, quotas and some targeted recruitment brought a very diverse group of participants, which was a feature highly praised by the international observers:

> one of the most impressive features of the G1000 was the diversity of participants in terms of gender, age, political preferences as well as social, professional and cultural background. We were also impressed by the inclusion

of diverse faith communities and the fair representation of Belgium's different language communities (G1000 2012: 102).

The selection of the issues to be discussed in the G1000 was also driven by the aim to give voice to citizens. Particularly in the first phase, everyone had the opportunity to propose issues: this openness of the agenda was possible because of the autonomy of the G1000. Contrary to the Irish and Icelandic cases, the G1000 was not mandated by public authorities and was not embedded in formal political processes. This high level of openness is positive in terms of input but it can also be an obstacle to implementation of the outcomes, thus weakening output legitimacy; we explore this issue in greater detail later in the chapter.

Throughput legitimacy

The G1000 focused strongly on the quality of the deliberative process. This process was organised and managed by volunteers with professional skills as facilitators; their task was to ensure, to the greatest extent possible, equal consideration of all opinions represented at the table. Each roundtable began with an introduction of all participants in order to create a setting conducive to respectful exchange. Experts were also invited to feed the discussion with substantive information at the plenary discussion. Their role was to provide a minimum context of common knowledge on the issues at stake but not to impose a specific framing. During the citizen-summit, two academics spoke on each of the three themes of the day. Nevertheless, according to the international observers, the presentations from the experts were not quite diverse enough. 'From what we have understood, we find that the keynotes were slightly biased; the experts who introduced the three themes approached the matter from a somewhat "left-wing" oriented perspective' (G1000 2012: 103). This is a key element because good deliberation needs to build on a plurality of points of view (Ryfe 2005). Yet the same observers pointed out that the impact of the experts on the discussions was not very substantial in the end and that the outcomes of the votes after the deliberation were not merely reflections of the experts' presentations. For the citizen-panel, the G32, the process was more open in terms of experts. Indeed the participants were invited to choose themselves whom they wanted to invite. This meant that they met not only academics but also members of lobbies and think-tanks as well as businessmen and representatives from a range of associations.

To be sure, time-constraints hindered the full development of deliberation over these three complex issues. Thus, in comparison to mini-publics that take place over several weekends, the throughput legitimacy assessment is lower for the G1000. It is also always difficult to grasp the quality of the deliberation. The Discourse Quality Index (DQI) is often used in this regard (Steiner *et al.* 2004). The coding using DQI of a random selection of tables at the G1000 did show an equal quality of deliberation across them (Caluwaerts and Reuchamps 2014b), due to the fact that each table was following the same script. Another measure is also possible: the Perceived Discourse Quality Index (PDQI). This index, built from the answers given by the participants to a *post facto* questionnaire, was quite high, with participants giving a positive evaluation of the quality of deliberation (Caluwaerts and Reuchamps 2014b). The perceived quality of deliberation was even higher during the three weekends of the G32, as participants had more time to ponder the issues at stake.

Finally, we have to look at the balance between aggregation and deliberation during the G1000 in order to evaluate a third dimension of throughput legitimacy. During the G1000, each table had to send all its ideas to a central desk, which then clustered them. But, as pointed out elsewhere, clustering is never a wholly neutral activity:

> after all, the experts at the central desk were asked to do a first clustering of the inputs from the tables in order to see which ideas were introduced and to facilitate the voting round. As such, some genuinely innovative and original ideas, which only appeared once or twice, did not make it to the final vote, and the post-test questionnaire indicated that some of the participants felt like their opinions were not taken seriously, because their ideas were not put to the vote (Caluwaerts and Reuchamps 2015: 161).

This is a risk that lots of deliberative mini-publics face because every discussion needs to be summarised to some extent. The crucial issue, therefore, is to make this step more transparent.

During the third phase, the thirty-two citizens were invited to write the proposals themselves. At each stage, people were invited to propose sentences for the proposals and also to critique and amend their wording. In this situation, there was little opportunity for the organisers to manipulate the process because participants could change the proposed text. Also, at the end of the process, votes were held on every proposal. All in all, the throughput legitimacy of the G1000 was quite good, especially if one takes into account all three phases and not only the citizen-summit.

Output legitimacy

What were the outputs of the mini-public? This is probably one of the most critical questions for any deliberative endeavour. Just a few days after the G1000, Edouard Delruelle, a Belgian philosopher, explained that the G1000 had no future because it was not about politics *per se*.[6] According to him, politics is about class conflict and is a struggle between organised groups. The question then becomes: has the G1000 had any influence on politics or policies in Belgium?

When looking at the possible uptake of mini-publics, we must clearly distinguish between two kinds of impact: on the public-policy content of different authorities and on agenda-setting with respect to the public debate. According to Goodin and Dryzek,

---

6. 'Le G 1000, maladie infantile de la démocratie postmoderne?', *RTBF*, 15 June 2011. All news reports referred to in the following footnotes are available through the websites listed after the References at the end of the chapter.

when it comes to the macro-political impact of micro-political innovations, mini-publics of the sort here in view rarely determine public policy (though more than direct impact on the content of public policy will turn out to be an issue, we shall be arguing). Generally they can have real political impact only by working on and through the broader public sphere, ordinary institutions of representative democracy, and administrative policy making (2006: 220–1).

It should not come as a surprise that, from its very conception, the G1000 was to be a citizen-led initiative, with no ties to formal decision-making institutions. The desire to stay independent from traditional political authorities reduced the likelihood that the conclusions of its deliberation would be translated into concrete public policies. There was no obligation for members of the government to take the report into account; no proposal for referendums; and no place for deliberation between participants and politicians. The presence of the presidents of the different parliaments of Belgium during the final session of the G1000 seems to be the only – weak – link with the formal process of political decision-making (Caluwaerts and Reuchamps 2015). Analysing causality in the content of public policy is always difficult but we can argue that the weight of the G1000's proposal was, in practice, negligible in the content of public policies in Belgium.

Does this imply that the G1000 was an island of deliberation largely isolated from the real politics that influence citizens in their everyday lives? Several elements show that the G1000 has influenced public debate in Belgium on one central topic: democratic renewal. That is the major justification provided by the initiators of the project (G1000 2012). The G1000 has given a clear example, which gained huge media attention. It embodied the demand for deliberative democracy. This role of agenda-setting is observable in different places and can be analysed using the classical distinction between the systemic and governmental agenda (Cobb and Elder 1983). The *systemic* agenda describes all the issues commonly perceived as important by members of the political community. Hereafter, we will show that the G1000 has received lots of attention from plenty of actors in Belgium, much more than previous deliberative mini-publics, in terms of media uptake, maxi-public uptake and social uptake. The *governmental* agenda consists of what is taken into account by public authorities at the international, national, regional or local levels, which we will refer to as conventional political uptake. The next sections analyse each of these uptakes. Thus, following the systemic approach to deliberative democracy (Parkinson and Mansbridge 2012), the aim of the remainder of this chapter is to analyse the interaction between the G1000 (its input and throughput) with the entire political system, by looking at the relationship with the media, public opinion, political parties and MPs and with other experiments in deliberative democracy (its output).

The media uptake

In order to grasp the character of media coverage of the G1000, we have analysed all the articles published in Dutch- and French-speaking newspapers in Belgium that covered the G1000, over the period from June 2011 (when the initiative was launched) to December 2013. This section is divided into three parts: first, the period before the citizen-summit of the G1000 period, that is, from 10 June to 10 November 2011; second, the period between 11 November 2011 and 10 November 2012, which corresponds to the second and the third phase of the G1000; third, the post-G1000 period.

Before the G1000 (10 June to 10 November 2011)

The G1000 was covered in all the major newspapers in the country on 10 June 2011.[7] The articles all mentioned the citizens' initiative, rooted in the perception that the inability of politicians to form a federal government for almost a year was not because of communal tensions but rather because Belgium's current form of democracy was unsuited to the twenty-first century. The next day, 11 June 2011, the presentation by the G1000 group of its Manifesto also received extensive media coverage.[8] In the following days, various articles mentioned the importance of launching such an initiative and the popular support for it.[9] In the weeks and months that followed, however, media interest decreased.

From the beginning of October and, to a greater extent, in November, the G1000 became the centre of media attention once again, with a multiplicity of articles focused on the upcoming event.[10] In the midst of this, some articles focused on the financial problems of the G1000,[11] which was a crowd-funded initiative (Caluwaerts and Reuchamps 2012).

The political context explains the large number of articles dealing with the G1000. When the G1000 was launched in June 2011, the country had been waiting for the formation of a federal government for almost one year (Deschouwer and Reuchamps 2013). This political situation opened a window of opportunity for the G1000, which positioned itself explicitly as a citizen-led alternative to the complete political stalemate. Moreover, despite the emergence of several protest

---

7. 'La journée', *La Libre*, 10 June 2011; '1 jaar politieke crisis: "Huidige democratie is als een koets op de E40" ', *De Morgen*, 10 June 2011; 'Un G1000 pour sortir de la crise', *Le Soir*, 10 June 2011; 'David Van Reybrouck lanceert politiek burgerinitiatief', *De Standaard*, 10 June 2011.

8. 'Belges, exprimez-vous!', *La Libre*, 11 June 2011; 'Le G1000 veut réunir mille citoyens le 11/11/11', *Le Soir*, 11 June 2011; 'Democratie 2.0', *De Standaard*, 11 June 2011; 'Droom', *De Standaard*, 11 June 2011; 'Burgerinitiatief rond David Van Reybrouck moet Belgische politiek hervomen', *De Standaard*, 11 June 2011; 'Manifest van de G1000', *De Morgen*, 11 June 2011.

9. 'Meer dan 2500 handtekeningen voor politiek burgerinitiatief', *De Standaard*, 13 June 2011; 'Zinnige burgerinspraak', *De Standaard*, 18 June 2011; 'Les grandes espérances du G 1000', *La Dernière Heure*, 23 June 2011.

10. 'Le G1000 est bien sur les rails', *La Libre*, 4 October 2011; 'Dernière ligne droite avec le sommet citoyen du G1000', *Le Vif*, 7 October 2011; 'Des Belges lancent le 'sommet citoyen' du G1000', *Le Soir*, 4 November 2011; 'G1000 buigt zich over sociale zekerheid, welvaart en immigratie', *De Standaard*, 8 November 2011.

11. 'G1000 zoekt nog 180.000 euro financiering voor werking', *De Standaard*, 8 November 2011; 'Un "petit déficit" de 28000 euros', *La Libre*, 9 November; 'Les gros sous du G1000', *Le Soir*, 9 November 2011.

movements (for example, SHAME; the Belgian Fries Revolution; Camping 16) during the government-formation process, the G1000 was one of the main initiatives that formulated clear demands and a clear alternative. These features triggered media interest.

During the G1000 (11 November 2011 to 10 November 2012)

The second phase should be divided into two distinct periods: coverage of the citizen-summit of 11 November 2011; and coverage of the citizen-panel, which did not receive as much media attention. The extensive media-coverage that preceded the citizen-summit continued after the event itself, with an overall positive slant: it was a 're-enchantment of Belgian democracy'[12] according to *Le Soir* and described as a 'successful first citizen-summit'[13] by *La Libre*. However, some did not hesitate to criticise 'the quality of sandwiches, coffee and the amount of toilets' and the low turnout for the event.[14] This topic raised different reactions. Indeed, there was a large difference in the number of participants according to various news sources: according to *Le Vif*, '850 participants'[15] attended the event, while the *Gazet van Antwerpen* reported that there were 'more than 1200 participants'.[16] According to the organisers of the G1000 there were 704 participants. These discrepancies are because some journalists included the volunteers that attended the event whereas others did not.

As the G1000 entered its third phase, thirty-two people were selected to further develop the results of the second phase but this sparked relatively little media interest.[17] Before this, there was a brief resurgence of G1000 media coverage on three separate occasions: the media covered problems of fundraising[18] and deliberations over where the G32 would take place and highlighted the dissolution of the G1000 and its formal integration into an existing Foundation.[19] However, these three topics of media interest were not directly related to the deliberation itself. Aside from these elements, the G32 was largely neglected by the media. This contrasts sharply with the enthusiasm of the media for the second phase of the G1000. There are two possible explanations for this. First, media interest in the G1000 might have derived from the absence of a federal government for such a prolonged period. On 6 December 2011, Elio Di Rupo was sworn in as

12. 'Le G1000 "réenchante" la démocratie belge', *Le Soir*, 12 November 2011.
13. 'Un premier sommet citoyen réussi', *La Libre*, 12 November 2011.
14. 'De G1000-democratie kampt met thuisblijvers', *De Standaard*, 12 November 2011.
15. 'G1000: Environ 850 participants présents à Tour & Taxis', *Le Vif*, 11 November 2011.
16. 'Meer dan 1.200 deelnemers voor G1000', *Gazet van Antwerpen*, 11 November 2011.
17. 'Slotweekend voor G1000', *De Standaard*, 10 November 2012; 'G1000 : le bout du tunnel', *Le Soir*, 14 November 2012; 'G1000: l'apothéose', *La Libre*, 9 November 2012.
18. 'Burgerinitiatief G1000 op zoek naar 75.000 euro', *De Morgen*, 6 March 2012; 'Le G1000 poursuivra l'effort', *La Libre*, 8 March 2012; 'Le G1000 en rade', *Le Soir*, 8 March 2012.
19. 'G1000 ruilt Burgertop in voor Stichting voor Toekomstige Generaties', *Knack*, 19 Augustus 2012; 'G1000-vzw opgeheven', *De Tijd*, 19 August 2012; 'Le G1000 dissous pour mieux se fondre dans une Fondation', *Le Soir*, 20 August 2012.

prime minister and Belgium finally had a federal government, which could have led to a gradual shift in media coverage. A second possible explanation is that the G1000 was a more interesting topic for the media to cover while it brought together a large number of people for one single day – the citizen-summit – than when it convened a small group of people for three weekends – the citizen-panel. This analysis is in line with Parkinson's (2006) evaluation of using media in deliberative democracy.

After the G1000 (11 November 2012 to 31 December 2013)

The last period starts with the presentation of the final report of the G1000. In the days following the G32, the media covered the content of the report and, more specifically, the willingness of participants to address some key political issues, such as automatic wage-indexation and the thorny issue of economic policy in Belgium.[20] After this, though a few articles still referred to the experience of the G1000,[21] overall, we note that with the exception of the week following the presentation of the report, the G1000 quickly disappeared from the Belgian media.

What can be concluded from this analysis of the media coverage of the G1000? It is possible to distinguish variation in the coverage according to the different G1000 phases. The 'before' phase was characterised by extensive media coverage. The 'between' phase started with strong exposure of the citizen-summit of 11 November 2011 but there was relatively little coverage of the G32 citizen-panel. The 'after' phase saw little coverage in the days succeeding the event and interest then evaporated due to the constant flow of new information on other topics. One crucial factor, the political crisis, seems to help explain the coverage of the G1000. As the G1000 was initiated in a context of high political tension it was seen as a possible alternative to traditional parliamentary politics. There was, therefore, a window of opportunity for the G1000 to capture media attention. Afterwards, media coverage reverted to its usual focus on formal politics.

The maxi-public uptake

Besides looking at how media reacted to the G1000, it is equally important to determine how much public support the G1000 garnered. After all, if the G1000 wants its results/proposals to be significant at a macro-political level, there has to be support for the G1000 in the wider public sphere. As Goodin and Dryzek argue

---

20. 'G1000 legt politici conclusies voor', *Het Belang van Limburg*, 11 November 2012; 'G1000 ziet geen heil in indexsprong', *De Standaard*, 11 November 2012; 'La fusée citoyenne belge est bel et bien sur orbite', *La Libre*, 12 November 2012; 'Le G1000 contre un saut d'index', *La Libre*, 12 November 2012; 'G1000 of de kracht van burgerdemocratie', *De Morgen*, 12 November 2012.

21. 'La démocratie change terriblement', *Le Soir*, 12 December 2012; 'G1000-bedenker Didier Caluwaerts trekt met onderzoeksbeurzen naar VS', *Knack*, 5 April 2013; 'Participatie is geen modegril', *De Morgen*, 13 October 2013.

(2006), only with large-scale public support can the proposals of any deliberative event reach the decision-making sphere; and only with a strong endorsement of the results in the wider public sphere can the mini-public legitimately claim to be heard. This is why we conducted a survey among the general public in Belgium in order to determine whether the *process* and *results* of the G1000 produced wider endorsement among the Belgian population. This survey was sent out to 1,000 randomly selected citizens from both sides of the linguistic divide, by a commercial polling firm bureau, which has a panel of over 110,000 individuals. Despite the fact that the pool is inevitably biased, the *ex post* controls showed that socio-demographic characteristics of our sample largely concurred with the socio-demographic distribution of the Belgian population.

Awareness of the G1000

In many European countries, participatory and deliberative events are usually very particular experiences, in the margin of the major political process and known only to a few people. Due to massive media coverage, the context of the Belgian political crisis and also the popularity of some of its organisers, however, the G1000 is known to more people than other similar initiatives. Table 4.1 shows that more than 52 per cent of respondents had heard of the G1000. We can also see that

Table 4.1: Awareness of the G1000

Have you heard of G1000?	Not at all	A little	Quite a lot	A great deal
Total	47.7%	39.8%	10.1%	2.4%
Region (p=0.000)				
Flanders	38.0%	45.9%	12.6%	3.5%
Wallonia	65.0%	30.9%	31.4%	0.6%
Brussels	52.3%	31.4%	15.1%	1.2%
Gender (p=0.010)				
Male	42.2%	43.1%	11.7%	3.0%
Female	52.4%	37.3%	8.5%	1.9%
Education (p=0.005)				
Low	53.4%	38.8%	6.8%	1.1%
Middle	49.5%	42.5%	9.2%	2.5%
High	40.0%	42.5%	14.0%	3.5%
Age (p=0.909)				
>= 34	47.9%	39.1%	10.5%	2.5%
34–54	46.3%	41.0%	09.6%	3.0%
55+	48.8%	39.5%	10.1%	1.6%

there were big differences between the north and the south of the country, with many more people in Flanders having heard of it. The more extensive Flemish media coverage, linked to the presence of famous Flemish personalities in the organisational team, are the most credible factors accounting for this difference. The second interesting element shown in Table 4.1 is that there is a positive link between levels of education, although it seems smaller than one would expect. Unlike other cases of deliberation, the G1000 was not known only to the better educated, who are often already convinced of the merits of democratic innovations (Gourgues and Sainty 2011). This suggests that the organisers succeeded in putting their initiative on the societal agenda and opening the door to a wider public debate on democratic innovation.

Support for the process of the G1000

Before turning to the popular evaluation of the results of the G1000, we will examine to what extent the respondents were in favour of the process by which it was conducted. In other words, do respondents support the way in which citizens were consulted in the G1000? And do they think the G1000 has had any significant impact on the functioning of politics in Belgium?

The results in Table 4.2 show that respondents had mixed feelings regarding the procedures applied by the G1000. On the one hand, a large majority wants to see a repeat of the G1000. After all, about 60 per cent of respondents agree that citizens should be involved in political discussions on important policy issues in the future while about 40 per cent of respondents declare themselves willing to partake in such a mini-public in the future. This suggests that the G1000 process

Table 4.2: Support for the process of the G1000

	Completely disagree	Disagree	Neither agree nor disagree	Agree	Completely agree
G1000 contributed to renewal of democracy in Belgium.	7.2%	16.6%	60.1%	15.4%	0.7%
Recommendations formulated by citizens at G1000 should be turned into law.	3.3%	6.3%	59.7%	28.0%	2.7%
In future, citizens should be gathered again to discuss political issues, as at the G1000.	2.8%	4.9%	32.6%	44.0%	15.7%
I would agree to participate in a G1000 if I were randomly selected in the future.	11.4%	10.9%	36.2%	29.8%	11.7%

was received with enthusiasm and considered legitimate. On the other hand, however, only 16.1 per cent feel that the G1000 changed anything for democracy in Belgium. Most people (60.1 per cent) neither agree nor disagree that the G1000 set democratic innovation in motion. So while there is widespread support for the G1000, there is also doubt about the difference it made.

It is also noteworthy that citizens are undecided about whether the recommendations of the G1000 should be binding. This is interesting in light of recent discussions among deliberative democrats concerning the reach that the proposals of mini-publics should have (see, for example, Goodin and Dryzek 2006; Smith 2009; Ryan and Smith 2014). Some scholars advocate automatic implementation whereas others see a more modest role for these recommendations because they think mini-publics should have a merely advisory function. The respondents in our survey are also undecided concerning the impact that the G1000 should have on the political and legislative process, even though the advocates of direct implementation (32.7 per cent) still outnumber those who are opposed (9.6 per cent).

Support for the results of the G1000

Finally, we turn to the question of specific results. In any deliberative process, it is important that the recommendations formulated by the mini-public receive some form of public endorsement. As Dryzek puts it: 'decisions still have to be justified to those who did not participate' (2001: 654). This means that the results from a deliberative endeavour should be put to the test of publicity once more, and receive public assent. This could be done by putting the results to a popular vote in a referendum. Such a process of public endorsement was not part of the G1000, which is why we rely on the survey data to see whether there is substantive support for its ideas or not (Table 4.3).

Of the first two items, on labour-market-related questions, both proposals received overwhelming support among the survey respondents. No less than 72.3 per cent agreed with making the labour market more flexible and 61.3 per cent were in favour of lowering income taxes. The automatic indexing mechanism, which increases salaries based on a consumption index, also received the support of 60.6 per cent of the wider public.

The other three proposals (retirees on the labour market, non-discrimination and a universal basic income) received weaker public endorsement. This is most likely because there has never been a real public debate on these issues. People's opinions thus have not yet crystallised. Another interesting perspective on these findings is that members of the wider maxi-public do not automatically endorse the decisions reached by the mini-public. This is the argument for deliberative polls: opinions announced after deliberation are different from common opinion because people have had the time and space to deliberate, exchange argument, hear different points of view and to develop a more 'enlightened' opinion (Fishkin 1992, 2009).

Table 4.3: Support for results of G1000

	Completely disagree	Disagree	Neither agree nor disagree	Agree	Completely agree
Labour market has to become more flexible so employees can move more easily between companies and organisations.	2.4%	5.6%	19.7%	47.3%	25.0%
Income taxes should be reduced and alternative sources of public finances must be found.	4.9%	9.6%	24.2%	40.5%	20.8%
Automatic indexing mechanism for salaries must be maintained.	5.1%	11.8%	22.5%	34.5%	26.1%
To prevent future generations from having to bear weight of ageing population, labour market should be opened more to retirees.	10.9%	16.7%	25.6%	34.4%	12.4%
Non-discrimination should be main principle for getting subsidies.	5.1%	12.2%	37.0%	32.6%	13.1%
A universal basic income should be implemented.	18.2%	25.6%	28.6%	21.4%	6.2%

The conventional political uptake

The effect of the G1000 on the policy process was non-existent in the short term but that does not mean that there were no influences from the G1000 on the major political actors of the country. This section analyses the reactions of political elites towards the G1000 and its idea of a different kind of democracy. First, we look at the manifestos of the political parties that are the main players in the Belgian political landscape (Deschouwer 2012). Second, we observe the discourses of members of Belgium's several parliaments and how they refer to the G1000.

Party manifestos

The notion of citizen political participation beyond the ballot box, including deliberation as well as sortition (drawing lots), became an important element in the discourse of some Belgian parties in the electoral campaign of 2014. We have analysed every manifesto of the thirteen parties[22] that won at least one seat in one of the parliaments directly elected in that year (European Parliament; House of Representatives; Flemish Parliament; Walloon Parliament; Parliament of the Brussels-Capital Region; Parliament of the German-speaking Community). All the manifestos published by the parties for the three elections (European, federal, and regional/community) were part of this comparison. Some parties, like the Francophone ecologists (Ecolo) and Flemish regionalists (N-VA), produced one manifesto for the three elections; whereas parties like the Francophone regionalists (FDF) had four different ones (federal, Walloon, Brussels and European). Moreover, we performed a thematic analysis on questions related to democratic innovations, participation and deliberation.

The analysis yielded a fourfold typology. The first group is composed of the Flemish regionalists (N-VA) and the Francophone Union (UF). The topics of participation or deliberation are not present in their manifestos. For the second group, these questions are present in the manifesto only by the institution of referendum. This is the case for the (radical) right-wing parties like the Francophone Populist Party (PP) and Flemish radical-right party (VB). Thirdly, the majority of party manifestos include general sentences asking for more participation, mainly at local levels, but without concrete propositions for institutions or the formalisation of this participation by citizens. This is the case for Francophone liberals (MR), radical left (PTB GO!), regionalists (FDF) as well as Flemish socialists (sp.a) and Christian-Democrats (CD&V). For instance, FDF explains in its Proposition 354 in the federal manifesto that 'It should also adopt a code of citizen participation at the provincial level according to the principle of participatory democracy' (FDF 2014: 148 [author's translation]) but the manifesto gives neither an explanation about the content of this code nor does it state if this principle is also necessary at other levels of governance.

Parties that seem more in favour of citizen-participation form the last group; some of these parties had propositions comparable to the ones defended by the G1000. This is the case for the two Green parties (Ecolo and Groen); the Francophone socialists (PS); the Francophone Christian-Democrats (cdH); and the Flemish liberals (Open Vld). This last group of parties all suggest delving into hot political issues by organising citizen-panels or citizen-juries, which would be in charge of formulating propositions. The Open Vld proposes the use of a form of participatory budgeting (page 48 of its manifesto). The three Francophone parties of this fourth group also recommend the use of sortition to select participants for such experiments.

---

22. CD&V (Flemish Christian Democrats); cdH (Francophone Christian Democrats); Ecolo (Francophone Ecologists); Groen (Flemish Ecologists); FDF (Francophone Regionalists); MR (Francophone Liberals); N-VA (Flemish Regionalists); Open Vld (Flemish Liberals); PP (Francophone Populists); PS (Francophone Socialists); PTB-GO! (Francophone Radical Left); sp.a (Flemish Socialists); VB (Flemish Radical Right); UF (Union of the Francophone in Flanders).

So what is the impact of the G1000 on these manifestos? In the previous elections, of 2010, there was no reference to citizen-panels or random selection in politics for the PS and Open Vld and the chapters on democratic innovation concentrated on the reinforcement of existing institutions (parliaments; petitions; use of public consultation). The G1000 is certainly not the only source of democratic innovation but it influenced the discourse of these parties on this topic. In a chronicle published in 2014, the President of the Francophone Socialists argued that the G1000 and the ideas defended by its organisers ought to inspire public authorities to organise randomly selected bodies of citizens to transform representative democracy.[23] For the other parties of the group, institutionalised participation by citizens had already been proposed in 2010 but we can see some links with the G1000 in the two Green parties' manifestos. In the Flemish Green Party manifesto, one sentence was, in fact, inspired by one of G1000's slogan: 'Democracy is more than colouring in a box every four, five or six years'. The manifesto of the Francophone Greens was the most influenced by the G1000. They take this experiment as an exemplar of good future practice:

Specifically, Ecolo calls for the development of citizens' conferences or deliberative panels such as panels of citizen-users to evaluate some policy; roundtables with experts and citizens or the G1000. In other words, investigation of an issue by a group of people randomly selected, through an improved public debate (particularly with regard to environmental issues, societal debates or other long-term issues) (Ecolo 2014: 000) [authors' translation].

This extract reveals the indirect impact of the G1000. The initiative acts as a point of reference, an argument, and an exemplar of best practice for parties that want to promote or organise participation in public deliberation among ordinary citizens. The G1000 is certainly not the only source of inspiration for them but it acts as an important element of the issue-framing for people both outside and inside the political arena. For instance, the President of the Study Centre of the Francophone liberal MR organised a conference on 15 March 2014 with the title 'Reinventing Democracy'. The MR invited one spokesperson from the G1000 to speak about the experience. One day before the conference, the President of this Centre gave an interview to the newspaper *Le Soir* to explain why the Belgian regime needed democratic innovation. Furthermore, he argued that deliberation among randomly selected citizens was a good means for achieving such renewal.[24] In an open letter, the President of the Francophone Brussels Parliament, Hamza Fassi-Firi (cdH), argued for the importance of making democracies more deliberative as they faced the major issues of the twenty-first century. He then organised a conference with another spokesperson of the G1000 (Fassi-Fihri 2014). In sum, several political leaders have used the G1000 as an exemplar of desirable democratic transformation.

23. Available online at: http://www.ps.be/Pagetype1/Actus/News/Chronique-de-Paul-Magnette-Contre-les-elections.aspx (accessed 9 February 2016).
24. 'La démocratie, avec tirage au sort', Richard Miller, *Le Soir*, 14 March 2014.

G1000 in the parliament

As mentioned earlier, the formal political uptake of the G1000 was limited. In the different parliaments of Belgium, the heart of representative democracy, a few MPs did speak about the G1000. For example, in the session on 9 May 2012 three MPs from the two Green parties in the House of Representatives presented a proposition for a resolution concerning the Treaty on Stability, Coordination and Governance in the Economic and Monetary Union. Opposed to the ratification of this agreement, they proposed to organise a large debate with social partners before proceeding to a vote. This large debate would use 'innovative ways to encourage reflection based on the G1000'.[25] Here, the G1000 was used by opposition MPs in support of their criticism of the negotiation process of the treaty and to insist on the idea that other forms of political process are possible.

In the Flemish Parliament, the Socialist MP Steve D'Hulster (sp.a) asked the Flemish Minister-President a question about the initiative.[26] He said that the content of the report should be analysed by the Flemish government and that the process could inspire other governmental initiatives. The Minister-President responded, in a very formal style, that he had not yet read the report. Nevertheless, he noted that this kind of initiative is very fruitful and that the participation of citizens is a very important component in the process.

The social uptake

Since its very conception, the dissemination of the idea of a more participatory and deliberative democracy was the aim of the G1000. That is the reason why, at the margin of the G1000 summit, two events were organised to broaden the scale of the project. With the G'Home, every citizen had the opportunity to participate in a simultaneous online deliberation. This gave the opportunity to 730 citizens, not randomly selected, to participate in the discussion and to exchange points of view. Also, local mini-publics, the G'Offs, were organised by volunteers across the country. In total, 356 participants met each other in fifty locations to discuss the same topics as in Brussels.

These two elements opened the G1000 to the outside world and gained the support of people who wanted to find new modes of political participation. Some people were interested by the idea and the method and became defenders of deliberative democracy. An example is very illustrative. A group of citizens organised a G'Off in Grez-Doiceau but they found the experience too short to have any real effectiveness. A few months later, joined by other inhabitants of the village, they decided to create their own democratic innovation in Grez-Doiceau. Their G100 took place three years later in 2014, gathering volunteers and randomly

---

25. Doc 53 2180/001, Chambre des représentants de Belgique, 9 May 2012, 'Proposition de résolution relative au Traité sur la stabilité, la coordination et la gouvernance au sein de l'Union économique et monétaire', déposée par MM. Georges Gilkinet et Stefaan Van Hecke et Mme Muriel Gerken, p. 12.
26. Vlaams Parlement, Handeling, Plenaire vergadering nr. 9 (2012–2013),14 November 2012.

selected people during one weekend to discuss and engage proposals for the future of the municipality.

It is always difficult to measure the influence of one specific event on the spirit of a time but several initiatives can be considered to be clearly the result of the G1000. The most evident example is the G1000 that was organised on 22 March 2014 in Amersfoort, a city just south of Amsterdam, three days after the municipal elections. The logo and the general atmosphere were similar to the ones in Brussels. The project was also organised by independent citizens but the major difference was that traditional political actors were more integrated with the process. Every discussion table was composed of randomly selected citizens alongside public officials and elected representatives, as in the case of Ireland.

Several initiatives were also born in Belgium in the wake of the G1000, mainly at the local level, such as the G100 organised by the cultural centre in Ath, K35 in Kortrijk or the local CD&V of Kuurne, who organised a G100. These experiences make the trajectory of the G1000 interesting to consider. Indeed, these grassroots events inspire more traditional political actors like political parties, and public and semi-public bodies. G1000 projects exist also in Uden and Rotterdam in the Netherlands, in France, in the United Kingdom and in Hungary.

All these elements can help us rethink the relation between deliberative small-scale democratic venues and democracy in the whole system (Chambers 2009). Goodin and Dryzek (2006) explain that mini-public deliberation can be used to inform the public debate; to test propositions for reform; and to legitimate policy. With the example of the G1000, we can add a new sort of output: the existence of a mini-public used by other political actors, traditional and non-traditional, as a reference to promote a more deliberative democracy. For them, while the content of the final proposition of the G1000 is not so relevant, the process remains crucial.

Conclusion

The G1000 was certainly an outlier in the Belgian political context. In a country in which not just political parties but also civil-society organisations are the backbone of the political system, such a citizen-led initiative was received with both great caution and great expectations. The G1000 received praise for its input and its throughput legitimacy because of its overall organisation and bottom-up approach. Moreover, this bottom-up approach was seen as especially successful as it was reinforced by a will to maintain wide inclusiveness that relied on random selection. However, on the output side, the G1000 failed to have an impact on short-term policy-making, despite the concrete proposals made by the G32 citizens after three weekends of deliberation.

Nevertheless, in the longer run, the political and social uptakes of the G1000 are increasing: most political parties now advocate some form of participatory and deliberative democracy. What is more, the G1000 sparked a debate in Belgium and in neighbouring countries about new ways of designing democracy. Therefore the weak output legitimacy assessment that was given immediately after the G1000 now needs to be nuanced. And this finding is interesting in light of the debate raised by this book.

To be sure, the G1000 cannot be described as a *constitutional* mini-public. It was not designed by any political bodies, let alone by any constitution-making ones. Above all, the aim of the G1000 was not reforming the Belgian constitution, even partially. Yet the G1000's macro-level political uptake, broadly understood, has been increasing steadily in the years since it happened. In fact, this citizen-led initiative sparked a more general debate about the nature of democracy in Belgium and, especially, about the role of citizens. The public authorities are not necessarily going to call for a constitutional convention inspired by the G1000 but this initiative has paved the way for this possibility in a country in which, because of the divide between the two main language-communities and the consociational legacy (Swenden 2013; Caluwaerts and Reuchamps 2014a), citizens are often kept away from political negotiations about the future of the country.

References

Caluwaerts, D., and Reuchamps, M. (2012) *The G1000: Facts, figures and some lessons from an experience of deliberative democracy in Belgium*, Brussels, BE: Re-Bel, available at: http://www.rethinkingbelgium.eu/rebel-initiative-files/events/seventh-public-event-g1000-european-citizens-initiative-malaise-democracy/G1000-Background-Paper.pdf (accessed 9 February 2016).

—   (2014a) 'Deliberative stress in linguistically divided Belgium', in Ugarriza, J. and Caluwaerts, D. (eds) *Democratic Deliberation in Deeply Divided Societies: From conflict to common ground*, Basingstoke, UK: Palgrave Macmillan.

—   (2014b) 'Does inter-group deliberation foster inter-group appreciation? Evidence from two experiments in Belgium', *Politics* 34(2): 101–15.

—   (2015) 'Strengthening democracy through bottom-up deliberation: an assessment of the internal legitimacy of the G1000 project', *Acta Politica* 50(2): 151–70.

Caluwaerts, D., and Ugarriza, J. E. (2012) 'Favorable conditions to epistemic validity in deliberative experiments: a methodological assessment', *Journal of Public Deliberation* 8(1).

Chambers, S. (2009) 'Rhetoric and the public sphere: has deliberative democracy abandoned mass democracy?' *Political Theory* 37(3): 323–50.

Cobb, R., and Elder, C. (1983) *Participation in American Politics: The dynamics of agenda building*, Baltimore, MD: Johns Hopkins University Press.

Crosby, N., and Nethercut, D. (2005) 'Citizens juries: creating a trustworthy voice of the people', in Gastil, J. and Levine, P. (eds) *The Deliberative Democracy Handbook*, San Francisco, CA: Jossey-Bass.

Deschouwer, K. (2012) *The Politics of Belgium: Governing a divided society*, Houndmills, Basingstoke, UK: Palgrave Macmillan.

Deschouwer, K., and Reuchamps, M. (2013) 'The Belgian Federation at a crossroad', *Regional & Federal Studies* 23(3): 261–70.

Dryzek, J. S. (2001) 'Legitimacy and economy in deliberative democracy', *Political Theory* 29(5): 651–69.

Ecolo (2014) *Programme 2014*, available at: http://www.ecolo.be/?-nos-priorites-et-notre-programme- (accessed 9 February 2016).

Fassi-Fihri, H. (2014) 'Pour une démocratie moderne: des panels citoyens tirés au sort', *Le Soir*, 21 January, available at: http://www.lesoir.be/407616/article/debats/cartes-blanches/2014-01-21/pour-une-democratie-moderne-des-panels-citoyens-tires-au-sort (accessed 23 February 2016).

FDF (2014) *Programme fédéral 2014*, available at: http://www.defi.eu/fdf/initiatives/archives/les-resultats-electoraux/elections-regionales-legislatives/le-programme-des-fdf-aux-elections/ (accessed 23 February 2016).

Fishkin, J. S. (1992) 'The idea of a deliberative opinion poll', *Public Perspective* 3(2): 26–7.

— (2009) *When the People Speak. Deliberative democracy and public consultation*, Oxford, UK: Oxford University Press.

Fung, A. (2007) 'Minipublics: deliberative designs and their consequences', in Rosenberg, S. W. (ed.) *Deliberation, Participation and Democracy: Can the people govern?*, Basingstoke, UK and New York, NY: Palgrave Macmillan.

G1000 (2012) *Final report: Democratic innovation in practice*, Brussels, BE: G1000, available at: http://www.g1000.org/documents/G1000_EN_Website.pdf (accessed 23 February 2016).

Garbe, D. (1986) 'Planning cell and citizen report: a report on German experiences with new participation instruments', *European Journal of Political Research* 14(1–2): 221–36.

Goodin, R. E., and Dryzek, J. S. (2006) 'Deliberative impacts: the macro-political uptake of mini-publics', *Politics & Society* 34(2): 219–44.

Gourgues, G., and Sainty, J. (2011) 'Does public participation only concern upper classes? The "social oligarchization" of new types of democracy', CIRES Working Papers.

Kies, R., and Nanz, P. (eds) (2013) *Is Europe Listening to Us? Successes and failures of EU citizen consultations*, Farnham, UK: Ashgate.

Open VLD (2014) *Programmacongres Vlaanderen vleugels geven*, available at: http://www.openvld.be/library/1/files/4505_definitief_programma___vlaanderen_vleugels_geven.pdf (accessed 23 February 2016)

Parkinson, J. (2006) 'Rickety bridges: using the media in deliberative democracy', *British Journal of Political Science* 36(1): 175–84.

Parkinson, J. and Mansbridge, J. (eds) (2012) *Deliberative Systems*, Cambridge, UK: Cambridge University Press.

Ryan, M., and Smith, G. (2014) 'Defining mini-publics', in Grönlund, K., Bächtiger, A. and Setälä, M. (eds) *Deliberative Mini-Publics: Involving citizens in the democratic process*, Colchester, UK: ECPR Press.

Ryfe, D. M. (2005) 'Does deliberative democracy work?', *Annual Review of Political Science* 8: 49–71.

Smith, G. (2009) *Democratic Innovations: Designing institutions for citizen participation*, Cambridge, UK: Cambridge University Press.

Steiner, J., Bächtiger, A., Spörndli, M. and Steenbergen, M. R. (2004) *Deliberative Politics in Action: Analyzing parliamentary discourse*, Cambridge, UK and New York, NY: Cambridge University Press.

Swenden, W. (2013) 'Conclusion: the future of Belgian federalism—between reform and swansong?', *Regional & Federal Studies* 23(3): 369–82.

News websites of articles referenced in the chapter

http://www.demorgen.be
http://www.dhnet.be
http://www.gva.be
http://www.hbvl.be
http://www.knack.be
http://www.lalibre.be
http://www.lesoir.be
http://www.levif.be
http://www.rtbf.be
http://www.standaard.be

Chapter Five

Constitutional Deliberative Democracy and Democratic Innovations

Brigitte Geissel and Sergiu Gherghina

Increasing numbers of scholars as well as citizens are pinning their hopes on participatory innovation as a means to cure democratic malaise. These scholars are convinced that the cure for democracies' ills is more democracy (for example, Dalton, Cain and Scarrow 2003: 251; Offe 2003; Warren 2003), because the attitudes of citizens towards the representative system should change for the better and policies should be improved if citizens are involved in the processes of will-formation and decision-making (Cain, Dalton and Scarrow 2003; Zittel and Fuchs 2007; Geissel and Newton 2012). At the same time, critical citizens demand more opportunities for direct involvement and claim an active part in political processes (Norris 1999; Dalton 2004). Following this logic, several governments at both national and local levels have gone down the participatory route and implemented various kinds of democratic innovation that allow citizens to make their voices heard.

In the wake of these developments, governments have increasingly granted popular involvement in processes of constitutional reforms as well. Constitutions set broad principles in political systems and societies by establishing the functions of institutions and the rights and duties of citizens, as well as setting limits to the interference of the state in areas of private life (Freeman 1990; Ackerman 1993; Dworkin 1995). Many authors argue that, at the normative level, constitutions must be forged through procedures that ensure the broad participation of citizens, whose lives are directly affected (Fossum and Menendez 2005). Among these authors, there is a consensus that the best form of popular involvement in the process of constitutional reform is not only via 'final approval' through popular referendum but through deliberation during the reform-process itself. The essence of such deliberation can be summarised as 'producing reasonable, well-informed opinions in which participants are willing to revise preferences in light of discussion, new information, and claims made by fellow participants' (Chambers 2003: 309). In practice, as illustrated by previous chapters of this book, citizens have increasingly obtained an opportunity for consultation and input during constitutional reform. The variety of these consultation processes leads to several inter-connected questions: how did these consultation processes work? What are the effects of these deliberative processes in comparative perspective? Do these effects match findings on participatory innovation in general?

This chapter seeks to provide some answers by embedding constitutional reform through popular involvement within the broader topic of democratic innovation. We start with a discussion of possible frameworks for the analysis and explain our decision to adapt the framework proposed by Reuchamps and Suiter in the introduction (2016, Chapter One of this volume). Then we comparatively evaluate the three case studies on constitutional deliberative procedures (Belgium, Iceland, Ireland), referring to input legitimacy, throughput legitimacy and output legitimacy. Finally, we embed the findings in the debate about the effects of democratic innovations in general.

Framework for the analysis

Although the call for a 'concise research agenda' to evaluate participatory innovations was made more than three decades ago (Sewell and Philips 1979) and has continued to resonate since then, it remained almost unheard for years (Rowe and Frewer 2004). However, frameworks for analysing (diverse categories of) democratic innovations have been developed more recently. In this sense, the studies conducted by Renn, Webler and Wiedemann (1995), Chess and Purcell (1999), or Rowe, Marsh and Frewer (2004) may be regarded as the first generation of frameworks. Following their pioneering examples, similar yardsticks have been elaborated, focusing on a variety of criteria (Abelson and Gauvin 2006; Geissel 2013).

Table 5.1 summarises the major frameworks available and illustrates that the majority of authors consider criteria such as inclusive participation, deliberative quality and political impact of participatory innovations to be crucial. For example, in his seminal work, Smith (2009) suggested the use of six criteria: inclusiveness; popular control; considered judgement; publicity; efficiency; and transferability. Inclusiveness means both access for different social groups to the participatory innovation *and* an equal opportunity to have a say in the process. Popular control – or impact, as defined in Table 5.1 – refers to deliberation having a meaningful effect on policies, that is, that the participatory process has a visible influence on the decision-making process. Considered judgement, a synonym for enlightenment as summarised in the table, refers to the increase of cognitive competence among those who participate in the deliberation process. Publicity ensures the visibility and openness of proceedings, both internally (among participants) and externally (for the broader public), while efficiency refers to 'the costs participation can place on both citizens and public authorities' (Smith 2009: 13). Finally, transferability means that participatory tools can be, and are, applied to other contexts than those for which they were initially designed.

In their turn, Michels (2011) and Geissel (2012) have identified somewhat different criteria in research on participatory innovations: inclusive participation; improvement of citizens' democratic skills; impact on public policies; quality of deliberation; legitimacy; and political satisfaction.[1] As can be easily observed, most of these frameworks – although often applying different terms

---

1. Further frameworks refer to the impacts of deliberative procedures (Goodin and Dryzek 2006); some assess constitution-making processes in general (Elster 1995; Wheatley and Mendez 2013); or scrutinise specific participatory constitution-making procedures (Moehler 2008; Wheatley and Mendez 2013). These frameworks can be taken into account only partly in this chapter.

Table 5.1: *Frameworks and criteria applied in studies evaluating participatory innovations*

	Renn et al. 1995	Chess and Purcell 1999	Rowe et al. 2004	Abelson and Gauvin 2006	Dalton et al. 2003	Papadopoulos and Warin 2007	Fung 2008	Smith 2009	Geissel 2009	Michels 2011	Geissel 2012
Inclusive participation ('input')	(x)	(x)	x	x	x	x	x	x	(x)	x	x
Quality of deliberation ('throughput')	(x)			x		x	x	x	x	x	x
Impact ('output')			x	x	(x)	(x)	x	x	(x)	x	x
Citizens' enlightenment ('output')	(x)	(x)		x				(x)	x	x	x
Perceived legitimacy ('output')	(x)	(x)	x	x					x	x	x
Other criteria (examples)	Fairness		Many[2]	Process rules	Transparency	Publicity, accountability		Transferability			

Notes: x = mentioned explicitly, although terms differ; (x) = mentioned implicitly
Source: Geissel 2013: 15.

2. The other criteria are: independence; early involvement; transparency; resource accessibility; task definition; and structured decision-making.

and conceptualisations – are explicitly or implicitly in line with the framework suggested in the introduction of this book: in other words, most of these criteria can be regarded as functional equivalents to input, throughput and output legitimacy. On the basis of this similarity, our chapter builds on the framework suggested by Reuchamps and Suiter and adds some specifications that brings their approach closer to the broader perspective of democratic innovations. In particular, we selected five criteria that fit the legitimacy dimensions.

Considering *input* legitimacy, we mainly refer to inclusive participation. Inclusive participation seems to be guaranteed in representative democracies – at least *de jure* – by election of political representatives on the basis of formal political equality. However, participation in elections has been declining in most consolidated democracies for years, because underprivileged groups in society increasingly refuse to take part (Schäfer 2009); so participation has become, *de facto*, rather exclusive. Obviously, facilitating more 'equality in input', 'representative input' or 'inclusive participation' is a topic of concern and the question of whether new participatory procedures could, and do, provide more inclusive participation has become a crucial topic in recent research. As suggested in Suiter and Reuchamps 2016, Chapter One of this volume, we also include the criterion 'agenda-setting', that is, the question of whether the agenda of a citizens' assembly is open or closed.

With reference to *throughput* legitimacy, our main focus is on the quality of deliberation.[3] Deliberation cannot be operationalised easily and standard measurements, such as the Discourse Quality Index (DQI), cannot be applied to evaluate the three case studies, due to the lack of data (see the later discussion).

The dimension of *output* legitimacy refers to the *impact* deliberative procedures have on the policy-areas they are concerned with. It means that the mini-publics should not be purely symbolic but actually 'make a difference'. In our chapter, output legitimacy comprises three criteria, namely: actual impact on the new constitution; influence on the 'enlightenment' of the broader or even the entire citizenry; and impact on citizens' attitudes towards political objects such as the political system and its institutions (so-called 'perceived legitimacy').

We differentiate for each criteria between *ex ante* design of the deliberation-event on the one hand and *ex post* reality, that is, its actual achievement in practice, on the other hand (*see* Table 5.2). Why do we take design into account, not only results? An appropriate design is a necessary condition for successful participatory procedures. If a criterion, for example, inclusive participation or quality of deliberation, is not considered in the design, its implementation and outcome will most likely fail. Our approach is intended to bring the theoretical framework closer to reality. The framework with the criteria and indicators to be applied is summarised in Table 5.2.

---

3. Deliberation has always played an important role in theories of democracy. However, it was limited to the political elite for a long time. In contrast, current democratic theories demand deliberation within civil society and among citizens.

Table 5.2: Framework for evaluating participatory innovations

Type of legitimacy	Criteria	Stage/phase	Indicator
Input legitimacy	Inclusive participation	*Ex ante* design	Who can take part?
		Ex post reality	Who takes/took part?
	Open or closed agenda/ agenda-setting options	*Ex ante* design	Agenda provided or topic of discussion?
		Ex post reality	Agenda created/ changed/followed
Throughput legitimacy	Quality of deliberation (e.g., 'equal voice'; mutual respect; empathy)	*Ex ante* design	Existence of moderator/ facilitator; rules for deliberation; Balanced information
		Ex post reality	Practice
Output legitimacy	Impact on new constitution	*Ex ante* design	Institutionalised connection to constitution making body; plan to put recommendations of mini-public to referendum
		Ex post reality	Real impact on constitution
	Visibility; improved citizens' 'enlightenment'/'awareness'.	*Ex ante* design	Connection to media; Plan for visibility of process
		Ex post reality	Achieved visibility; achieved enlightenment/ awareness
	'Perceived legitimacy'	*Ex ante* design	Incorporated in plan? e.g. *ex ante* and *ex post* survey of participants (and whole citizenry)
		Ex post reality	Change in attitudes

How did we assess the *ex ante design considering legitimacy (input, throughput, and output)*? Looking at the indicators for input legitimacy, we evaluate whether the initial design included systematic planning for inclusive participants' recruitment. If participants are self-selected, there is never inclusive participation and the 'usual suspects' will dominate. Inclusive participation is only reached in procedures designed with random or other types of participant-selection mechanisms. The second question concerning input legitimacy is – according to this volume's framework – the question of whether the agenda was set beforehand or not (openness of the agenda). In terms of throughput legitimacy, high-quality deliberation can only develop with clear rules and a moderator or facilitator. Along these lines, we consider it relevant to check the extent to which each of these was planned in the design of the process. When it comes to output legitimacy, we look for the institutionalisation of strong links to constitution-making bodies and to the broader public; it is already well known that deliberative mini-publics 'only have some impact on public policies if they are connected to political decision-making bodies', that is, political representatives or popular decision-making via referendum (Geissel 2012: 212).

All these indicators of legitimacy in design have then to be weighed against the practices. We examine the extent to which the design was put into reality. Along these lines, we have developed matching *ex post reality criteria* that reflect the reality of the deliberative procedures. For example, referring to inclusiveness (input legitimacy) the *ex ante* 'who can take part?' aspect of the design has an *ex post* equivalent in the form of 'who took part?'. There are three empirical possibilities: 1) consistency between the design and practice, that is, implementation of plans; 2) inconsistency between design and practice because some design-aspects were not properly implemented; and 3) practices that went beyond the initial design, that is, the actual process surpassed the initial plans.

Evaluation of the three country studies: Iceland, Ireland and Belgium

The three country studies presented in this volume will be compared according to the framework outlined in Table 5.2. Their comparison is useful from several methodological and empirical points of view. First, following the definition used in the introduction to this book, they are all cases of constitutional deliberation in which ordinary citizens were involved and carried on a dialogue aiming at developing (guiding principles for) their society's constitution. Second, the fairly similar timing of these deliberative processes (2010–12) makes it possible to analyse them without a major threat of 'contagion' (learning effect) from one to another. Quite often, successful deliberative experiments serve as reference points for similar processes and the passage of time favours this (the longer the distance between events, the higher the likelihood of learning). Third, there is some variation in the reasons for which each of these deliberation-processes emerged; the form they took; and their initial goals. Such diversity allows a better understanding of constitutional deliberative democracy.

Our assessment of legitimacy will compare the *ex ante* design, that is, the intentions of the organisers, against the *ex post* reality, to see the extent to which the design criteria were implemented. Starting with *ex ante inclusive participation*, we focus on who was supposed to take part in the deliberation and on the existence of a selection-mechanism envisaged to ensure some form of representativeness. In all three countries, the selection mechanisms were oriented towards the creation of inclusive participation (*see* Table 5.3) but the means differed. In Belgium, the aim was not to organise a representative mini-public but a randomly selected one: every inhabitant of the country was supposed to have the same probability of being chosen for the citizen-summit (G1000) and the citizen-panel (G32). Iceland had a similar approach towards ordinary citizens and aimed at choosing 1,000 people by random selection (stratified sampling) for their so called National Forum. In addition, two more bodies were created. The first was the Constitutional Committee, consisting of seven members who were supposed to collect information, analyse the core issues discussed by the Forum and propose ideas for constitutional revision. A second body was the Constitutional Assembly, consisting of twenty-five elected members (*see* Bergmann 2016, Chapter Two in this volume). This body was expected to revise Iceland's constitution using proposals coming from the Forum and from the Committee. In Ireland, inclusiveness was ensured by a random selection of ordinary citizens aimed at gender, age, and regional representativeness.

In all three cases, the initial plans were implemented to a great extent. In Belgium, a company was hired to randomly select participants and it used Random Digit Dialling based on phone numbers. About 3 per cent of the contacted persons agreed to join the deliberation-day in Brussels to participate in the deliberative event. The organisers also used gender, territorial (province-based) and language quotas to obtain better descriptive representation. To increase inclusiveness, 10 per cent of the seats were reserved for marginalised demographics such as homeless people or immigrants (chosen by a mixture of random selection and targeted recruitment). To reach these groups, the G1000 asked local associations to help with contacts for this segment of the population. In Iceland, the three-layered selection process worked in practice and the deliberation included a mix of randomly selected citizens, appointed experts and nationally elected individual representatives. In Ireland, a polling company was hired to do the random sampling using a face-to-face approach. Individuals who agreed were contacted by the Convention and there was a substitute for each participant (that is, twice as many potential participants were lined up as were going to be needed). In addition, the deliberation included politicians who were nominated by their parties (*see* Sutter, Farrell and Harris 2016, Chapter Three of this volume, for details). In terms of composition, at a working table (the discussions were divided into such tables) there were always more citizens than political representatives.

The *ex ante agenda-setting options* were similar in the three countries. Iceland and Ireland had clear and precise agendas to which topics could be added. In Iceland, all three deliberative forums (National Forum; Constitutional Committee; Constitutional Assembly/Council) had the task of revising the mechanics of the existing constitution, which no longer reflected the Icelandic political system, for example, the division of power between state institutions. On top of this, they had the freedom to include other constitutional matters on the agenda. In Ireland, the agenda was also clear and specific providing similar room to manoeuver. The legislature allowed the Convention to consider other relevant amendments, apart from those stipulated in the terms of reference. In Belgium, the agenda was not determined by the organisers. The agenda-setting process was very open and took place via broad public consultation. Three issues were identified as crucial by the public and put on the agenda for the citizen-summit as well as for the citizen-panel (*see* Jacquet, Moskovic, Caluwaerts and Reuchamps 2016, Chapter Four of this volume, for details).

However, the *ex post* reality of agenda-setting presents great variation. At one extreme, in Belgium, the deliberation followed the initial agenda and did not alter it in any substantial manner. Such a result is unsurprising since the initial agenda-setting was achieved via public consultation and adjusted before each phase. This dynamic is particular to the G1000 process and was not observed in the other two countries. At the other extreme, in the case of Iceland, the agenda was completely altered. While the initial idea was to revise constitutional provisions, during deliberations, the Council arrived at the conclusion that the old constitution could not be adjusted to contemporary realities and decided to write a new one. Ireland is the middle case and the recommendations that resulted from deliberation there did not follow the previously set agenda closely (*see* Suiter, Farrell and Harris 2016, Chapter Three of this volume, for details).

Let us now turn to throughput legitimacy and assess the *quality* of deliberation. In the *ex ante* design, this aspect was mainly the responsibility of a facilitator or moderator. In all cases, facilitators or moderators were, in fact, provided. The involvement of professional facilitators was meant to foster respect for dialogue (such as listening to other participants); allow equal consideration of all opinions represented at the table; and guarantee openness towards and inclusion of all opinions around the table. In Ireland, discussions were organised in tables of from six to eight participants and each table had a trained facilitator and a note-taker. The facilitators were provided with a list of rules designed to ensure that all those at the table had the opportunity to have a say, not allowing one voice to dominate. Iceland is a more complicated case due to its multi-layered structure: Forum, Committee and Council. The presence of moderators was either difficult (Forum) or not required (Committee and Council). Regarding the latter, the relatively small number of participants and the type of discussions were thought to be functional without a moderator.

This similarity of the *ex ante* designs is also reflected in the *ex post* realities. In Belgium and Ireland, the design was carefully implemented to ensure quality of deliberation and no deviations from it were observed. Practical components were added to ensure the rules functioned properly. The Icelandic case, with its multi-layered structure, provides a mixed picture.

The first indicator of the output legitimacy of these mini-publics is their impact on any new constitution or constitutional amendments. To this end, we look at their institutionalised connections to constitution-making bodies, that is, whether their designs included plans to submit the recommendations of the mini-publics for legislative consideration or to a referendum. There is variation between the three deliberative processes: no institutional connection and no plans for referendum (Belgium), and institutional connection and referendums (Iceland and Ireland). The G1000 began as a citizen-initiative to improve representative democracy by breathing new life into it. Its aim was to stay independent from political and state institutions (no formal ties) and so there was no plan to put the recommendations of the mini-public to referendum. In Iceland, the entire process was developed in a relation to the national legislature and the plan was that the draft resulted from deliberation would go to Parliament. In Ireland, the deliberation process was also set up by the government and the plan was for all issues to be discussed by the legislature, with a view to deciding which to put to referendum. The terms of reference explicitly stated that 'the Government will provide in the Oireachtas [houses of parliament] a response to each recommendation of the Convention within four months and, if accepting the recommendation, will indicate the timeframe it envisages for the holding of any related referendum'.

The actual impact of the mini-publics on the three constitutions also varied somewhat, with no real effect in Belgium and potentially large but actually mixed effects in Iceland and Ireland. The desire of the G1000 creators to remain independent of traditional political authorities reduced the likelihood that this debate would be translated into concrete public policies. There was no obligation for members of the government to take the report of the deliberation into account and neither proposals for a referendum nor for any deliberation between participants and politicians. In Iceland, the crowd-sourced draft constitution was sent to Parliament in 2011 and subjected to a referendum in 2012. The draft constitution was approved by the popular vote and the new constitution was expected to come into force. However, the 2013 legislative elections were won by opponents of the new constitution and the entire process was put on hold. Nevertheless, the deliberative procedure and the non-binding referendum did leave their marks. In Ireland, parliament debated the first three reports and referendums were held in May 2015. However, a number of the Convention reports have yet to be debated in Parliament.

The planned public visibility of the deliberation processes was limited in each of the three countries. In Belgium, before the deliberation, the manifesto of the G1000 was published in the four major newspapers of the country. After that, there were no formal ties but several press releases were sent to the media. Three spokespersons were also selected. Similarly, in Iceland, there were no specific plans in the design to increase the publicity of the process but, given the salience of the event, the media were expected to cover it. In Ireland, there was also no specific design to ensure media interest. In spite of this poor planning, however, in practice, each deliberative event was the object of extensive media exposure and interest. Jacquet et al. (2016, Chapter Four of this volume) provide detailed accounts of the Belgian media coverage; the key point is that the event received high levels of attention. In Iceland, the deliberation received increased media attention and a similar situation could be observed in Ireland, where each weekend of deliberation was reported extensively on the main evening news and in the major newspapers.

The final indicator of output legitimacy is the increased approval of the citizenry towards both the political system and its institutions. In Belgium, there was no real plan to improve the political attitudes of the participants or to enhance perceived legitimacy. Instead, the ambition was to show that citizens are able to deliberate and provide meaningful opinions. In Iceland, the deliberation was planned as a healing process after the financial crisis. To some extent, therefore, we can say that this process was aimed at changing citizens' attitudes towards the political system.

Table 5.3: Empirical evidence of constitutional revisions through deliberation

Criteria	Stage/phase	Belgium	Iceland	Ireland
Inclusive participation	*ex ante* design	✓	✓	✓
	ex post reality	✓	✓	✓
Agenda-setting options	*ex ante* design	✓	✓	✓
	ex post reality	✓	x	x/✓
Quality of deliberation	*ex ante* design	✓	✓	✓
	ex post reality	✓	✓	✓
Impact on new constitution	*ex ante* design	x	✓	✓
	ex post reality	x	→	→
Citizens' awareness	*ex ante* design	x	x	x
	ex post reality	?	?	?
Improved perceived legitimacy	*ex ante* design	x	✓	✓
	ex post reality	?	?	?

Note: ✓ = (mostly) fulfilled; x = not intended/not fulfilled; → = pending, partly fulfilled; ? = data missing.

In Ireland, changing the attitudes of citizens towards the political system was part of the reasoning for creating this deliberation as well. Unfortunately, without a measurement of attitude-change, the *ex post* reality cannot be assessed.

Table 5.3 summarises these findings. The three cases reveal a complex picture of deliberative processes and their legitimacy. In Belgium, the G1000 can be praised for its input and throughput legitimacy but had little or no output legitimacy. It failed to effect real constitutional reform. Iceland and Ireland score quite highly on all three aspects of legitimacy, though with some differences between them. In Iceland, the aim was to regain the lost legitimacy of democratic politics through a 'healing' dialogue, while in the Irish case deliberation was well connected to decision-making bodies, including referendums.

Findings in the context of the democratic-innovation literature

How do the comparative results of the three cases fit into the overall debate within current scholarship in the field of democratic innovation? How do the findings on input, throughput, and output legitimacy match results of democratic innovations in general? The following discussion embeds the findings presented in the previous section within the broader context of democratic-innovation literature.

To begin with, there are no 'general findings' on the impacts of democratic participatory innovations, because any impact depends heavily on the type of innovation and on the specific context. Several *types* of democratic innovation can be classified, for example, deliberative *versus* direct democratic procedures or top-down procedures, organised by governmental authorities, *versus* bottom-up ones, organised by civil society (see Geissel and Newton 2012). Another difference is in the degree of citizens' decision-making power, ranging on a continuum between no-say, shared decision-making and full citizen final decision-making power (Smith 2009; Newton 2012; Talpin 2012). The innovations discussed in this edition are deliberative; two were organised by governmental authorities (Ireland, Iceland) and one by civil society (Belgium). All of them were designed for consultation, to bring up well thought-out suggestions.

The *context of the innovations* discussed in this book is also very specific. The events took place at the national level and they were destined to provide suggestions for long-standing guiding principles for the entire society – whereas most deliberative innovations are concerned with local problem-solving. Participatory procedures at the national level are hard to find. Among the few are Brazil's National Public Policy Conferences (Pogrebinschi and Samuels 2014). However, Brazil's Conferences were expected to provide policy-suggestions for specific policy-areas, not for the constitution. The notion that citizens are able to deliberate on far-reaching, abstract constitutional topics is rather new.

The attempt to compare findings on national, constitutional, value-focusing, deliberative mini-publics with findings on local, problem-solving ones is demanding. The task of identifying the main values on which the constitutional drafting should be based is very different from finding a solution for a local public problem (Elster 1995). So, what do we learn, when we embed the findings on constitutional deliberative democracy within the research on democratic innovations in general?

Regarding *input legitimacy*, the empirical evidence presented in this book mainly confirms the findings of the democratic-innovation literature. Increasingly, it is recognised that 'democratic innovations, *per se*, do not guarantee equal, inclusive participation. Quite the contrary: without special and continued endeavors, democratic innovations are likely to result in exclusive and unequal participation' (Geissel 2012: 211). In all three cases, efforts were made to achieve some form of descriptive representativeness within the participatory constitutional assemblies. Random selection was the primary mechanism in all three. However, there were some interesting, innovative variations. The mixture of random and targeted selection used in Belgium as well as the extraordinary public election for the Constitutional Assembly in Iceland are both instructive in this regard. And the Irish Convention is also an interesting case, since it was made up of 100 members consisting of sixty-six citizens, thirty-three elected legislators and a chair. The *ex post* reality mostly fulfilled the request for descriptive representation. The second aspect of input legitimacy, agenda-setting options, however, can hardly be discussed in the general context of democratic innovations. Research in this topic is too new to provide good data.

Considering *throughput legitimacy*, that is, the quality of deliberation, all three procedures were designed with deliberative rules and included moderators to guide the discussion. The case studies cannot provide much information about the actual quality of deliberation, however. Adversarial debates were obviously not rare but, in the end, participants generally came to terms on their final suggestions (*see* Talpin 2016, Chapter Six in this volume, for a more detailed discussion of this).

What did we learn about *output legitimacy?* We considered three different aspects of output, namely, 1) the impact on the final constitution or on constitutional reform; 2) increased awareness and enlightenment among citizens in the wake of the publicity of the process; and 3) whether the perceived legitimacy of the political systems as a whole was enhanced. In two cases (Ireland and Iceland) close connections between the deliberative mini-public and the constitution-making bodies were institutionalised. In Ireland, politicians were involved in the debates and the parliament was expected to respond to each recommendation of the Convention within four months. In Iceland, several mechanisms were applied to guarantee the linkage. In the case of G1000, this was never the intention. In Ireland and Iceland, however, the *de facto impact* seemed to be rather small, although some suggestions found their way into the two constitutions. The Irish parliament debated the first three reports and a referendum on two proposed amendments to the Constitution of Ireland was held in 2015.[4]

The lack of macro-effects of deliberative constitutional procedures is not surprising: so far, deliberative procedures have been, with very few exceptions, consultative, with 'little or even no impact on public policies' (Geissel 2012: 212). Even if they are connected to the decision-making bodies, as was the case in Iceland and Ireland, their actual impact on policies and constitutional reforms is generally small.

However, in most cases, social effects beyond actual changes of the constitution were expected. For example in Iceland, the deliberative procedure was meant to provide 'recovery' and to 'heal' the community after severe shocks and crisis. The prerequisite for such effects on the public is some form of publicity, meaning the public receives a substantial amount of information about the procedure. There is not much data in the chapters about whether and how the design of the different procedures institutionalised publicity mechanisms and connections with the media. Sometimes, such a connection was built up during the process, for example, in Ireland a professional public-relations company was eventually hired. In all cases, *de facto* publicity was relatively high. Surprisingly, procedures with no impact on constitutional reforms, such as the G1000, scored well in this field. Publicity and support for the G1000 among citizens and politicians increased during the procedure and nowadays many parties advocate participatory instruments. G1000 'sparked the debate'. Jacquet *et al.* (2016, Chapter Four of this volume) are confident that 'the G1000 seems to indicate that this experience has fostered some sort of constitutional deliberative democracy broadly defined'. However, we know little about the actual impact on citizens' political understanding. Unfortunately, surveys about changes in citizens' political attitudes were not conducted in any

---

4.   One visible result is the adoption of marriage-equality in the constitution, following a referendum.

of the cases, so expert impressions are the only source of information. The same is true for '*perceived legitimacy*', the attitudes of citizens towards their political systems, institutions, constitutions and representatives. Again, these findings are in line with research on democratic innovations in general. Expectations about impact on citizens are high but actual data is difficult to find.

Conclusion

In this chapter, we have tried to embed the findings on citizens' involvement in deliberative constitution-making within the broader background of democratic-innovation research. Most findings in this edition go hand in hand with results on other forms of participatory, deliberative innovations. For example, the lack of impact on actual decision-making, be it on constitutional reform, regional policies or local problem-solving, can be found in almost all deliberative procedures. However, comparison of the cases in this volume with other cases of deliberative involvement reveals a clear research gap. Until now, research in democratic innovations has seldom compared the effects of democratic innovations taking place at different political levels and in different contexts. This is surprising, because it is intuitively convincing that, for example, deliberation on national *versus* sub-national topics as well as concrete problem-solving *versus* abstract, constitutional questions will most likely require different deliberative structures and generate different results.

Research in this field is just starting to tackle emerging normative as well as empirical questions, such as: should citizens (only) be involved in local decisions, because local topics are 'closer to their lives'? Are they 'more competent' to discuss local, 'down-to earth' topics? Should they be involved in deliberation and decision-making considering the abstract guiding principles of a society, that is, the constitution? Is it more important to involve citizens in decisions about a society's value-frame, manifested in its constitution? Should different forms and structures of deliberation be applied in these different contexts? How do the results of participatory deliberative procedures in these different contexts differ according to input, throughput and output legitimacy?

In addition to all these normative and empirical questions, another, future-oriented, conceptual realm of research has just begun. What would comprehensive systems, combining deliberative structures with direct-democratic instruments in a systematic way, look like? How can democratic innovations escape their limitation of being sporadic events? How can representative democratic institutions be more systematically connected to participatory innovations? No innovation can cure all the malaises of current representative democracies (Joas 2013) and this is also true for deliberative procedures in the context of constitutional reforms. The hopes pinned on deliberative procedures can only be fulfilled if participatory innovations are combined in such a way that their respective weaknesses and strengths can be balanced. One of the disadvantages of deliberative procedures is their small number of participants. They may be able to produce high-quality deliberation but it is obvious that they cannot legitimately make binding decisions about constitutional reform; these require a subsequent referendum or legislative action. With popular votes, the problem is the reverse: the entire electorate can take part but preferences might not be well thought through. Thus, neither deliberative procedures nor the aggregation of preferences ('voting') are optimal. However, intelligent, systematic combinations and 'sequencing' (Smith 2009) of different procedures could mitigate some of the weaknesses of each (Saward 2000).

The political impact of mini-publics is currently one of the most crucial issues within deliberative-democracy research. For example, studies describing and analysing the most famous example, the Citizens' Assembly on Electoral Reform in British Columbia, Canada, discuss the impact of this mini-public (Warren and Pearse 2008; Fung, Warren and Gabriel 2011). Fournier *et al.* (2011), comparing citizens' assemblies on electoral reform in British Columbia, Ontario and the Netherlands, point out the limits of deliberative mini-publics and argue for a more 'down to earth' approach. The authors not only asked sceptical questions, such as whether these assemblies really provided descriptive representation or unbiased will-formation, they also elaborated the challenges of connecting mini-publics with society and actual political decision-making, be it by political representatives or by citizens via popular vote. They also demonstrated that mini-publics are always embedded in a specific society with particular political arrangements. These societal and political contexts are responsive to mini-publics to different degrees (see, for example, Fournier *et al.* 2011).

All cases discussed here are interesting and instructive democratic innovations. However, they are trapped in the logic of representative systems with sporadic participatory procedures. Theoretical and conceptual considerations about what *participatory systems* could look like has only just started (for example, Parkinson and Mansbridge 2013).

References

Abelson, J., and Gauvin, F.-P. (2006) *Assessing the Impacts of Public Participation: Concepts, evidence and policy implications*, Ottawa, Canada: Canadian Policy Research Networks (CPRN).

Ackerman, B. (1993) *We the People*, vol. 1: *Foundations*, reprinted edn, Cambridge, MA: Belknap Press.

Bergmann, E. (2016) 'Participatory constitutional deliberation in the wake of crisis: the case of Iceland', in Reuchamps, M. and Suiter, J. (eds) (2016) *Constitutional Deliberative Democracy in Europe*, Colchester, UK: ECPR Press.

Cain, B. E., Dalton, R. J., and Scarrow, S. E. (eds) (2003) *Democracy Transformed? Expanding political opportunities in advanced industrial democracies*, Oxford, UK: Oxford University Press.

Chambers, S. (2003) 'Deliberative democratic theory', *Annual Review of Political Science* 6(1): 307–26.

Chess, C., and Purcell, K. (1999) 'Public participation and the environment: do we know what works?', *Environmental Science & Technology* 33(16): 2685–92.

Dalton, R. J. (2004) *Democratic Challenges, Democratic Choices: The erosion of political support in advanced industrial democracies*, Oxford, UK: Oxford University Press.

Dalton, R. J., Cain, B. E., and Scarrow, S. E. (2003) 'Democratic publics and democratic institutions', in Cain, B. E., Dalton, R. J. and Scarrow, S. E. (eds) *Democracy Transformed?* Oxford, UK: Oxford University Press, p. 250–75.

Dworkin, R. (1995) 'Constitutionalism and democracy', *European Journal of Philosophy* 3(1): 2–11.

Elster, J. (1995) 'Forces and mechanisms in the constitution-making process', *Duke Law Journal* 45(2): 364–96.

Fossum, J. E., and Menendez, A. J. (2005) 'The constitution's gift? A deliberative democratic analysis of constitution making in the European Union', *European Law Journal* 11(4): 380–410.

Fournier P., van der Kolk, H., Carty, R. K., Blais, A., and Rose, J. (2011) *When Citizens Decide: Lessons from the citizen assemblies on electoral reform*, Oxford, UK: Oxford University Press.

Freeman, S. (1990) 'Constitutional democracy and the legitimacy of judicial review', *Law and Philosophy* 9(4): 327–70.

Fung, A., Warren, M., and Gabriel, O.W. (2011) 'British Columbia, Canada: Citizens' Assembly on Electoral Reform (BCCA)', Gütersloh, DE: Bertelsmann Stiftung, available at: http://participedia.net/sites/default/files/case-files/653_303_Case_Study_British_Columbia.pdf (accessed 22 March 2016).

Geissel, B. (2009) 'How to improve the quality of democracy? Experiences with participatory innovations at the local level in Germany', *German Politics & Society* 27(4): 51–71.

— (2012) 'Democratic innovations: theoretical and empirical challenges of evaluation', in Geissel, B. and Newton, K. (eds) *Evaluating Democratic Innovations*, London and New York: Routledge, pp. 209–214.

— (2013) 'Introduction: on the evaluation of participatory innovations – a preliminary framework', in Geissel, B. and Joas, M. (eds) *Participatory Democratic Innovations in Europe: Improving the quality of democracy*, Opladen, DE: Barbara Budrich, pp. 8–31.

Geissel, B., and Newton, K. (eds) (2012) *Evaluating Democratic Innovations: Curing the democratic malaise?*, London, UK: Routledge.

Goodin, R. E., and Dryzek, J. S. (2006) 'Deliberative impacts: the macro-political uptake of mini-publics', *Politics & Society* 34(2): 219–44.

Jacquet, V., Moskovic, J., Caluwaerts D., and Reuchamps, M. 'The macro political uptake of the G1000 in Belgium', in Reuchamps, M. and Suiter, J. (eds) (2016) *Constitutional Deliberative Democracy in Europe*, Colchester, UK: ECPR Press.

Joas, M. (2013) 'Conclusions. An evaluation of democratic innovations in Europe', in Geissel, B. and Joas, M. (eds) (2013) *Participatory Democratic Innovations in Europe. Improving the quality of democracy?* Opladen: Barbara Budrich, pp. 249–62.

Michels, A. (2011) 'Innovations in democratic governance: how does citizen participation contribute to a better democracy?', *International Review of Administrative Sciences* 77(2): 275–93.

Moehler, D. C. (2008) *Distrusting Democrats: Outcomes of participatory constitution making*, Ann Arbor, MI: University of Michigan Press.

Newton, K. (2012) 'Curing the democratic malaise with democratic innovations', in Geissel, B. and Newton, K. (eds) *Evaluating Democratic Innovations: Curing the democratic malaise?* London, UK: Routledge, pp. 3–20.

Norris, P. (ed.) (1999) *Critical Citizens: Global support for democratic government*, Oxford, UK: Oxford University Press.

Offe, C. (2003) *Die Demokratisierung der Demokratie: Diagnosen und Reformvorschläge [The Democratization of Democracy. Diagnoses and Reform Proposals]*, Frankfurt-am-Main, DE: Campus.

Papadopoulos, Y., and Warin, P. (2007) 'Are innovative, participatory and deliberative procedures in policy making democratic and effective?', *European Journal of Political Research* 46(4): 445–72.

Mansbridge, J., and Parkinson, J. (eds.) (2013) *Deliberative Systems: Deliberative democracy at the large scale*, Cambridge, UK: Cambridge University Press.

Pogrebinschi, T., and Samuels, D. (2014) 'The impact of participatory democracy. evidence from Brazil's National Public Policy Conferences', *Comparative Politics* 46(3): 313–32.

Renn, O., Webler, T., and Wiedemann, P. (eds) (1995) *Fairness and Competence in Citizen Participation: Evaluating models for environmental discourse*, Dordrecht, NE: Kluwer Academic Publishers.

Rowe, G., and Frewer, L. J. (2004) 'Evaluating public-participation exercises: a research agenda', *Science, Technology, & Human Values* 29(4): 512–56.

Rowe, G., Marsh, R., and Frewer, L. J. (2004) 'Evaluation of a deliberative conference', *Science, Technology, & Human Values* 29(1): 88–121.

Saward, M. (ed.) (2000) *Democratic Innovation: Deliberation, representation and association*, London and New York: Routledge/ECPR Studies in European Political Science.

Schäfer, A. (2009) 'Alles halb so schlimm? Warum eine sinkende Wahlbeteiligung der Demokratie' ['It is not so bad? Why turnout decreases in democracy'], in *MPIfG Jahrbuch 2009–2010*, Köln, DE: Max-Planck-Institut für Gesellschaftsforschung, pp. 5–10.

Sewell, D., and Philips, S. (1979) 'Models for the evaluation of public participation programmes', *Natural Resources Journal* 19: 337–58.

Smith, G. (2009) *Democratic Innovations: Designing institutions for citizen participation*, Cambridge, UK: Cambridge University Press.

Suiter, J., and Reuchamps, M. (2016) 'A constitutional turn for deliberative democracy in Europe?', in Reuchamps, M. and Suiter, J. (eds) (2016) *Constitutional Deliberative Democracy in Europe*, Colchester, UK: ECPR Press.

Suiter, J., Farrell, D., and Harris, C. 'The Irish Constitutional Convention: a case of "high legitimacy"?', in Reuchamps, M. and Suiter, J. (eds) (2016) *Constitutional Deliberative Democracy in Europe*, Colchester, UK: ECPR Press.

Talpin, J. (2012) 'When democratic innovations let the people decide. An evaluation of co-governance experiments', in Geissel, B. and Newton, K. (eds) *Evaluating Democratic Innovations: Curing the democratic malaise?* London, UK: Routledge, pp. 184–206.

Warren, M. E. (2003) 'A second transformation of democracy', in Cain, B. E., Dalton, R. J. and Scarrow, S. E. (eds) *Democracy Transformed? Expanding political opportunities in advanced industrial democracies*, Oxford, UK: Oxford University Press, pp. 223–49.

Warren, M. E., and Pearse, H. (eds) (2008) *Designing Deliberative Democracy: The British Columbia Citizens' Assembly*, Cambridge, UK: Cambridge University Press.

Wheatley, J., and Mendez, F. (eds) (2013) *Patterns of Constitutional Design: The role of citizens and elites in constitution-making*, Aldershot, UK: Ashgate.

Zittel, T., and Fuchs, D. (eds) (2007) *Participatory Democracy and Political Participation – Can participatory engineering bring citizens back in?*, London, UK: Routledge.

Chapter Six

How Can Constitutional Reforms Be Deliberative? The Hybrid Legitimacies of Constitutional Deliberative Democracy

Julien Talpin

Deliberation has been used to draft constitutions at least since the eighteenth century (Elster 1999). Until recently, however, it was reserved to elected officials and experts. The novelty of current practices of constitutional deliberative democracy, thoroughly analysed in the first three chapters of this book, does not lie so much in the use of deliberation itself for drafting a constitution as in the involvement of the public in the process. While citizens have generally been activated to ratify constitutional reforms through the ballot, their participation is now increasingly required for the definition of the reforms themselves. The deliberative turn in constitutional reform is, therefore, also a participatory turn. Beyond the cases presented here, democratic innovations are spreading on institutional and even constitutional issues. The British Columbia Citizens' Assembly proved that citizens' voices could be included in complex institutional matters. It has since been replicated in Ontario and the Netherlands. Similarly, in Denmark – for deciding on joining the eurozone – and in Australia – on the move from a constitutional monarchy to a republic – advisory deliberative mini-publics have been organised before (binding) referendums (Fishkin 2009).

The increasingly frequent inclusion of the public in the discussion, writing or validation of constitutional reforms indicates the powerful attraction embodied by the deliberative ideal. This inclusion takes place in a context of deep political disaffection towards elected officials. In Iceland, Ireland and Belgium it was in a context of both political and economic crisis that these innovative democratic processes were envisaged. As politicians are no longer seen as role models, lay citizens are increasingly perceived as competent enough to give their views on even technical issues and, sometimes, on important political matters. This process is grounded on the increased educational level of most citizens but also in the capacity of democratic innovations to make participants competent enough to construct informed opinions on complex issues. The rise of deliberative experiments in drafting constitutional reforms attests, therefore, to the growing legitimacy of deliberative devices that have already proved, at a more local level, that they were capable of producing informed collective decisions.

While increasingly dealing with important political stakes, deliberative experiments aim at strengthening their legitimacy to ensure political outputs. The aim of this chapter is to tackle the conditions for legitimising constitutional reforms through wide public involvement. To put it simply: how can constitutional reforms be deliberative? We will analyse how the three case studies presented in this book answer this question by maximising input, throughput and output legitimacy. Who is involved, or not, in making such a process democratically legitimate? How are the participants helped to become competent enough to express informed views on complex constitutional matters? What are the effects in terms of constitutional change and institutional reforms of the development of constitutional deliberative democracy? From this perspective, an important question remains: how can the intensity of micro-level deliberative processes be connected to the wider public sphere, to create sufficient legitimacy to ensure significant political changes? More precisely, how are the mini-publics connected to the maxi-public? I develop this important issue by exploring how deliberation can be stimulated in the public sphere. The deliberative roles of the media and political campaigns will be given special emphasis. The systemic turn taken by the deliberative-democracy literature recently has, indeed, emphasised the need to analyse deliberation beyond mini-publics and formal settings by looking at opinion-formation in the public sphere (Chambers 2012). When it comes to constitutional reforms in particular, mini-publics have a hard time producing sufficient legitimacy to ensure democratic ratification. The picture offered by the three case studies presented in this book, therefore, is that of a complex process of legitimacy-building, involving different settings and actors. Considering this potential fragmentation, the connection between deliberation in mini-publics and in the (maxi) public sphere needs to be conceptualised more thoroughly. What does deliberation mean in this case? Can the same term describe both controlled practices taking place in formal settings and informal discussions happening in the public sphere?

Deliberation can be defined as the weighting of the pros and cons of a certain course of action before taking a decision (Cohen 1989). Minimally, it requires both a discursive process of reason-giving and a practical orientation. These criteria have led scholars to exclude informal conversations from the scope of deliberative democracy (Schudson 1997; Remer 2000), as they do not necessarily entail a process of reason-giving and are not generally oriented towards a decision. I argue, however, that while all conversations in the public sphere are not deliberation, some of them are (see also Mansbridge 1999). Certain conversations are indeed based on an exchange of reasons oriented practically; when arguments aim at influencing the voting behaviour of fellow-citizens, for instance (Chambers 2012).[1] From this perspective, discursive interactions (through the media, public meetings or face-to-face) taking place in the framework of political campaigns can be thought of as instances of deliberation. They can be more or less deliberative, however, depending on the level of reason-giving and the inclusiveness of the discussion. From this perspective, exchange of arguments in mini-publics and in the public sphere should be seen not as two different kinds of deliberation but as two poles of a continuum of discursive practices that can be more or less deliberative, depending on a set of factors. Constitutional reforms can, therefore, be more or less

---

1.   In this case, the decision is the vote and the discussion that precedes can be characterised – if it is based on reasons – as deliberation.

deliberative too, depending on how much deliberation (and by whom) is entailed in the drafting and the ratification processes. The articulation between these different arenas and forms of legitimacy is at the heart of this chapter.

Input legitimacy: mini-publics and beyond

In the three cases presented in this book, the aim was to include ordinary citizens in discussion of constitutional or other important political matters. In all cases, this was achieved through the use of randomly selected mini-publics. All three experiments stemmed from an alliance between civil-society activists and political scientists. In both Iceland and Ireland, the official processes were preceded by 'quasi-experimental' events, organised by such civil-society actors and social scientists. From this perspective, the cases presented in this book embody a significant turn in the emergence of deliberative innovation. In Iceland, Ireland and Belgium, the mini-publics and constitutional reforms were indeed incepted from below by civil-society actors, rather than top-down by public officials or institutions. Academics, intellectuals and certain civil-society organisations were essential brokers in the process of transferring democratic innovations (Lee and Polletta 2009). The bottom-up nature of these processes makes the articulation between the mini- and maxi-publics all the more crucial, however. Once granted a form of scientific legitimacy (political scientists, in particular, play an important role in connecting the academic and political fields), these experiments were taken up at another level by elected officials and institutional actors. In many ways, the Belgian G1000 process remained at this experimental and bottom-up stage, even if it also had important political consequences. The other cases were more directly connected to traditional politics, which had significant consequences in terms of their output legitimacy.

While all based on random selection, the mini-publics in the three countries each had a different shape. In Iceland, the National Forum gathered 950 randomly selected citizens. The Irish Constitutional Convention gathered sixty-six randomly selected citizens (in addition to thirty-three elected legislators). In Belgium, the second phase of the G1000, the citizen-summit, included 704 randomly selected participants. The sample-sizes therefore vary a great deal, which has an impact on the statistical representativeness of the panels. In Iceland, a country of only 300,000 residents, such a large panel gave the process an important socio-demographic legitimacy that the Irish process could not claim. Despite these differences, most mini-publics – beyond the cases presented in this volume – appear fairly representative of the population in terms of age, gender and, sometimes, in terms of political orientation, linguistic group and social class. Stratified random selection of the public appears as the gold standard of democratic inclusion, therefore. It ensures the participation in the process of actors and viewpoints that might otherwise have been marginalised.

Even when stratified, however, random selection is insufficient to ensure by itself the input legitimacy of deliberative processes. One of the reasons for this is the very low response-rates to most random-selection procedures (between 3 and 5 per cent), which could cause sortition to collapse into self-selection. As a matter of fact, randomly selected citizens can always refuse to take part in the experiment. All individuals are not equally equipped to respond positively to such solicitations. The more aloof from the public sphere and less socialised to political participation might simply say no. Targeted recruitment of certain low-income or minority groups alleviates some of these shortcomings, as in the G1000 case.

Given these shortcomings, randomly selected mini-publics never appear sufficient to ensure the representation of all viewpoints in the process by themselves. Beyond the mini-publics, therefore, other arenas of participation are often opened, in the hope of reaching out beyond the small number of actually participating citizens. The internet is a powerful tool from this perspective. In Belgium, the citizen-summit was preceded by a public-consultation phase, during which 6,000 people formulated 2,000 ideas, out of which a list of twenty-five themes were selected; three of them were then ranked through online voting. This deepened the input legitimacy of the G1000 by enlarging the public involved in the experiment and allowing a deliberative agenda-setting process. The Irish Constitutional Convention received 2,500 submissions, some of them embodying detailed proposals and ideas. In Iceland, the internet was used after the mini-public to enrich the constitutional draft proposed by the Convention (3,600 inputs were posted on Facebook alone). While thousands of inputs were attracted through various digital media, Bergmann emphasises that it cannot be considered a 'crowd-sourced constitution', as the Convention was not able to include or discuss systematically all the ideas expressed online (Bergmann 2016, Chapter Two of this volume). Despite this difficulty, the use of the internet in these cases – either before the mini-public, to set its agenda, or after, to refine its proposals – enabled more voices to be included in the process. The legitimacy of deliberative experiments does not depend only on the actual inclusion of people but on the broad discursive representation (Dryzek and Hendrycks 2012) of all views on an issue.

Beyond the digital publics, more traditional face-to-face assemblies have also been organised. In Ireland, a submission process was opened, after the initial topics had been covered, through regional meetings across the country, attended by more than 1,000 people. Perhaps for practical reasons, such devolution of the deliberative process is not systematic, however. The enlargement of the public for deliberative constitutional reform can also happen after the mini-public, for informing the maxi-public of the results of the discussions that took place at the micro-level. Thus, in British Columbia, public hearings have been organised across the province, allowing randomly selected citizens who had participated in the Citizens' Assembly to defend the reform they had drafted (Warren and Pearse 2008). The enlargement of participation beyond mini-publics also allows the inclusion of civil-society organisations and NGOs in the deliberation. This is all the more important since mini-publics have often been criticised as artificial democratic devices, cut off from the real world of power and politics (Hendriks 2012; Lee 2014). They are sometimes used to channel or avoid contestation coming from social movements or interest-groups. In the three cases presented in this book, inputs from civil-society actors were made possible through either online or face-to-face participation. In the Irish case, additionally, such actors were also given room to explain their views.

The input legitimacy of deliberative innovations therefore depends on their capacity to articulate different forms of legitimacy, coming from the intensity of the preferences of civil-society actors or the selfless nature of the preferences of randomly selected lay citizens on certain topics (Bobbio 2010). Considering the diversity of the forms of participation presented in this book, it appears that there is not one public for deliberative constitutional reforms but several. They are activated through different tools and methods, generating several different forms of legitimacy. From this perspective, the Irish process embodies a real innovation in the (recent) history of mini-publics. While they generally only gather lay citizens, in the Irish case 33 per cent of the participants were elected officials. Their inclusion could have biased the deliberative process, such qualified actors being able to frame or dominate the discussion, as has been observed in French neighbourhood councils, for instance (Talpin 2011). Does the Irish Constitutional Convention indicate similar forms of domination? Suiter, Farrow and Harris argue, on the contrary, that politicians showed a great deal of respect towards lay citizens, encouraging them to speak up (Suiter, Farrow and Harris 2016, Chapter Three of this volume). This might be linked to the design of the process, the small groups facilitating more egalitarian discussions than the town-hall-meeting type prevailing in French participatory devices. The way elected officials were engaged in the process – on a voluntary basis – also spurred a co-operative attitude that is not always found in the French neighbourhood councils, which are imposed from above by a national law.

A final difference between the three cases in terms of input legitimacy lies in the role devoted to these deliberative experiments in the broader process of constitutional reform. In the Icelandic case, the public was involved in defining the main values that should guide the future constitution (National Forum) and in commenting on the constitutional draft. In Ireland, citizens could make specific policy- or political-reform proposals, on a set of issues that had been defined beforehand. While the first session of the Constitutional Convention allowed the remit of the mini-public to be enlarged, it remained strictly constrained. Irish citizens could then comment on the proposals and finally express their views through a referendum. In the Belgian case, the public was involved in selecting the most important themes to be discussed and the orientation to be given to each of these policy issues, which were then the subject of more detailed discussion at the G1000 and even more so at the G32. The public were included at various stages, therefore, but in discussing very different matters.

Throughput legitimacy: making the public competent to make constitutional decisions

The legitimacy of constitutional deliberative democracy also depends on the quality of the process of participation. In this regard, beyond a well organised deliberative design, what matters is the information provided to the participants before they make up their minds. The epistemic completeness of the experiment appears crucial for its legitimacy. Public participation in deliberation on technical and abstract matters such as constitutional issues embodies a real challenge for deliberative democracy. Most participatory processes deal with rather local and close-to-home issues, in which citizens can use their local knowledge. This is not to say that deliberation is impossible on extra-local issues; but it requires a serious information phase. Constitutional deliberative democracy can only be deemed legitimate if the public can be shown to be competent on such complex issues. In the case of the British Columbia Citizen Assembly, for instance, participants felt they had gone through a 'crash course in electoral systems', provided by law and political-science professors as well as certain interest-groups (Lang 2007; Warren and Pearse 2008).

The shape of these training sessions appears largely standard across mini-publics. This is linked to the way democratic innovations are transferred and circulate – through specific brokers, amongst whom academics play an important role – in a rather small and closed market (Lee 2014). Often, informational material (booklets, brochures and so on) is sent to the participants before the mini-public, in order for them to acquire basic knowledge on the issue at hand. But the real epistemic input takes place during the experiment, through the intervention of experts holding contradictory opinions or interest-groups presenting – and sometimes discussing – the different sides of a subject. Epistemic diversity is at stake here, to ensure that one side is not privileged over the other. A post-discussion survey in the Irish case indicates that experts were deemed impartial by the participants. It was perhaps less so with the G1000. While each theme was introduced by a presentation by two (theoretically) opposing experts, the way the questions were framed surely influenced the debates.[2] In the first discussion session, both experts emphasised that social security was important for national solidarity and neither introduced the difficult question of the necessary trade-offs implied by the financing of the system. In the second session, the two experts both spoke from a 'regulationist' perspective, defending the importance of regulation, taxation and redistribution for fighting the financial crisis and ensuring a just society, a position that is far from representative of the diversity of ideas on the matter. Finally, in the third discussion session, both experts stressed that 'migrations were a chance not a problem', and that 'we should have a balanced perspective between opening the doors and closing them to immigrants'. Rather than expressing diverging opinions on the issues at stake, experts presented shared liberal views. Concerning migration, for instance, a more internationalist perspective could have been defended ('we cannot close the doors to migrants given their life conditions in their own countries'), as well as a more protectionist one ('we cannot accept all the poor people of the world'). This framing of the discussion by the experts might have influenced the participants; some of them criticised the process along these lines.

---

2. The author of this chapter observed the G1000 as a member of the 'international experts' team.

Deliberative processes are not ideal-speech situations and, despite all the energy put into their organisation, they might score higher or lower on an impartiality scale. In particular, in the G1000 case, the design of the experiment – three very broad topics, each to be discussed over a single day – made it difficult to ensure sufficient neutrality in the transmission of information. Despite this limitation in the Belgian case, however, participants generally came out of deliberative experiments dealing with constitutional or other matters better informed than they were beforehand (Fishkin 2009). Moreover, the epistemic completeness of constitutional deliberative democracy experiments should not be assessed on the basis of only one of their stages; a more holistic perspective is needed. The G1000 was, indeed, followed by a thirty-two-member citizen-panel, who worked in much more detail on specific and concrete proposals. The G32 was also informed by the cross-examination of different experts and stakeholders. This complex process ensured that the epistemic quality of the proposals formulated in the end was robust enough to pass the test of their publication. Similarly, in Iceland, while the randomly selected citizens deliberated on the basic values and ideas that should permeate the constitution, the draft was really worked upon by the Constitutional Assembly. While none of its twenty-five members were professional politicians, they were knowledgeable enough on public matters to ensure the work was serious. The epistemic completeness of the Icelandic process stems from the articulation between deliberation and personal competence: members of the Constitutional Assembly were elected by the general public, so election acted as a filter for selecting (and therefore also excluding) those deemed by voters more capable of producing an informed opinion, as it has since the eighteenth century (Manin 1997).

The throughput legitimacy of constitutional deliberative democracy depends mostly on the quality of the deliberation during the experiment. While none of the research teams could carry out a precise discourse-quality analysis of the content of the deliberation in each case, they all stress that, in terms of information received, learning and opportunity for speaking, these experiments score highly. Two elements need greater analysis, however: the length and the extent of these processes. First, time is important when it comes to opinion-formation, learning and the epistemic completeness of an experiment. Then, the role of deliberation in constitutional reforms cannot be limited to discursive interactions in mini-publics: deliberation at all the stages of the experiment (even if more informal) should also be considered in evaluating the legitimacy of constitutional deliberative democracy.

While the methods of reaching epistemic completeness appear similar in the three cases, they diverge in one important aspect: time. The G1000 and the Icelandic National Forum offered only one day of deliberation; the G32 consisted of three weekends; while the Irish Constitutional Convention lasted for ten weekends. This makes a crucial difference: with more time, experts can develop their points and participants can digest the inputs they get. While in the Irish case, the diversity of the issues to be tackled required such a lengthy process and did not ensure that participants had the time to assimilate all the new information that was provided, it appears difficult to imagine a thorough deliberative process on important and complex constitutional matters in only a few hours. As in the British Columbia Citizens' Assembly case, learning and understanding requires time. This might conflict with the need to take fast decisions in a context of crisis.

Output legitimacy: the macro-political uptake of constitutional deliberative democracy

The connection of the different experiments presented in this volume to their respective political systems explains their distinct trajectories. The G1000, as a purely bottom-up process, was completely disconnected from the political process. While some recommendations were transmitted to the parliament, the latter had neither engagement nor obligation to debate or take action on them.

In contrast, the Icelandic experiment was *too* dependent on the political system, so that the reform process was subsequently stalled by elected politicians, including the President, who had felt excluded from the process (both from the National Forum and the Constitutional Assembly). The Icelandic process probably went too far in getting rid of traditional political actors, who had enough resources to impose their will again after a few years of turmoil.

The Irish case falls between these two poles of total autonomy from and significant dependence on the political system. The inclusion of a few politicians as participators in the deliberative process created sufficient connection to the parliamentary system to ensure political uptake. For example, a referendum, directly stemming from the Constitutional Convention, has recently legalised same-sex marriage in Ireland. The Irish Constitutional Convention certainly embodies a powerful legitimacy mix – between the electoral legitimacy of the politician-members, the socio-demographic diversity of the citizens and the epistemic legitimacy of proposals agreed upon after thorough discussion. The Irish process appears, therefore, to be standing on solid democratic ground.

Such unique political and symbolic change was made possible by the original design of the Irish constitutional-reform process. In contrast, processes solely based on deliberative legitimacy might have more difficulty in altering public policies or constitutional arrangements. The Irish outcome cannot be explained solely by the design of the constitutional-reform process, however. It is also linked to the political context. The 2011 'electoral earthquake', which saw the defeat of the historically dominant party of Irish political life, made room for innovation. The newly elected coalition had, additionally, some faith in deliberation. And in addition to this electoral change, the Irish constitutional reform-process was also strengthened by the scientific legitimacy of the previous experiments and the political scientists that followed the process all the way through.

We should not conclude that deliberative experiments which fail to have a policy-impact have no consequences at all, however. The Icelandic process appeared to act as a 'healing exercise', a form of catharsis for an island deeply affected and shocked by the economic crash. In some sense, the constitutional process embodied a form of national re-foundation. More pragmatically, it also highlighted expectations among the citizenry of greater public participation in decision-making processes. Similarly, in Belgium, the G1000 contributed to the legitimacy of deliberative democracy more broadly; and it inspired other deliberative experiments, especially at the local level; and proposals for other such experiments began to be included in political parties' platforms. Large-scale constitutional deliberative democracy events could, therefore, contribute to shaping the political culture of a polity.

From controlled mini-publics to deliberation in the public sphere: towards deliberative constitutional reforms

Despite the procedural sophistication aimed at maximising the epistemic completeness of deliberative experiments, the case-studies presented in this volume indicate that mini-publics are never sufficient, by themselves, to ensure the legitimacy of political decisions – especially such important ones as are involved in the drafting of a new constitution. While this is open to normative discussion (Leib 2006; Smith 2009), few mini-publics have ever taken directly binding public decisions (*see* Geissel and Gherfina 2016, Chapter Five of this volume). Different options exist to ensure the political uptake of deliberative experiments. The first and most common one is to grant an advisory role to mini-publics: they make recommendations transmitted to elected officials, who take the decisions, influenced (in theory) by the information received from lay citizens. This is what happened after the Belgium G32, which produced a report transmitted to MPs and ministers. While the political uptake of mini-publics cannot be brought down to this communication – (Suiter, Farrell and Harris 2016, Chapter Three of this volume) indicate other forms of influence through the media and the shaping of the political debate – little effect is generally produced by such indirect links.

Another channel, with more direct decision-making power, is to submit the proposals produced by the mini-public to a referendum. It is the easiest way; especially considering the history and tradition of constitutional ratifications in Western democracies: people expect to have a direct say in the definition of the fundamental charter of a polity. Due to civic culture and the entrenchment of a conception of democratic legitimacy based on consent, it is hard to produce collective agreements on merely epistemic grounds (Manin 1997). This prevents mini-publics from being really empowered; but it also provides a bulwark against the government of experts and technocrats, which is the quintessential form of epistemic government (Estlund 2009). The criticisms addressed by public opinion to non-directly-elected bodies – such as the European Commission or metropolitan governments in France – or to 'technical governments' conducted by technocrats, indicate that the most common conception of democratic legitimacy does not rest merely on competence and expertise but also on direct popular participation (Neblo *et al.* 2010).

A fully deliberative constitutional reform could therefore include both a randomly selected convention – discussing the draft of the constitution – producing a proposal that would be ratified by referendum. Such a process has never taken place. The closest real-world experience is the British Columbia Citizens' Assembly but that dealt with provincial electoral reform, not a national constitution. In Iceland, a referendum followed the mini-public but it was advisory and the constitutional draft was then submitted to MPs and ministers, who have stalled the project. In Ireland, only a couple of the proposals of the mini-public – dealing with marriage-equality and the length of the presidential term – have been submitted to referendums so far.

Deliberative democrats have therefore tried to elaborate on the articulation between deliberation and direct democracy, based on the consideration that constitutional or important institutional reforms have to be ratified through referendum. Gastil and Richards (2013) have mapped out five types of randomly selected deliberative mini-publics that can be added at different stages of referendum or initiative processes, three of which would be suitable for deliberating on constitutional reform.

1. 'Design panels' are randomly selected devices aimed at improving the text of an initiative. In the framework of a constitutional reform, such a mini-public could evaluate and amend a constitutional draft coming from an elected constitutional assembly.

2. The second device, the citizen-assembly, is aimed at drafting a specific policy or text, to be ratified by referendum afterwards, as in the British Columbian case. It is of particular interest here, as a 'Citizens' Assembly is ideal for addressing issues on which the legislature has a conflict of interest (e.g., term limits and campaign reform)' (Gastil and Richards 2013: 268), which might well be the case with constitutional reforms.

3. Finally, the citizen-initiative-review is a panel aimed at assessing the pros and cons of a proposed reform and transmitting balanced information to the public before it casts its vote. In 2011, the state of Oregon instituted such citizen-initiative-reviews: citizen-panels provide a pre-vote assessment of the subject of forthcoming referendums (referendums are very frequent in Oregon). Eighteen to twenty-four randomly selected individuals meet for a maximum of five days to deliberate on the topic of the referendum. Members of the panel hear from political parties and interest-groups advocating or rejecting the measure; consult policy-experts; and then draft a 'Citizens' Statement' highlighting the most important elements of the ballot measure. The Statement also includes the result of the final vote of the members of the panel. This document is then communicated to the voters of the state as a neutral piece of information to help them make up their minds (Gastil, Richards and Knobloch 2014). This process increases the deliberativeness of direct-democratic procedures.

These three different devices have different functions and could eventually be organised successively. The first two deal with the deliberative drafting of the constitutional reform; the last one with the organisation of deliberation in the public sphere.

A fundamental problem with the mini-public/referendum combination – and one that has been little discussed so far in the literature (see, nevertheless, Chambers 2009) – is that such a design gives the final word to an un- (or little-) informed public. While mini-public participants may have had the chance to construct a sophisticated opinion on a complex matter after weeks of discussions, the general public usually makes up its mind with little information. What matters, therefore, is the organisation of information and communication in the public sphere. While mini-publics such as citizen-initiative-reviews can play a role from this perspective, other important measures to increase the epistemic completeness of constitutional deliberative democracy should also be taken into account in the design.

A crucial matter, from this perspective, is the role of the media. The first three chapters of this volume describe media coverage of the mini-publics and constitutional processes. They all mention how much the media broadcast the events and which parts were covered; all stress the positive attitude of journalists. The Belgian case emphasises, as well, the role of the political context in the way deliberative events are covered. The political vacuum at the head of the Belgian government at the time favoured a positive media treatment of the G1000, which faded away with the return to normality a few months later, at the time of the G32. Other chapters in this volume deal with another aspect of media coverage – more qualitative than quantitative – namely how deliberative experiments infuse the public debate. In the Belgian case, the G1000 influenced some political parties' platforms by legitimising the very idea of deliberative democracy. The content of the discussions that took place within the mini-public had little impact on the Belgian public sphere, however, as the survey conducted a few months after the G1000 indicated: it showed (as expected) a wide discrepancy between the opinions of the general public and those of the mini-public participants.

The discussions and proposals of the mini-public need to shape public opinion, at least minimally, to ensure sufficient connection between the mini- and the maxi-public for the latter to make a sufficiently well informed decision. One can wonder, for instance, whether the way marriage-equality positions were expressed during the Irish Constitutional Convention influenced public discussions on this issue afterwards, especially during the referendum campaign. Suiter and her colleagues stress that the fact that the referendum was on a proposal that came from the Constitutional Convention increased its legitimacy in the eyes of the general public and therefore its chances of success (Suiter, Farrell and Harris 2016, Chapter Three of this volume). It is not clear, however, whether this was linked to a positive attitude towards deliberative democracy in general or to the form deliberation took in the Constitutional Convention.

The effectiveness of the connection between mini- and maxi-publics depends mostly on the way the media cover deliberative events: do they report the debates taking place inside the mini-public, the arguments that are exchanged and the opinion-change potentially experienced by some participants? Or do they mostly focus on the organisation of the process and the innovative aspect of mini-publics, as in the case of the G1000? Exchange of arguments might be difficult to render on screens or in newspaper columns (Parkinson 2006) but it makes a decisive difference concerning the macro-uptake of mini-publics. The deliberativeness of a constitutional reform requires both that it be drafted deliberatively and that voters' choices expressed through referendum be well enough informed before they cast their ballot.

While the logic of the media might be at odds with that of deliberation, a distinction should be made between the daily coverage of politics – which often emphasises strategic behaviour and personal matters – and that of referendums. In the latter case, reports might be less personalised[3] and more focused on the issue on the ballot. The question is not only about the way media cover and present politics but also about the way media coverage is received and apprehended by the citizenry. It is not certain that a media-outlet doing a serious job of covering the content of the deliberation in mini-publics (as they sometimes do for the debates in the parliament) would reach a large audience. Hence, the idea put forward by some political theorists of organising 'Deliberation Days' (Ackerman and Fishkin 2004) before elections, to ensure voters have a minimum level of information before casting their votes. While Ackerman and Fishkin do not argue in this direction, one could defend making attendance at these deliberations compulsory (so everyone can be exposed to the different viewpoints held by those with whom they are deliberating). While compelling political participation might seem inappropriate to democracy, some countries do still practise compulsory voting. This could be replaced by an obligation of becoming (minimally) informed about the issues at stake (the responsibility of voting or not then depending on free choice).

Beyond media-coverage and deliberation days, what matters is the dynamic of political campaigns. The linkage between the mini- and the maxi-public operates more broadly through political campaigns and deliberation in the public sphere. Campaigns can be more or less deliberative, depending on several factors (LeDuc 2002). Campaigns have a deliberative impact as at least some people change their minds between the beginning and the end, sometimes significantly (Kriesi 2012). They can be more or less deliberative, however, depending on the type of election, the country, the structure of the political system and so on. When it comes to referendum-campaigns, the issue at stake is also decisive. It appears that there is more opinion-change when actors do not have a pre-set preference on the issue on the ballot (LeDuc 2002). Referendum campaigns on constitutional projects should, therefore, be more deliberative than on marriage-equality or the death-penalty for instance, where the strength of deep-seated opinions might reduce discussion to mere polemic. The level of deliberativeness of a campaign is crucial for assessing

---

3.   Referendums and direct democracy can have very different meanings and dynamics, depending on political traditions. While in France they are often seen in an authoritarian way, due to their instrumental use by Napoleon Bonaparte and General de Gaulle – who personalised the vote, embodying a direct decision of the people in the person of the ruler – this is not the case in all countries. In contrast, referendums are also sometimes seen as a counter-weighting tendency to the personalisation of politics.

whether a reform is the product of the aggregation of uninformed votes or of an enlightened public opinion. There is, however, a lack of research on deliberation in political campaigns and in the public sphere in general.

The complex legitimacies of constitutional deliberative democracy

The systemic turn in deliberative democracy scholarship (Mansbridge and Parkinson 2013) acknowledges the multiplicity of the sites of deliberation in the public sphere. In so doing, it overcomes the procedural emphasis that had previously characterised the deliberation literature, to contemplate the political consequences of discursive activities in the public sphere. There is no single perfect tool or device to ensure the legitimacy of political reform and the richness of a democracy depends on the diversity of its sites of discursive interactions. To go beyond the 'salad bowl' view of the deliberative system – emphasising its heterogeneous and disorganised nature (Dryzek 2009) – however, we need to conceptualise the forms of articulation between these different sites of democratic interactions more thoroughly. This volume, by focusing on constitutional deliberative democracy, offers a significant step forward from this perspective.

The cases presented in the volume embody different forms of the legitimacy required to reshape the principal institutions and rules of political systems. They all, to various extents, articulate four forms of legitimacy. First, the *epistemic* legitimacy granted to experts and scientists. They can either intervene to provide information during the deliberation itself or advise on the organisation of the deliberative process as such. Then, a '*common sense*' legitimacy, coming from ordinary citizens' input into mini-publics and in the other arenas (either online or face-to-face) that can be opened to include a variety of voices in the deliberative process. Third, a *democratic* legitimacy, based on numbers, can be granted by referendums, in which all citizens can have their say through the ballot. Finally, there is a *representative* legitimacy, that of elected officials, who play a role both in the deliberation itself and in connecting these different forms of legitimacy within the political system. Depending on how they are articulated, these different forms of legitimacy can give rise to more or less deliberative constitutional reforms.

There is still a need, however, to grasp more precisely the deliberative potential and weaknesses of one of the central moments of democratic life, namely, political campaigns. Despite the spread of democratic innovation and the deliberative turn taken by representative democracy, elections remain the central device for allocating political goods. From this perspective, the campaigns that precede elections could become instances of deliberation in the public sphere, that is, of exchanges of arguments oriented towards a decision (a voting choice). While deliberative democrats have tried to re-conceptualise democratic legitimacy by expanding participation opportunities beyond the ballot box, the study of deliberation in political campaigns is a new field of inquiry.

References

Ackerman, B., and Fishkin, J. (2005) *Deliberation Day*, Yale, CT: Yale University Press.

Bergmann, E. (2016) 'Participatory constitutional deliberation in the wake of crisis: the case of Iceland', in Reuchamps, M. and Suiter, J. (eds) (2016) *Constitutional Deliberative Democracy in Europe*, Colchester, UK: ECPR Press.

Bobbio, L. (2010) 'Types of deliberation', *Journal of Public Deliberation* 6(2): article 1.

Chambers, C. (2012) 'Deliberation and mass democracy', in Mansbridge, J. and Parkinson, J. (eds) *Deliberative Systems: Deliberative democracy at the large scale*, Cambridge, UK: Cambridge University Press, pp. 52–71.

Chambers, S. (2009) 'Rhetoric and the public sphere: has deliberative democracy abandoned mass democracy? *Political Theory* 37(3): 323–50.

Cohen, J. (1989) 'Deliberation and democratic legitimacy', in Hamlin A. and Pettit, P. (eds) *The Good Polity*, Oxford, UK: Basil Blackwell.

Dryzek, J. (2009) *Foundations and Frontiers of Deliberative Governance*, Oxford, UK: Oxford University Press.

Dryzek, J., and Hendriks, C. (2012) 'Fostering deliberation in the forum and beyond', in Fischer, F. and Gottweis, H. (eds) *The Argumentative Turn Revisited*, Durham, NC: Duke University Press, pp. 31–57.

Elster, J. (1999) 'Arguing and bargaining in two constituent assemblies', *University of Pennsylvania Journal of Constitutional Law* 2: 345–.

Estlund, D. (2009) *Democratic Authority: A philosophical framework*, Princeton, NJ: Princeton University Press.

Fishkin, J. (2009) *When the People Speak: Deliberative democracy and public consultation*, Oxford, UK: Oxford University Press.

Gastil, J., and Richards, R. C. (2013) 'Making direct democracy deliberative through random assemblies', *Politics & Society* 41(2): 251–83.

Gastil, J., Richards, R. C., and Knobloch, K. R. (2014) 'Vicarious deliberation: how the Oregon Citizens' Initiative Review influenced deliberation in mass elections', *International Journal of Communication* 8: 62–89.

Geissel, B., and Gherghina, S. (2016) 'Constitutional deliberative democracy and democratic innovations', in Reuchamps, M. and Suiter, J. (eds) (2016) *Constitutional Deliberative Democracy in Europe*, Colchester, UK: ECPR Press.

Hendriks, C. (2012) *The Politics of Public Deliberation. Citizen engagement and interest advocacy*, London, UK: Palgrave MacMillan.

Kriesi, H. P. (2012) (ed.) *Political Communication in Direct-Democratic Campaigns: Enlightening or manipulating?* Basingstoke, UK: Palgrave.

Lang, A. (2007) 'But is it for real? The British Columbia Citizens' Assembly as a model of state-sponsored citizen empowerment', *Politics & Society* 35(1): 35–69.

LeDuc, L. (2002) 'Referendums and elections: how do campaigns differ?', in Farrell, D. and Schmitt-Beck, R. (eds) *Do Political Campaigns Matter? Campaign effects in elections and referendums*, London, UK: Routledge.

Lee, C. (2014) *Do it Yourself Democracy: The rise of the public engagement industry*, Oxford, UK: Oxford University Press.

Lee, C., and Polletta, F. (2009) 'Deliberative democracy practitioners survey: what is the state of the field?', Lafayette University, available at: http://sites. lafayette.edu/ddps/files/2010/01/Results2009.pdf (accessed 18 February 2016).

Leib, E. (2006) 'Can direct democracy be made deliberative?', *Buffalo Law Review* 54: 903–26.

Manin, B. (1997) *The Principles of Representative Government*, Cambridge, UK: Cambridge University Press.

Mansbridge, J. (1999) 'Everyday talk in the deliberative system', in Macedo, S. (ed.) *Deliberative Politics: Essays on democracy and disagreement*, Oxford, UK: Oxford University Press.

Mansbridge, J., and Parkinson, J. (eds.) (2013) *Deliberative Systems: Deliberative democracy at the large scale*, Cambridge, UK: Cambridge University Press.

Neblo, M., Esterling, K., Kennedy, R., Lazer, D. and Sokhey, A. (2010) 'Who wants to deliberate – and why?', *American Political Science Review* 104(3): 566–83.

Parkinson, J. (2006) 'Rickety bridges: using the media in deliberative democracy', *British Journal of Political Science* 36(1): 175–83.

Remer, G. (2000) 'Two models of deliberation: oratory and conversation in ratifying the constitution', *Journal of Political Philosophy* 8(1): 68–90.

Schudson, M. (1997) 'Why conversation is not the soul of democracy', *Critical Studies in Mass Communication* 14(4): 297–309.

Smith, G. (2009) *Democratic Innovations*, Cambridge, UK: Cambridge University Press.

Suiter, J., Farrell, D., and Harris, C. 'The Irish Constitutional Convention: a case of "high legitimacy"?', in Reuchamps, M. and Suiter, J. (eds) (2016) *Constitutional Deliberative Democracy in Europe*, Colchester, UK: ECPR Press.

Talpin, J. (2011) *Schools of Democracy: How ordinary citizens (sometimes) become competent in participatory budgeting institutions*, Colchester, UK: ECPR Press.

Warren, M., and Pearse, H. (eds) (2008) *Designing Deliberative Democracy: The British Columbia Citizens' Assembly*, Cambridge, UK: Cambridge University Press.

Chapter Seven

Designing Mini-Publics for Constitutional Deliberative Democracy

Kimmo Grönlund

Why mini-publics for constitutional reforms?

From a theoretical point of view, constitutional questions should be ideal for deliberative problem-solving. A constitution is a framework for how a country is governed. These profound rules of democratic government ought not be changed without a thorough reflection on the consequences of such amendments. Put in other words: constitutions are written to last for long periods of time and they should not be changed whenever power shifts between political parties. Thus, constitutions should not reflect ideological fluctuations in power. In practice, however, constitutional reform tends to be a parliamentary process and therefore in the hands of the political elite.

Even though parliamentarians can be seen as experts in deliberation, the downside of letting them decide on constitutions lies in their partisanship. Politics as policy-making is basically about trying to solve conflicts between justified claims and interests. In the policy-making process, political parties and MPs act, at least partly, as representatives of the groups who support and elect them. Thus, political parties and other gatekeepers tend to consider the pros and cons of all law-making in terms of their gains and losses. Even though the ideal of the common good might guide meta-level parliamentary processes, the gains and losses are defined from the points of view of the political party and its supporters. Contrary to policy-making, decisions on constitutions should not be based on political actors' calculations of short-term gains and losses: '[a] prudent principle of a constitutional design is that decisions about rules that affect who is elected should not be controlled by individuals who have a preponderant interest against (or for) change in the membership of the institutions' (Thompson 2008: 24).

From a democratic point of view, just and fair constitutions that guarantee equal opportunities for all citizens and their associations are normatively highly desirable. Therefore, trying to decipher what an informed public opinion looks like is even more important when it comes to constitutional reform than when it comes to policy-decisions. For this reason, the goal of institutionalising deliberative mini-publics for constitutional questions is both theoretically interesting and democratically pressing.

The general idea of deliberative mini-publics was most famously put forward by Robert Dahl (1989).[1] Since then, academics and policy-makers all over the world have implemented, often in collaboration with each other, many different kinds of mini-publics. *The term deliberative mini-public refers to forums in which lay citizens representing different viewpoints are gathered together to deliberate on a particular issue in small groups.* In fact, the earliest designs resembling deliberative mini-publics were planning cells (Germany) and citizens' juries (United States) in the 1970s and 1980s. The development of these formats was motivated by the need to bridge the observed gap between citizens and policy-makers. Although the basic ideas and formats of deliberative mini-publics were elaborated by democratic theorists and practitioners before the 'deliberative turn' in the 1990s (Dryzek 2002), scholarly interest in mini-publics has been boosted by developments in democratic theory (Grönlund, Bächtiger and Setälä 2014). There has been a growing interest in developing methods for engaging citizens in reasoned and balanced deliberation. Deliberative Polling® (DP), developed by James Fishkin and Robert Luskin in the early 1990s, was designed to address the problems of measuring public opinion through raw opinion polls. DP aims to provide a method of measuring informed and reflective public opinion by allowing people to gain information and deliberate on a political issue in small groups. In fact, Fishkin's (2009: 81) idea of creating a 'microcosm' of the people through random sampling resembles Dahl's original idea.

Deliberative Polling® is by no means the only design in existence but it has become something of a gold-standard for mini-publics (Grönlund, Bächtiger and Setälä 2014: 2). Typically, DPs measure opinions before and after deliberation but do not include any common decision-making process for the participants. Instead, individual post-deliberation opinions are aggregated in order to measure informed opinion. When it comes to policy-decisions, an aggregated post-deliberation opinion might be an adequate way to decipher how people reason but, in constitutional matters, some kind of a common verdict is desirable. Constitutions are frameworks for which the whole truly is more than the sum of its parts.

Thus far, not many mini-publics have addressed constitutional questions. The typical mini-public, whether organised by researchers or governments, has been policy-oriented. Perhaps the most prominent examples of constitutional mini-publics come from Canada, where the provinces of British Columbia (Warren and Pearse 2008) and Ontario (http://www.citizensassembly.gov.on.ca, accessed 22 February 2016) have organised 'Citizens' Assemblies' on electoral reform. In both cases, the setup was similar. A sample of almost randomly selected citizens from different regions within the provinces was chosen to discuss the need for electoral reform. The goal was to compare the existing single-member plurality system with more proportional system and to come up with a recommendation that would be put to a referendum in the province. The Citizens' Assemblies were assisted by civil servants and briefed thoroughly by experts on different electoral systems

---

1. His original term was mini-populus; later he also talked about a mini-demos.

and their advantages and disadvantages. Some European mini-publics pertaining to constitutional issues and with some policy-impact have also been organised. The Irish Constitutional Convention in 2013 (Suiter, Farrell and Harris 2016, Chapter Three of this volume) and the Icelandic Constitutional Assembly in 2011 (Bergmann 2016, Chapter Two of this volume) are recent examples of European counterparts, although the Icelandic Assembly was chosen through election, not randomly.

The goal of the present chapter is to discuss whether and how mini-publics can be institutionalised in a democratic system. The empirical evidence provided comes from the population-based experiments with deliberative mini-publics that my team has carried out in Finland. In the following, I describe these experiments, their research questions, design and major findings. Thereafter, I try summarise what we have learned about mini-publics as a decision-making method and discuss how this knowledge could be used in designing mini-publics for constitutional decision-making.

The Finnish mini-public experiments

So far, we have organised five experiments in citizen-deliberation. They have been population-based, that is, the participants have been recruited from the general public. Our goal has been to increase the external validity of the experiments by involving 'lay' citizens in deliberations, instead of using convenience samples drawn from students, for example. This way, we hoped to be able to deduce how mini-publics could be used in democratic decision-making in the real world.

The participants in each mini-public were recruited by taking a simple random sample from the population registry but participation was, naturally, voluntary. We used two modes for deliberation. Three mini-publics deliberated face to face and two were online replications of a face-to-face mini-public. There three themes: mini-publics #1 (face-to-face) in the autumn of 2006 and #2 (online) in the spring of 2008 deliberated on energy policy, with a specific focus on nuclear power. Mini-public #3 (face-to-face, spring 2012) dealt with immigration, whereas the newest mini-publics #4 (face-to-face) and #5 (online), both in the autumn of 2014, concerned the status of the Swedish language in Finland. In terms of the scope of the present book, the overall impression given by these mini-publics is that randomly selected citizens indeed possess the will and capabilities to act as responsible and reflective 'politicians'. Our experiments confirm the common wisdom that people who take part in mini-publics and receive the 'deliberative package' (Mutz 2006: 61) – that is, are first informed about the subject and then deliberate in small groups – reflect on the issue and change their opinions as a result (Suiter, Farrell and O'Malley 2014; Grönlund, Strandberg and Himmelroos 2009; Setälä, Grönlund and Herne 2010; Grönlund, Bächtiger and Setälä 2014; Luskin, Fishkin and Jowell 2002). Moreover, we have traced clear, positive side-effects, especially in terms of learning but also when it comes to increased trust in politicians and democratic institutions as well as increased satisfaction with democracy (Grönlund, Setälä and Herne 2010).

Experiment #1: nuclear power

Our first population-based experiment took place in November 2006. Its experimental design was inspired by the tension between the consensual ideal of deliberative democracy and the realism of real-life politics in which decisions often need to be reached through voting. Thus, two experimental treatments were applied. Half of the twelve small groups voted on the issue of a commissioning a sixth Finnish nuclear-power plant through secret ballot ('vote-treatment'); in the remaining six groups, the decision was made by formulating a commonly accepted statement ('common statement-treatment'). The participants were randomly assigned to these small groups. In the vote-treatment, members could vote 'yes', 'no' or cast an empty ballot. In the common statement-treatment, a final statement on which all group members could agree was written. The procedure did not aim for consensus in a strict sense but emphasised the search for a 'meta-consensus' on the viewpoints and facts related to the nuclear-power decision (cf. Dryzek and Niemeyer 2006).

The recruitment of participants was carried out as a three-stage procedure. First, a random sample of 2,500 persons was drawn among all eligible voters in the constituency of Varsinais-Suomi. A preliminary invitation to take part in citizen-deliberation was sent out with the first survey. The participants were promised a remuneration of 100 euros, free meals during the day and compensation for their travel costs. This first survey was answered by almost one-fourth of the sample (n = 592). Of the respondents, 244 agreed to participate in the event. At the third stage of the recruitment process, the number of participants was cut down so that the target sample of 144 people, that is, twelve small groups consisting of twelve persons each, could be reached. We invited 194 of the 244 volunteers to take part in the citizen-deliberation event. Of the invited, 135 participants showed up.

The deliberation day started with a quiz. After, the participants were asked to read briefing material on nuclear energy. Thereafter, an expert panel was questioned in a plenary session. The panel consisted of two experts supporting nuclear energy and two experts opposing it. Each member of the panel made a short presentation, after which the participants were allowed to pose questions to the experts. The actual deliberation took place in twelve small groups consisting of between ten and thirteen members. The discussions were moderated and the participants were asked to follow specific rules that emphasised respecting other participants' viewpoints, the importance of giving reasons to justify their views and of self-reflection. The deliberations lasted for three hours, after which the groups were asked to make a decision on whether a sixth nuclear-power plant should be built in Finland. The sessions ended with a survey. In February 2007, a follow-up survey was conducted.

Our results show that treatment did not have any systematic impact on the development of opinions on energy-policy in the experiment. Moreover, we found that there were neither indications of group-pressure among the participants in general, nor significant differences between the two treatments in this respect. The participants became more critical of the use of coal and peat in energy production and somewhat more critical of nuclear power; whereas there was increased support for saving energy and belief in other people's willingness to save energy if asked to do so (Setälä, Grönlund and Herne 2010). When it comes to gains in energy-related knowledge, participants in the common statement-treatment learned somewhat more than participants in the vote-treatment. Also, regarding political efficacy, the common statement-treatment produced a higher sense of external efficacy after deliberation whereas no such change could be traced in the vote-treatment (Grönlund, Setälä and Herne 2010). The reports written by the moderators show that the participants were both motivated and serious about their task of deliberating and reaching a decision. All deliberations were also audio-recorded and transcribed. The transcriptions of group discussions indicate that, in accordance with our theoretical expectations, the deliberative process was more thorough in the common-statement groups than in the secret-ballot groups (Himmelroos 2012). Our conclusion is that the common-statement procedure, which resembles a consensual ideal, seems to produce more 'deliberative' outcomes than a treatment that uses a secret ballot (Grönlund, Setälä and Herne 2010; Setälä, Grönlund and Herne 2010).

Experiment #2: nuclear power (online)

A replica of the citizen-deliberation experiment on nuclear power was organised online in 2008. Simultaneously, it was a pilot experiment, seeking to test how online deliberation works, with the help of live webcam streaming and audio. With the exception of the online mode, the procedure was fully identical with the 2006 face-to-face experiment. Therefore, groups in the common statement-treatment ended their deliberation by writing down a statement containing the topics all participants considered to be most important regarding nuclear power. In the vote-treatment groups, the deliberative session ended with secret voting, in which the participants voted either in favour of or against a sixth nuclear-power plant in Finland.

First, a simple random sample of 6,000 Finnish adult citizens was invited to participate. The participants were offered webcam equipment and a gift certificate for their participation. Alas, only 147 citizens volunteered to take part. Of these, seventy-nine participants completed the actual deliberation. Some volunteers did not show up and some just dropped out during the experiment. The participants were allocated randomly into the two treatments and groups within them. Both treatments consisted of six small groups. On the whole, the 147 participants in the experiment were fairly representative of the general Finnish population in terms of education, gender, age and political interest (Strandberg and Grönlund 2012).

The actual deliberation-events were carried out at weekends in April and May 2008 via a special online platform. Each small group had one session. The participants took part in theirs, by logging in via the website (Grönlund, Strandberg and Himmelroos 2009). Prior to the discussion session, participants read balanced information material on nuclear power and watched the recorded expert-panel discussion from the 2006 experiment. The actual deliberation-events were carried out with the use of videoconferencing technology; both live audio and webcam streaming were used in the discussions. Trained moderators were used in all discussion groups.

The actual deliberation sessions included twelve groups, consisting of from four to eleven participants. The number of participants was not intended to vary but, participants often did not show up. In order to avoid cacophony, only one participant could talk at a time. There was also a text-based chat option, in case any participants experienced problems with audio- or video-streaming. This text-chat was also used by the moderator for technical information. The discussion room also contained a whiteboard window in which the moderator listed the topics suggested by the participants. It was also used for writing the common statements. The online discussions lasted for a couple of hours, varying mainly according to group-size (Strandberg and Grönlund 2012).

Despite technical problems, the participants completed the surveys in a similar manner to the face-to-face experiment. The main finding of the online is that the patterns found in terms of opinion-change and knowledge-gain were very similar to the offline experiment. Overall, the participants grew more critical of coal, peat, and nuclear power (Grönlund, Strandberg and Himmelroos 2009). Regarding treatment-effects in the online mode, the common statement-treatment produced more statistically significant opinion-changes than the vote-treatment. The control group did not show any significant opinion-change (Strandberg and Grönlund 2012).

Experiment #3: immigration

Whereas the first two experiments were typical deliberative mini-publics (Grönlund, Bächtiger and Setälä 2014), in which participants with different views discussed in small groups, the third experiment, in part, extended our research agenda into new territory. In designing it, we were inspired by the concern, most notably expressed by Cass Sunstein (2002, 2007, 2009), about the future of democracy when people only discuss politics in like-minded groups. This 'enclave-deliberation' may lead to group-thinking, with more extreme views and an amplification of cognitive errors as a result. The phenomenon of the development of more extreme views in enclave deliberation is called 'group-polarisation'; it occurs when deliberation in a group of like-minded participants reinforces the attitudes and opinions prevailing in the group at the outset. Sunstein (2009: 3) defines group-polarisation as follows: 'members of a deliberating group usually end up at a more extreme position in the same general direction as their inclinations before deliberation began.' Like-minded discussion may also lead to an amplification of cognitive errors (Sunstein 2007: 80–95, 140–3), which means that people's false factual beliefs are strengthened. One of the key features of deliberation is the inclusion of different viewpoints in the process of exchanging arguments. Indeed, the presence of conflicting viewpoints is often regarded as a necessary condition for deliberation (Thompson 2008: 502). However, the term 'enclave-deliberation' has been used to refer to any discussion among like-minded people.

The topic, immigration policy, was chosen as one of the most contentious among contested contemporary issues. The participants' opinions on immigration were measured before and after deliberation. In the first survey, respondents with negative attitudes to immigration formed a con-enclave, whereas respondents with a positive view on immigration formed a pro-enclave. Since the main research interest was enclave-deliberation, we manipulated the group-composition in order to compare deliberation in two types of groups: 1) groups of people like-minded on immigration; and 2) groups of people with different opinions on immigration. Thus, the participants were randomly assigned to like-minded groups, mixed groups and a control-group. The treatment-groups deliberated, whereas the control-group only filled in surveys at home.

A short survey was first mailed out to a simple random sample of 12,000 adults in the region of Turku (Åbo). Every fourth person in the addressed sample responded to the first survey, which consisted of fourteen items measuring the respondents' attitudes on immigration. Since the design of the experiment required people with clear views on the immigration issue, we excluded moderates (n=631), that is, those respondents whose opinions on immigration were close to the median value of the frequency distribution (see Grönlund, Herne and Setälä 2015 for a detailed description of the process). Thus, the second survey (T2), which also included an invitation to take part in a deliberation-event, was sent out to 2,601 people. Half of the invited sample consisted of people with pro-immigration and the other half of those with anti-immigration (con) views. At this stage, it was made clear that only some of those who had volunteered could be included in the deliberation-event and that the choice would be made by lot. Each participant who completed all the stages was compensated with 90 euros; the control-group received 15 euros each.

Eventually, 805 people volunteered and 366 were invited to take part in the deliberation-event. The target sample was 256 participants, that is, thirty-two small groups of eight participants each. This was not achieved and only 207 people showed up. People in the con-enclave, especially, tended to abstain at this final stage, even though there were no indications of this kind of a bias at the earlier stages of the recruitment process. At the deliberation-event, random assignment was used within the con- and pro-enclaves. Eventually, we could form ten like-minded pro-groups, five like-minded con-groups and eleven mixed groups. Because of the need for balance between the enclaves, each mixed group consisted of exactly eight participants, four from each enclave, whereas the group-size was allowed to vary between seven and nine in the like-minded groups. This was due to attrition at the last stage. The control-group consisted of 369 people.

The deliberation event took place during one weekend in the spring of 2012. Each participant took part during one day. The setup was identical each time. The day started with a fifteen-item knowledge quiz, after which the participants were briefed about some basic facts related to immigration in Finland. The briefing was designed to be balanced and focused on basic facts. It was also given as a written hand-out out to the participants.

People deliberated in their small groups for four hours, including a forty-five-minute lunch break. In each group, a trained moderator facilitated the discussion and made sure that specific rules – emphasising respect for other people's opinions; the importance of justifying one's opinions with reasons; and openness to others' points of view – were followed. The discussion was free and the moderators interfered only if any of the either group-members dominated or completely withdrew from the discussion. After deliberation, a post-experiment survey was filled in.

The main result of the experiment was that participants in the anti-immigration enclave became more liberal. This was especially true in the mixed-group treatment, in which the small groups consisted of four anti- and pro-immigration participators each; but it was also true in the groups consisting of only participants with an initially negative view of immigration. Within the pro-immigration enclave, participants in the mixed treatment did not change their preferences, whereas a slight polarisation in a liberal direction could be traced in the like-minded pro-groups. Those pro-immigration participants in like-minded groups who did not show any measureable, became polarised, that is, even more liberal, in the post-deliberation measurement (Grönlund, Herne and Setälä 2015).

The results support a central theoretical assumption in deliberative democracy: that all arguments should not have an equal weight in the process of public reasoning. Reasonable arguments appealing to generalisable moral principles are expected to be powerful whereas arguments based on attitudes such as prejudice should be 'laundered' in the course of deliberation (Goodin 1986). Thus, our interpretation of the outcome of the experiment is that deliberation is different from other kinds of talk. The deliberative package with informational material and discussion-rules emphasising respect, equality and reflection can be particularly useful in hindering group-polarisation in like-minded contexts (Grönlund, Herne and Setälä 2015).

Experiments #4 and #5: Swedish language (face-to-face and online)

Inspired by the outcome of the third experiment, we designed new experiments with two modes in order to re-test and possibly replicate its main finding, according to which deliberative norms alleviate the well known pattern of group-polarisation in like-minded groups. In the design of the fourth and the fifth experiments, we specifically wanted to test the impact of deliberative discussion-rules. Moreover, we wanted to test how the mode of deliberation affects the outcome, bearing in mind the concern expressed by Sunstein (2007, 2009) that group-polarisation is a phenomenon especially observed on the internet, where people have a tendency to seek the company of other people with similar views to their own.

The chosen topic was similar, but not identical, to the third experiment. The participants in the fourth (face-to-face) and the fifth (online) experiment were invited to deliberate the status of the Swedish language in Finland. Even though the Swedish language is an official language in Finland, it is only spoken by a small minority: 290,000 people or 5.3 per cent of the population. At the time of the experiment, the topic was highly contested due to a forthcoming vote in the Parliament on a citizen-initiative suggesting that teaching Swedish in schools should be made voluntary.[2] Our main purpose was to compare the effects of discussion in like-minded groups with or without facilitated deliberation. Thus, the participants were randomly assigned either to groups with facilitated deliberation or groups lacking it (Grönlund, Himmelroos and Strandberg 2016).

The recruitment process for the fourth and the fifth experiments was similar to the third experiment. First, an initial survey measuring opinions on the Swedish language with seventeen items was mailed to two simple random samples drawn from the Finnish-speaking population aged 18 to 80. For the face-to-face experiment, the sample was 20,000 persons and for the online mode it was 15,000. Of the surveyed samples, 5,797 persons responded to the survey in the face-to-face experiment and 1,509 persons in the online experiment. With the help of a factor analysis, fourteen items were eventually used when creating a sum-variable to measure the respondents' opinions on the Swedish language. Each statement was on a Likert scale and was recoded into a scale ranging from 0 to 1; the latter value was always the most positive attitude toward the Swedish language. Thus, the sum-variable could range from 0 to 14. Respondents whose value on the sum-variable was less than 6.01 formed an 'anti-Swedish' enclave, whereas those who scored greater than 8.0 formed a pro-Swedish enclave. Since we wanted to replicate the enclave design of the third experiment, the respondents who did not have a clear opinion for or against the issue, were not invited to take part in deliberations.

In the face-to-face mode, 537 respondents were interested in taking part in the deliberative event and there were 264 interested participants in the online mode. They were all invited to take part in deliberation. All who took part were promised compensation (a gift voucher worth 90 euros) and the travel costs of participants in the face-to-face mode were reimbursed. Among these invited, a final total of N = 312 participants actually turned up for the deliberation; 202 of these were in the offline mode and 110 in the online mode.

Similarly to the pattern in the third experiment on immigration, the participants from the anti-Swedish enclave who eventually showed up were somewhat more positive towards the Swedish language than citizens were within the same enclave in the earlier stages of the recruitment process. This tendency was most evident in the face-to-face mode. For some reason, it appears to be harder to attract citizens with the most extreme anti-Swedish attitudes to show up for deliberation in public. This phenomenon might be associated with social desirability: people who feel that their opinion differs from the 'politically correct' view seem to be hesitant to take part in a scholarly event, even though it is framed very neutrally (see also Grönlund, Herne and Setälä 2015).

---

2.   The Finnish citizen-initiative institution is indirect and was implemented through an amendment to the Constitution of Finland in 2011. According to the amendment, an initiative requires signatures of 50,000 eligible voters in order that the Parliament will consider it. The institution is indirect since there is no referendum and the final decision is made by the Parliament. The particular initiative on the Swedish language was defeated in the Parliament 134–48; but a majority (93–89) of the MPs supported regional trials in which other languages could replace Swedish.

The actual deliberation event in the fourth experiment (face-to-face mode) took place during one weekend, 22–3 November 2014, in the city of Tampere, with participants from the whole of Finland. The online deliberations of the fifth experiment were held in November 2014. In both modes, each participant only took part in one session. Upon arrival at the face-to-face deliberation experiment, the participants filled in a survey measuring socio-economic variables. They also received briefing material on the Swedish language in the form of a four-page leaflet. The briefing material was designed to be balanced and fact-based. In both experiments, the small groups consisted of six participants. In the online mode, the surveys were filled in online and the briefing material was available to participants when they logged in to our deliberative platform. The deliberation itself lasted for two hours. The online discussions were set up in Adobe Connect and used live webcam feeds as well as audio and text-messaging.

Each group either employed facilitated deliberation (the 'rules-treatment') or totally free discussion (the 'no-rules treatment'). Both treatments had a representative from the organisers present in the room but she did not interfere with the discussion in the no-rules treatment. Moreover, the deliberative discussion-rules for the rules-treatment groups were identical with the third experiment. After the discussion, all participants filled in a survey which contained, among others, the same questions on opinions on the Swedish language that had been included in the pre-test survey.

What did we find? In accordance with our expectations, group-polarisation occurred in the no-rules treatment. Moreover, group-polarisation did not occur in the rules-treatment. Finally, we expected group-polarisation tendencies to be more evident in the online mode. However, in fact, modality did not have an impact and the results were similar in both modes of the experiment (Grönlund, Himmelroos and Strandberg 2016).

Based on the third, fourth and fifth experiments, we can conclude that the phenomenon of group-polarisation, that views in groups which consist of like-minded people become more extreme in the course of discussion, can be alleviated if deliberative norms are used. In the experiment on immigration (#3), especially, anti-immigration participants also became more liberal in the like-minded-group treatment. In the 'all-enclave' experiments on the Swedish language in Finland, groups in the deliberative treatment were not polarised, whereas the participants in the non-deliberative (no-rules) treatment became more extreme, just like in previous, non-deliberative experiments. This finding highlights the possibility of using deliberative discussion-rules in contexts that are not designed as mini-publics or in mini-publics that suffer from participant biases (cf. Morrell 2014). This is an important finding since like-minded groups, that is, enclaves, can be valuable for political articulation and mobilisation, especially for groups who are traditionally politically disadvantaged, have low levels of political efficacy and are demobilised from the political sphere (see, for example, Karpowitz, Raphael and Hammond 2009; see also Sunstein 2007: 76–7). Mansbridge (1994: 63), has called for 'enclaves of protected discourse and action' as an element of a just society. One of the criticisms of deliberative forums is that unequal socio-economic status (SES) easily leads to unequal participation-levels in deliberation (Thompson 2008: 509; Karpowitz, Raphael and Hammond 2009). The possibility of boosting the internal efficacy of people with low SES through deliberation in like-minded groups is promising when it comes to the goal of effective participation in deliberative democracy. If their internal efficacy is boosted, it may also increase their readiness to participate in political debates with conflicting viewpoints.

Summary of the Finnish experiments

The design and the main findings of the five Finnish experiments in citizen-deliberation are summarised in Table 7.1. The table lists the main topic of deliberation; the treatments studied; the common features, that is, the variables that were held constant; the number of deliberating participants; the mode for deliberation; the year in which the experiment was organised; and the main outcome of each experiment; as well as the main conclusion that we have reached based on the experiment.

Even though we have not kept them secret, none of our deliberative mini-publics has had a direct policy-impact. The first experiment was the only one for which the press were invited to the actual event. This was also the only time we had an expert-panel present in an experiment. On the other occasions, we organised press conferences with some initial results after the events had been held. This has made it possible to increase the awareness of the Finnish media and the general public of our work, in which the emphasis has been, broadly defined, on democracy-development. The Finnish democracy is something of an anomaly – high levels of education, social and political trust are not reflected in participation-levels when it comes to the traditional partisan forms of political participation. Both electoral turnout and party-activism are at much lower levels than in the Scandinavian neighbouring countries (Grönlund and Setälä 2007; Bengtsson et al. 2013). Thus, there is an interest in democratic 'cures' in Finland and the mini-publics experiments have definitely fallen into this category. Members of the research team have also informed media, civil servants, politicians and the general public on several occasions, using both our data and data from abroad as examples of how lay citizens can be involved in political debate and, possibly, decision-making.

Our data consist mainly of survey responses but also of audio-recordings (and video-recordings from the online experiments) from all small-group deliberations. So far, almost all group-discussions have been transcribed and the content of many of them has been analysed (for example, Himmelroos 2012; Lindell 2015; Grönlund, Herne and Setälä 2015). Twice (#2 and #5), we have organised citizen-deliberation online in small groups. These deliberations have been synchronous, using webcams and microphones on a tailor-made platform. Otherwise, they have replicated designs from face-to-face deliberations, enabling us to analyse modal differences.

Since 2006, all in all, people have participated in our deliberations. Their evaluations of the experiments have been very positive and – even though our

Table 7.1: Comparison of Finnish experiments with mini-publics

	Theme	Question	Treatments	Common features	N	Mode	Year	Outcome	Conclusion
#1	Energy, nuclear power	Should Finland build 6th nuclear-power plant?	Secret-ballot and common-statement	Information package; expert-panel; rules; moderators.	135	F2F	2006	Treatment not important to opinion change but common statement-treatment had more positive side-effects.	Information and deliberation change opinions. Consensus produces positive side-effects.
#2	Energy, nuclear power	Replication of #1	Secret-ballot and common-statement	Replication of #1	79 (147)	Online	2008	Similar to #1	Similar to #1
#3	Immigration	Should Finland have more immigration?	Like-minded and mixed groups	Information package; rules; moderators.	207	F2F	2012	Like-minded anti-immigrant groups did not become more extreme.	Deliberation seems to 'launder' preferences. Deliberative norms alleviate opinion-polarisation.
#4	Minority language (Swedish)	What is the role of the Swedish language in Finland?	Like-minded groups with or without deliberative discussion rules	Information package; moderators.		F2F	2014	Groups with no rules became more extreme; groups with rules did not become more extreme.	Deliberative norms alleviate opinion-polarisation.
#5	Minority language (Swedish)	Replication of #4	Like-minded groups with or without deliberative discussion-rules	Replication of #4		Online	2014	Similar to #4	Similar to #4

primary interest has been scientific and not educative – all these people have had the opportunity to engage in political discussion. Many of them had no previous experience of organised political deliberation. Each mini-public has focused on one major topic. This means that the deliberations have been focused, also thanks to the fact that they have attracted participants with an interest in the topic at hand.

The costs related to organising the events have been high, several tens of thousands of euro per experiment, not including the salaries of the research staff. The costs consist of printing and postage for surveys and invitations; rent of rooms for group-discussion, remunerations for taking part in the event; food and drink; and travel costs. Moreover, software development for the online platform and hardware purchases have been costly.

Experiments #4 and #5 were the only ones that directly dealt with a *constitutional* issue, the status of the Swedish language in Finland. According to the Finnish Constitution:

> The national languages of Finland are Finnish and Swedish. The right of everyone to use his or her own language, either Finnish or Swedish, before courts of law and other authorities, and to receive official documents in that language, shall be guaranteed by an Act. The public authorities shall provide for the cultural and societal needs of the Finnish-speaking and Swedish-speaking populations of the country on an equal basis.

According to our first survey in experiments #4 and #5, a vast majority of the Finnish-speaking population in Finland is in favour of the bilingualism of the country. This support, however, is less obvious when asked in specific policy-terms. In particular, support for mandatory study in the Swedish language has declined: only one in four Finnish-speakers was in favour in October 2014. It should be kept in mind that the experiments on the status of the Swedish language were not organised as traditional mini-publics: we recruited opinion-enclaves to talk amongst themselves. They then deliberated with deliberative rules or discussed freely without specific rules. They were not 'constitutional deliberative mini-publics' wherein differing opinions met.

Thus, we cannot say what happens when a mini-public with heterogeneous views deliberates on a constitutional question. What we can conclude, however, is that *deliberative rules do make a difference*. This is good news for deliberative democracy in general and deliberative mini-publics in particular. Many of the normative assumptions made by deliberative democrats can be fulfilled with simple rules emphasising reasoning, openness, respect and reflection.

Conclusion

Above, I have described the five deliberative experiments that we have organised since 2006. They have all been population-based mini-publics with clear scientific goals. We have had an interest in a) different decision-making methods;

b) different group compositions; c) different modes; and d) the impact of deliberative rules in alleviating polarisation in like-minded groups. Even though only the last experiments dealt with a constitutional issue, we have learned a lot about deliberative mini-publics and the possibilities of using them in democratic decision-making. Thus, the knowledge gained of mini-publics is used as a reference below, where I discuss the possibility of using deliberative mini-publics in constitutional decision-making in real-world politics.

I start with recruitment and the problem of representation. Creating a representative sample or a 'microcosm' of the population (Fishkin 1997) is the goal of most mini-publics. This goal follows the logic of survey-research and aims at fulfilling the ideal of external inclusion. Therefore, most mini-publics use random selection in recruiting participants (Brown 2006). Random sampling may, however, lead to unrepresentative samples if the sample-size is small. Contrary to Dahl's original idea of approximately 1000 participants, most mini-publics are much smaller: often, fewer than 100 participants gather for deliberation. When a small probability-sample is drawn from a population of millions of people, sampling errors become huge and the randomly drawn mini-public might be anything but a 'microcosm' of the population. Still, random sampling is an appropriate technique for obtaining sufficient cognitive diversity, which is crucial for epistemic fruitfulness (Bächtiger, Setälä and Grönlund 2014: 230).

Yet, there may be good reasons for over-sampling certain social groups to ensure their presence, sometimes in higher numbers than their proportion in the broader population would warrant. For example, a critical mass of participants from minority social groups may be needed to ensure their voice is recognised and heard (James 2008; Derenne 2012: 27). When it comes to constitutional decision-making, different national minorities should be included in a mini-public if their interests are at stake. These minorities might reflect 'vertical' conflicts (Lipset and Rokkan 1967) that is, ethnic, linguistic or religious cleavages in society, but they can also reflect the social diversity of contemporary societies: for example, they could be based on sexual orientation when discussing fundamental rights such as gay-marriage.

It is important to consider the pros and cons of probability-sampling when recruiting participants to a mini-public. The main rule is that probability-sampling can be used if the sample-size is large enough. If the mini-public is small, the issue of representativeness should be addressed separately, especially if the mini-public is to be used as a proxy for the informed public opinion of a larger population. Further, attrition related to self-selection needs to be thought of. It may be difficult to attract people with low levels of political efficacy or political interest. Therefore, stratification and over-sampling should be considered in order to guarantee external inclusion, especially when the sample-size is small. Lastly, representation should not only cover different social groups but also different viewpoints (Dryzek and Niemeyer 2006). One of the reasons for this is that people will always belong to multiple statistical categories and it is to know in advance how each individual ranks his or her various identities (Brown 2006: 218; Lafont 2015: 49). A combination of (stratified) probability-sampling and opinion-based recruitment might be an option (Bächtiger, Setälä and Grönlund 2014). Opinion-based recruitment is a process in which a probability-sample is first surveyed on the issue at hand. After this, the organiser can create strata based on opinions and apply a further recruitment-method within the opinion strata. At this stage, random selection can be applied anew (see Grönlund, Herne and Setälä 2015 for a detailed description of a process using opinion-based probability-sampling).

Can the judgment of a mini-demos be 'the verdict of the demos itself' as Dahl (1989: 340) suggested? Parkinson (2006: 34) argues that representation by random selection can only be legitimate when its aim is to gather information, or when it is used as part of a 'wider deliberative decision-making process that involves the people more generally'. He compares randomly selected representatives with experts whose role is to inform representatives, selected through a popular vote at elections. The elected representatives act with formal bonds of accountability and authorisation. According to his view, only elected representatives should have collective decision-making power on behalf of everyone else. In this sense, his view resembles Fishkin's (1997) who thinks that Deliberative Polling® should be used in order to find out the informed opinion of the demos.

If the mini-public is treated as a 'trusted information proxy' (MacKenzie and Warren 2012) of the public will, who should have the final say on constitutional issues? Thompson (2008) provides strong arguments against politicians making decisions on the electoral system. He favours a combination of a citizen-assembly – the British Columbia Citizens' Assembly is an example – which gives a verdict that is used as a voting recommendation in a referendum. His particular constitutional example, the electoral system, is so complex that a mere referendum without a body 'where citizens who serve on such a body could act as representatives of their fellow citizens' (Thompson 2008: 29), is not enough. Citizens cannot be expected to walk around with detailed knowledge of electoral systems. A mini-public, on the other hand, can set up criteria for a just and fair electoral system, read facts, hear experts, and finally reach, through public reasoning, a recommendation on a system that fulfils these criteria. The BC experience shows that lay citizens are capable of deliberating and forming an informed opinion on a complex issue such as the electoral system. Our Finnish experiments lead to similar conclusions (see also Suiter, Farrell and O'Malley 2014 and Suiter, Farrell and Harris 2016, Chapter Three in this volume). Even though facilitated deliberation tries to achieve 'an ideal-speech situation', we know that some participants talk less whereas others are more active. Still, self-reported experience of other participants' dominance is very rare. Moreover, the more silent participants in our experiments have not expressed less satisfaction with the deliberative sessions in anonymous surveys. To sum up, ordinary citizens do not lack the competence to discuss complex issues, including constitutional questions.

Randomly selected mini-publics are not accountable in the traditional sense, in which citizens can reward or punish representatives at elections for their actions and decisions. In contemporary democracies, we tend to think of elections only as a democratic selection-mechanism for representative institutions. Thus, the primary mechanism for selecting representatives in the ancient Athenian democracy, lottery, is not even considered to be democratic any more (Manin 1997).[3] The underlying assumption seems to be: a representative body cannot act responsibly without electoral accountability. This assumption is strong, almost a conviction, and is seldom questioned. It should, however, be scrutinised theoretically and tested empirically, preferably with experimental methods.

In a recent book-chapter, we discuss the future of deliberative mini-publics and their role in representative democracy and reach a conclusion (Bächtiger, Setälä and Grönlund 2014):

> Even though electoral democracy will continue to form the basis of representative government, changes in character of political issues, forms of governance and citizens' political behaviour call for institutional reforms (cf. Warren 2003). In order to enhance the role of mini-publics in policy-making processes, we recommend institutionalisation of their use and developing forms of public communication between mini-publics and elected representatives and other policy-makers.

This was a general recommendation. Constitutional questions, on the other hand, might call for the demos to have a stronger impact, because of the stakeholder position of elected politicians, especially concerning electoral systems (as previously discussed).

The Irish Constitutional Convention (*see* Suiter, Farrell and Harris 2016, Chapter Three in this volume) is a very promising endeavour within the area of deliberative constitutional decision-making. By design, it was not a traditional mini-public in which only citizens discuss among themselves. It brought together randomly selected citizens and elected representatives in joint deliberations that ended with recommendations, some of which were put to referendums in Ireland.[4] Whereas pure mini-publics consisting of randomly selected citizens might encounter legitimacy problems in the eyes of the general public and, at least in the short run, also have to struggle with getting their recommendations put on to the agenda of decision-making bodies, such as parliaments or referendums, the Irish combination of citizens and politicians who have already been elected in free and fair elections is a true democratic innovation worth investigating further.

Even though promising, however, the Irish model might also raise some questions. The most obvious has to do with effective participation: how to achieve equal participation and equal possibility of influencing the process at a convention

---

3. This is a paradox, since opinion-polls are based on the idea of representative samples and are often drawn as simple random samples of the electorate.

4. The newest example being the referendum on same-sex marriage, which was a recommendation from the Constitutional Convention and won the popular vote by a large margin (62 per cent in favour) in a referendum on 22 May 2015.

consisting of citizens and politicians.[5] When (mostly) unaccustomed citizens enter an assembly to deliberate with professional politicians, the ideal of equal participation is in danger. Modern politicians are politicians by profession. They are trained or have at least practised in rhetoric. They are used to conflicting views and cross-cutting exposure, whereas most lay citizens tend to avoid political conflict (Mutz 2006: 7–11). In order to guarantee equal participation, lay citizens could first gather among themselves in order to form an informed view on an issue. This is especially important to those with low socio-economic status, less experience of political discussion and low levels of political efficacy. Based on our experimental experience, these people might, in fact, gain from like-minded deliberation before entering the cross-cutting environment. Thus, enclave deliberation might be an answer to some of the criticism claiming that deliberative democracy is an elitist model of democracy (Jacobs, Lomax Cook and Delli Carpini 2009: 15).

In conclusion, fundamental decisions on the democratic system, that is, constitutional questions, should involve citizens directly. A deliberative mini-public consisting of a representative sample of the demos is an ideal participatory forum for such an endeavour. The outcome of a mini-public, a concrete standpoint on a constitutional issue, will work as an informed opinion-proxy of the public will. Moreover, be debated in public with the goal of 'actually improving the deliberative quality of the political discourse in the broad public sphere' (Lafont 2015: 59).

---

5. For discussion on effective participation within mini-publics of citizens, see O'Flynn and Sood 2014.

References

Bächtiger, A., Setälä, M., and Grönlund, K. (2014) 'Towards a new era of deliberative mini-publics', in Grönlund, K., Bächtiger, A., and Setälä, M. (eds) *Deliberative Mini-Publics: Involving citizens in the democratic process*, Colchester, UK: ECPR Press, pp. 225–45.

Bengtsson, Å., Hansen, K. M., Harðarson, Ó., Narud, H. M., and Oscarsson, H. (2013) *The Nordic Voter: Myths of exceptionalism*, Colchester, UK: ECPR Press.

Bergmann, E. (2016) 'Participatory constitutional deliberation in the wake of crisis: the case of Iceland', in Reuchamps, M., and Suiter, J. (eds) *Constitutional Deliberative Democracy in Europe*, Colchester, UK: ECPR Press.

Brown, M. B. (2006) 'Survey article: citizen panels and the concept of representation', *Journal of Political Philosophy* 14(2): 203–25.

Dahl, R. D. (1989) *Democracy and Its Critics*, New Haven, CT and London: Yale University Press.

Derenne, B. (2012) *G1000 Final Report: Democratic innovation in practice*, Legal deposit D-2012-8490-09, Brussels, BE: G1000.

Dryzek, J. (2002) *Deliberative Democracy and Beyond: Liberals, critics, contestations*, Oxford, UK: Oxford University Press.

Dryzek, J., and Niemeyer, S. (2006) 'Reconciling pluralism and consensus as political ideals', *American Journal of Political Science* 50(3): 634–49.

Fishkin, J. S. (1997) *The Voice of the People: Public opinion and democracy*, 2nd edn, New Haven, CT: Yale University Press.

—— (2009) *When the People Speak*, Oxford, UK: Oxford University Press.

Goodin, R. E. (1986) 'Laundering preferences', in Elster, J., and Hylland, A. (eds) *Foundations of Social Choice Theory*, New York, NY: Cambridge University Press, pp. 132–48.

Grönlund, K., and Setälä, M. (2007) 'Political trust, satisfaction and voter turnout', *Comparative European Politics* 5(4): 400–22.

Grönlund, K., Bächtiger, A., and Setälä, M. (2014) 'Introduction', in Grönlund, K., Bächtiger, A., and Setälä, M. (eds), *Deliberative Mini-Publics: Involving citizens in the democratic process*, Colchester, UK: ECPR Press, pp. 1–8.

Grönlund, K., Herne, K., and Setälä, M. (2015) 'Does enclave deliberation polarize opinions?', *Political Behavior* 37: 995–1020, online, DOI 10.1007/s11109-015-9304-x.

Grönlund, K., Himmelroos, S., and Strandberg, K. (2016) 'Can deliberative norms prevent group polarization in like-minded groups?', paper prepared for the MPSA Annual Meeting, Chicago, 7–10 April.

Grönlund, K., Setälä, M., and Herne, K. (2010) 'Deliberation and civic virtue: lessons from a citizen deliberation experiment', *European Political Science Review* 2(1): 95–117.

Grönlund, K., Strandberg, K., and Himmelroos, S. (2009) 'The challenge of deliberative democracy online – a comparison of face-to-face and virtual experiments in citizen deliberation', *Information Polity* 14(3): 187–201.

Himmelroos, S. (2012) *Det demokratiska samtalet – en studie av deliberativ demokrati i ett medborgarforum*, Åbo, FI: Åbo Akademi University Press.

Jacobs, L. R., Lomax Cook, F., and Delli Carpini M. X. (2009) *Talking Together – Public deliberation and political participation in America*, Chicago, IL: University of Chicago Press.

James, M. R. (2008) 'Descriptive representation in citizen assemblies', in Warren, M. E., and Pearse, H. (eds) *Designing Deliberative Democracy: The British Columbia Citizens' Assembly*, Cambridge, UK: Cambridge University Press.

Karpowitz, C. F., Raphael, C., and Hammond, A. S. (2009) 'Deliberative democracy and inequality: two cheers for enclave deliberation among the disempowered', *Politics & Society* 37(4): 576–615.

Lafont, C. (2015) 'Deliberation, participation, and democratic legitimacy: should deliberative mini-publics shape public policy?', *Journal of Political Philosophy* 23(1): 40–63.

Lindell, M. (2015) *Deliberation och åsiktsförändring – en studie av individegenskaper och gruppkontext*, Åbo, FI: Åbo Akademi University Press.

Lipset, S. M., and Rokkan, S. (1967) 'Cleavage structures, party systems and voter alignments: an introduction', in Lipset, S. M., and Rokkan, S. (eds) *Party Systems and Voter Alignments*, New York, NY: Free Press, pp. 1–64.

Luskin, R. C., Fishkin, J. S., and Jowell, R. (2002) 'Considered opinions: deliberative polling in Britain', *British Journal of Political Science* 32(3): 455–87.

MacKenzie, M., and Warren, M. (2012) 'Two trust-based uses of minipublics in democratic systems', in Mansbridge, J., and Parkinson, J. (eds) *Deliberative Systems: Deliberative democracy at the large scale*, Cambridge, UK: Cambridge University Press, pp. 95–124.

Manin, B. (1997) *The Principles of Representative Government*, Cambridge: Cambridge University Press.

Mansbridge, J. (1994) 'Using power/fighting power', *Constellations* 1(1): 53–73.

Morrell, M. (2014) 'Participant bias and success in deliberative mini-publics', in Grönlund, K., Bächtiger, A., and Setälä, M. (eds), *Deliberative Mini-Publics: Involving citizens in the democratic process*, Colchester, UK: ECPR Press, pp. 157–175.

Mutz, D. C. (2006) *Hearing the Other Side: Deliberative versus participatory democracy*, Cambridge, UK: Cambridge University Press.

O'Flynn, I., and Sood, G. (2014) 'What would Dahl say? An appraisal of the democratic credentials of deliberative polls and other mini-publics', in Grönlund, K., Bächtiger, A., and Setälä, M. (eds) *Deliberative Mini-Publics: Involving citizens in the democratic process*, Colchester, UK: ECPR Press, pp. 41–58.

Parkinson, J. (2006) *Deliberating in the Real World: Problems of legitimacy in deliberative democracy*, Oxford, UK: Oxford University Press.

Setälä, M., Grönlund, K., and Herne, K. (2010) 'Citizen deliberation on nuclear power: a comparison of two decision-making methods', *Political Studies* 58(4): 688–714.

Strandberg, K., and Grönlund, K. (2012) 'Online deliberation and its outcome – evidence from the virtual polity experiment', *Journal of Information Technology & Politics* 9(2): 167–84.

Suiter, J., Farrell, D. M., and Harris, C. (2016) 'The Irish Constitutional Convention: a case of "high legitimacy"?', in Reuchamps, M., and Suiter, J. (eds) *Constitutional Deliberative Democracy in Europe*, Colchester, UK: ECPR Press.

Suiter, J., Farrell, D. M., and O'Malley, E. (2014) 'When do deliberative citizens change their opinions? Evidence from the Irish Citizens' Assembly', *International Political Science Review*, online, DOI: 10.1177/0192512114544068, 1–15.

Sunstein, C. (2002) 'The law of group polarization', *Journal of Political Philosophy* 10(2): 175–95.

— (2007) *Republic.com 2.0*, Princeton, NJ: Princeton University Press.

— (2009) *Going to Extremes: How like minds unite and divide*, Oxford, UK: Oxford University Press.

Thompson, D. F. (2008) 'Who should govern who governs?', in Warren, M. E., and Pearse, H. (eds) *Designing Deliberative Democracy: The British Columbia Citizens' Assembly*, Cambridge, UK: Cambridge University Press, pp. 20–49.

Warren, M. E. (2003) 'A second transformation of democracy?', in Cain, B. E., Dalton, R. J., and Scarrow, S. E. (eds) *Democracy Transformed? Expanding political opportunities in advanced industrial democracies*, Oxford, UK: Oxford University Press, pp. 223–49.

Warren, M. E., and Pearse, H. (eds) (2008) *Designing Deliberative Democracy: The British Columbia Citizens' Assembly*, Cambridge, UK: Cambridge University Press.

Chapter Eight

Legitimacy without Visibility? On the Role of Mini-Publics in the Democratic System

Stefan Rummens

Mini-publics are often presented as a promising means for revitalising democratic systems at a time when there is a widespread feeling that more traditional parliamentary institutions are losing much of their efficacy, as well as their appeal to voters. The innovations with mini-publics discussed in this book are fascinating; and deliberative processes such as these undoubtedly have a significant democratic potential. At the same time, we should also appropriately temper our expectations. In this chapter, I focus on what I consider to be the main weakness of mini-publics: the fact that they lack visibility to the wider audience of citizens. Since these citizens do not actually participate in the deliberation, for them, the mini-public necessarily remains a kind of 'black box'. They do not have the opportunity to hear and discuss all of the relevant arguments and, as a result, it will be unclear to them why the outcomes of these deliberations should be accepted as democratically legitimate.

Below, I develop my concerns in the form of a series of six interrelated theses that I think should be taken seriously when discussing the proper role of mini-publics in the democratic process as a whole. My arguments aim to clarify, for instance, that it is not a coincidence that the case-studies discussed in this book suggest that mini-publics work best when they are properly connected with – and even integrated into – the conventional representative decision-making processes. If there is a future for deliberative assemblies in democratic systems, it is not as a replacement for ordinary parliamentary institutions. Instead, they should be thought of, and designed, as complementary tools that can help to mitigate some of the weaknesses of traditional parliamentary politics.

Thesis 1: Democratic legitimacy is a quality of the democratic system as a whole

The analyses of the case-studies presented in the earlier chapters of this book proceed on the basis of a theoretical model – developed in the introduction (Suiter and Reuchamps 2016, Chapter One of this volume) – which makes use of the important distinction between input, throughput and output legitimacy and which applies this threefold account of legitimacy to the mini-public as such (Schmidt 2013; Caluwaerts and Reuchamps 2015). Input legitimacy is concerned with the representativeness of the participants, the openness of the agenda and the epistemic completeness of the process. Throughput legitimacy concerns the quality of participation, the quality of decision-making and the contextual independence of the mini-public. Finally, output legitimacy refers to the social and political uptake of the debates in the mini-public by the larger public of citizens as well as by the more formal political or constitutional actors in the political system.

I believe that this threefold conceptual framework is very useful and suitable for analysing the deliberative legitimacy of mini-publics as deliberative events. At the same time, I think that it is very important to keep in mind that this framework only provides a local and partial measure of deliberative legitimacy, precisely because it focuses only on the mini-public as such rather than on the democratic system as a whole.

Recently, several leading authors have emphasised the importance of a systemic approach to deliberative democracy (Goodin 2005; Parkinson 2006; Parkinson and Mansbridge 2012). They rightly point out that the ideal of reasonable face-to-face deliberation, which inspires the whole deliberative paradigm, cannot be institutionalised directly in any straightforward manner in the large-scale political communities of today. An authentic deliberation between millions of citizens is simply not feasible. Yet the question of how to devise a democratic system that is suitable for our contemporary societies and which, at the same time, realises the underlying ideals of deliberative democracy as closely as possible, is an urgent matter that has not so far been given adequate attention in the flourishing debate of the past two decades.

A more systemic approach to deliberative democracy requires a shift: from the currently more common micro-analyses of the deliberative quality of singular deliberative events to a macro-analysis of the deliberative quality of the democratic system as a whole. An empirical assessment of the overall deliberative quality of democratic systems is highly challenging, however. An essential part of the problem, in this regard, is that a convincing theoretical framework for such an assessment has not yet been developed. The criteria we use for analysing the rationality of face-to-face discourse cannot simply be extrapolated to the macro-level. For example, on the micro-level, we insist that strategic behaviour on the part of participants is unacceptable. From a macro-perspective, however, strategic behaviour could, in some circumstances, be considered highly beneficial (Mansbridge et al. 2010). In order to bring a hitherto neglected issue on to the public agenda, it is important to think strategically about how to attract attention. You will probably need to protest, to rally in the streets, perhaps to exaggerate your concerns somewhat or present them in a particular and one-sided manner. This kind of behaviour is clearly at odds with the calm and orderly behaviour expected of rational discussants from a micro-perspective. At the same time, such behaviour might be necessary to put important new issues on the agenda and thus to guarantee the inclusive nature of the democratic process as a whole.

Before I discuss the proper conceptualisation of the macro-deliberative quality of the democratic system in the second thesis, two additional remarks are in order.

First, in the conceptual framework used in the previous chapters of this book, concerns about the macro-perspective are incorporated into the 'output' dimension of the legitimacy of mini-publics, in the sense that output legitimacy refers to the uptake of the deliberative event by the larger social and political system (Goodin and Dryzek 2006). This reference to the larger context is very important but, in itself, insufficient to deal with the prior but fundamental question regarding the contribution mini-publics *should* make to the democratic process as a whole. Should these outcomes, ideally, have a binding force and be translated directly into legal and constitutional decisions? Should they be used as the basis for a referendum? Should they be submitted to the formal representative institutions for approval? Or should they simply be used as informal contributions to the public debate?

Second, when thinking about the contribution mini-publics should make to the overall deliberative quality of the democratic system, it is important to bear in mind that there are other contenders in the debate about the proper institutionalisation of the deliberative ideal. Although much of the empirical work on deliberative democracy has, for reasons of feasibility, focused on the use of mini-publics, some of the leading theorists in the deliberative paradigm, including, most notably, Jürgen Habermas (1996), have argued from the start that the deliberative ideal should be realised within the context of the *traditional parliamentary system*. Habermas advocates a two-track model of the public sphere, in which the deliberative quality of the system depends on the quality of the debates in the informal public sphere as well as on the extent to which these informal deliberations actually influence the debates in the formal sphere of parliament and government. Other authors, in turn, argue that the ongoing rise of governance networks provides an interesting opportunity for institutionalising deliberative democracy. They suggest that the deliberative ideal should be properly realised in the form of *deliberative networks* connecting all of the relevant stakeholders through national and transnational governance structures (Cohen and Sabel 1997, 2004; Bohman 2007).

In my view, we do not have to make an exclusive choice between mini-publics, parliaments or networks. The optimal realisation of the deliberative ideal in contemporary circumstances will probably require a democratic system which, in one way or another, combines these different modes of institutionalisation. At the same time (as I have argued elsewhere (Rummens 2012) and will explain again below) I also believe that traditional representative institutions will continue to play a key role in this optimal configuration. Most probably, the best way of moving forward is to retain the idea of a political system centred on a formal sphere of parliament and government and to investigate how the use of mini-publics and/or deliberative networks could further strengthen this system and help to deal with some of the challenges it currently faces.

Thesis 2: The macro-deliberative quality of the democratic process is determined by epistemic and motivational criteria

In the introductory chapter of a recent volume on deliberative systems (Mansbridge *et al*. 2012: 10–13), the contributing authors attempt to give a sketch of the normative requirements any adequate deliberative system has to meet. They identify three main criteria. On the *epistemic* level, a deliberative system should produce preferences, opinions and decisions that are adequately informed by a careful consideration of all the relevant facts and arguments. On the *ethical* level, the system should promote mutual respect amongst citizens as autonomous agents. On the *democratic* level, the system should promote an inclusive political process on terms of equality.

Although there is nothing wrong with these three criteria in themselves, I believe that they are somewhat redundant, as well as incomplete. They are redundant in the sense that a proper understanding of the epistemic structure of democratic deliberation reveals that the first (epistemic) criterion necessarily implies the other two (ethical and democratic) criteria. At the same time, the three criteria are incomplete because none of them focuses on the importance of a genuine motivational commitment of citizens to the outcomes of the deliberative process. In order to maintain the integrity of the political community, citizens should be sufficiently motivated to uphold the law. For that to happen, as I shall further explain below, it is necessary that citizens can actually *see* for themselves that their concerns are effectively taken up by the deliberative system.

In order to amend these shortcomings, I propose two alternative criteria. I submit that the macro-deliberative quality of the democratic system as a whole should essentially be assessed in both *epistemic* and *motivational* terms. I discuss these two criteria in turn.

On the *epistemic level*, the deliberative ideal implies that democratic deliberation should be understood as the construction of a moral 'we-perspective' (Habermas 2003). This means that laws and policies should conform to an ideal of impartiality: they should give equal consideration to the interests and values of all citizens affected by them. This ideal of impartiality is thereby explicitly modelled as a first-person-plural ('we') perspective. This implies, as further explained, for instance, by Seyla Benhabib (1992), that citizens should be respected as 'concrete others' each having their own specific needs and values. If we want to do justice to this specificity, it is impossible for policy-makers or philosophers to know in advance what the proper 'impartial' solution will be for the problems that arise in our societies. An impartial solution requires an explicit exchange of arguments between all people affected, in which these people can learn from one another and discuss together which solution is acceptable, from their own particular point of view.

If the epistemic structure of the deliberative process is understood as the construction of an impartial we-perspective, it becomes clear why the first 'epistemic' criterion suggested by Mansbridge *et al.* (2012) automatically implies the other two criteria they propose. First of all, the ethical criterion of 'respect for citizens as autonomous agents' seems to be guaranteed. As Habermas (1996) explains, the deliberative ideal of impartiality translates into an abstract scheme of basic rights, which forms the normative core of every democratic state and which guarantees, amongst other things, the greatest possible amount of equal basic liberties for all citizens as autonomous agents. For example, it seems plausible to claim that the ideal of impartiality is incompatible with a state-imposed religion but requires, in contrast, the fullest recognition of the freedom of religion of all citizens (Rummens 2006). An objection, at this point, might be that Mansbridge *et al.* (2012) do not simply wish to argue in favour of the constitutional protection of individual rights but that their criterion of 'respect for citizens as autonomous agents' should rather be seen as a truly 'ethical' criterion, referring to the respect we owe one another in all of our interactions as citizens. Although I agree that their criterion could be interpreted in this manner, I believe that such a truly 'ethical' reading would be at odds with the systemic approach. Such a criterion would reintroduce micro-requirements ('respect') on individual interactions. It could, as such, come into conflict with more basic macro-requirements. As I have argued elsewhere, in line – notably – with earlier work by Jane Mansbridge herself, the use of 'rough' speech (which might be insulting or even hateful) could, in some circumstances, play an important epistemic role by revealing underlying grievances that should urgently be addressed by the political system. To that extent, such 'rough' interactions should be legally protected as unpleasant but important elements of the democratic process as a whole (Sottiaux and Rummens 2012). Second, the requirement to take the actual needs and values of citizens into consideration also explains the need for an inclusive democratic process, in which the citizens concerned can actually participate (the democratic criterion). Citizens have, of course, an epistemically privileged access to their own needs and values and only they themselves can provide the information and arguments needed to come to an impartial decision. The need for citizen-participation is, therefore, not simply a matter of 'respect'; it is an essential and ineliminable epistemic presupposition of the deliberative model and its constructivist account of rightness (Rummens 2007).

On the *motivational level*, which is the second criterion for assessing the macro-deliberative quality of the democratic system as a whole, it is crucial that the outcomes of the deliberative process are not simply 'right' in the epistemic sense of the word. It is equally important that they are *seen* to be right by the citizens themselves. In the deliberative model, deliberation is understood as a process of transformation in which an exchange of arguments induces a learning process in the citizens concerned. They learn, through a process of 'role-taking', to balance their own concerns and values with the equally legitimate concerns and values of others (Habermas 1996, 2003). This process is not simply essential from an epistemic point of view: it is simultaneously essential from a motivational point of view. Citizens who go through this process afterwards understand *why* the accepted outcome is indeed the proper outcome and why it embodies an impartial result, which gives equal consideration to everybody's concerns. This understanding ensures that these citizens are willing to withdraw their more unreasonable demands ('I now understand that I should not impose my own religious standards on everybody else') and that they are motivated to uphold the outcomes of the deliberative process as democratically legitimate decisions.

The importance of this motivational identification of the citizens at large with the outcomes of the democratic process is twofold. From a pragmatic perspective, it is important for maintaining the integrity of the political community: if people fail to identify with the political process and its outcomes, support for the political system itself might, in the long run, be dangerously weakened. From a normative perspective, this identification is needed to guarantee the political autonomy of citizens. The whole concept of '*auto-nomy*' refers to the idea that people can see themselves not simply as the *subjects* of law but, at the same time, as the *authors* of law, who agree that the law is as it should be and that it is what it is for the right reasons.

Thesis 3: The visibility of the political struggle in the traditional parliamentary system helps to ensure its macro-deliberative quality

As I have argued more extensively elsewhere (Rummens 2012), the typically oppositional dynamics of traditional representative institutions bestow on the political debate a kind of visibility that is highly beneficial in terms of the macro-deliberative quality of the democratic process. The 'visibility' of the public debate refers to the fact that this debate is generally structured around a limited number of topics as well as around a limited number of recognisable political players, who each defend their own position on the political stage. These political players can be actual politicians but can also be representatives of civil-society organisations. A public debate that is visibly staged by the media in this manner (I further discuss the role of the media below) has a narrative structure with recognisable antagonists and storylines which make it accessible and appealing to the larger audience of citizens.

The fact that the oppositional dynamics of representative politics support the visibility of the debate is due to the incentive-structure of such an electoral system. Political players aiming to gain political power have an incentive to take to the public stage with appealing arguments that challenge the arguments of their political opponents. In a well functioning public sphere, the public political struggle is a never-ending struggle, in which both established players and newcomers are motivated to present political projects that can convince citizens to support them with their vote in the next elections.

In order to further explain the importance of the visible staging of the oppositional political struggle, we can look at the epistemic and motivational impact of this staging on the democratic system. From the *epistemic point of view*, the oppositional dynamics of the parliamentary system help to open up a space of political reasons, in which individual citizens can then try to find their own bearings. Citizens are informed about the different policy options and the reasons for supporting them. Political actors are thereby continuously motivated to try to present proposals that are responsive to the genuine interests and concerns of the citizens, as well as to try to find and expose the weaknesses of their adversaries' proposals. The ongoing presence of a minority opposition on the public stage operates as a form of 'epistemic reservoir' or 'epistemic reminder'. Even though the ideas of the opposition are currently not being translated into policy, these ideas remain present in the debate and remind everybody of the fact that some citizens feel that the current majority's policies do not adequately take into account their concerns and values.

From the *motivational point of view*, the visibility of the debate allows the citizens to go through a form of learning process. Although most citizens do not actively participate in the mediatized debate themselves, they are able to participate in the public debate in a more passive way. They learn about the different views and arguments; they have the opportunity to discuss these with their families, friends and colleagues; and they are forced, as voters, to make up their own minds. The visible staging of the debate by recognisable political actors also helps to ensure the identification of the citizen with the political process. Precisely because different identifiable political actors defend different positions, there will generally be at least some political actors with whom a citizen can agree and therefore politically identify. This identification is maintained even if the citizen in question disagrees with the current majority's decisions. Precisely because there are recognisable majority-actors who can be held accountable and who can be 'punished' by voting for equally recognisable minority-actors, the citizen feels that her point of view is 'represented' on stage and that she has at least some minimal form of (electoral) control over the process. She can, moreover, legitimately foster the hope that her point of view will convince more of her fellow-citizens in the future and perhaps one day become the majority position.

As many authors have emphasised, the possibility of citizens identifying with political actors who visibly represent an opposition against current majority policies is crucial to the legitimacy of the political system as a whole. If citizens feel that they cannot oppose the political system from within, they easily tend to turn against the system itself. The system is experienced as an alienating form of political rule, over which citizens feel they have no control. In this context, the rise of populism has been analysed as a response of citizens to the overly consensual nature of contemporary politics. Here, some of the citizen's anti-establishment resentment has been understood as a reaction against the blurring of the left–right distinction in so-called 'third-way politics' (Mouffe 2005: 64–76). More recently, the rise of eurosceptic parties throughout the European Union has been connected – and I believe rightly – with the absence of any recognisable opposition within the European political system (Neunreither 1998: 439; Føllesdal and Hix 2006: 549; Mair 2007: 6). The European system appears, in the eyes of voters, as a kind of 'black box', out of which spill anonymous political decisions. Because there is no visibly staged European political debate, citizens are not adequately informed about possible policy alternatives; they are not presented with recognisable majority actors who can be held accountable for their decisions and they are not presented with a recognisable opposition for which they could vote if they would like to change the course of European decision-making.

Thesis 4: Political communication with the public at large has to conform to the dramaturgical logic of the media

Bernard Manin argues in his famous book, *The Principles of Representative Government*, that we have witnessed, in the past couple of decades, a transition from a 'party-democracy' to an 'audience-democracy' (Manin 1997: 193–235).

A party-democracy is characterised by a relatively stable party-landscape formed by a limited number of ideological mass-parties. The social-democratic parties rising to power around the beginning of the twentieth century provide the paradigm cases for this type of mass-party. They had extensive networks throughout the whole of civil society and succeeded in securing the ideological allegiance of a vast number of voters, by providing these voters, amongst other means, with all kinds of services within these networks. In some countries, this type of ideological network even resulted in the formation of rigidly divided, so-called 'pillarised societies'.

As a result of the increasingly rapid and profound cultural changes taking place in most western societies in the sixties of the previous century, the ideological loyalty of voters to these traditional mass parties was severely weakened. This cultural process of individualisation marked the beginning of the gradual transition to our contemporary 'audience-democracy'. This new type of democracy is characterised by a much more dynamic party-landscape, in which the success of political parties now significantly depends on the presence of a charismatic leader who succeeds in attracting the attention and the votes of increasingly volatile voters. This new personalisation of politics goes hand-in-hand with a further mediatization of politics. Whereas politicians could previously rely on their mass-party's network to communicate with voters and to secure their support, they now have to rely much more heavily on their ability to communicate via the mass-media and to present a political project that appeals to the electorate.

Manin himself remains reluctant to assess the transition from party-democracy to audience-democracy in normative terms – as either progress or a backwards step (Manin 1997: 232–4). Although the 'mediatization of politics' is often portrayed as a problematic evolution and even as one of the main sources of the current sense of crisis with regards to our democratic system, I believe that the transition to an audience-democracy constitutes an important step forwards in terms of the epistemic quality of the democratic system. The fact that voters are now much more 'volatile' and less loyal to political parties should not necessarily be seen as a sign of political disaffection. It could indicate, on the contrary, that voters are now much more critical than was the case a couple of decades ago. Rather than always voting for the same party (often the party their parents before them also voted for), they are now much more concerned about the actual proposals politicians put forward. The more dynamic nature of the party-landscape has thereby put an end to the often sterile ideological stalemates of earlier days. And although, no doubt, there are large differences between countries, it seems that the political debate in western countries is now more lively and more open to the introduction of new issues and ideological concerns than it was, say, in the fifties of the previous century.

Although the transition to an audience-democracy seems to mark progress in terms of the epistemic quality of the public debate and the epistemic responsiveness of the political process, Manin is, of course, right when he points out that the identification of the voters with the political system (the motivational dimension) has become more fragile in the new context. In the absence of rigid ideological networks and as a result, perhaps, of exaggerated expectations *vis-à-vis* the democratic system, some citizens are indeed easily disappointed and turn their backs on the political system as a whole. In an audience-democracy, politicians face the daunting task of convincing voters time and again of the value and feasibility of their political projects. Loyalty to the system is now no longer simply given but has to be earned over again by politicians every day. Although the new fragility of the political trust of citizens can be deplored, I think it is the price we have to pay for the emancipation of voters from the ideological straitjackets of the mass-parties of the old days.

In the times of party-democracy, the connection between politics and citizens was made through extensive and ideological party-networks. In view of the cultural processes of individualisation our societies have experienced, such networks can no longer exist today. As a result, there seems to be no readily available alternative to the central role played by the mass-media as the medium through which politicians communicate with the larger public of citizens. It may be a lack of imagination on my part, but I believe that the mediatization of politics is a characteristic of our political lives that we will simply have to accept and deal with for the foreseeable future. Again, in spite of the many misgivings about this mediatization, I believe that this evolution is not necessarily problematic. On the contrary, the media play a crucial role in 'staging' the public debate and, thereby, in making this debate visible and accessible to the wider audience.

The mediating role of the media, which is crucial from the democratic point of view, can be understood as follows. The media are characterised by a certain dramaturgical logic that dovetails very nicely with the agonistic and oppositional dynamics of parliamentary politics (Parkinson 2006: 99–123; Hajer 2009: 66). Because the media have to capture the attention of a wide audience, they aim to provide a telling story and, thus, focus on events and messages that can be staged as narratives. This means, for example, that the media are generally much more interested in conflict than in consensus; it means that the media want a story or an argument to be presented by a recognisable person; it means that messages have to be short, to the point and preferably presented by means of a captivating metaphor and some humour. Although these constraints are perhaps, in a certain sense, regrettable, parliamentary politics, with its agonistic and personalised structure, can easily adapt to this format. And, indeed, this is exactly what politicians have done in the course of the past decades (Esser and Strömbäck 2014). They have understood that the media are essential if they want to reach a large audience and they have learned to communicate in a way that is attractive to and in line with this dramaturgical logic. Importantly, however, this adaptation remains essentially an adaption in form. The mediatization of politics implies little, if anything, concerning the content of the messages that politicians can bring to the larger audience. If some voters are disappointed about the lack of inspiring ideological projects presented by their politicians, and if politics nowadays often seems barren of ideas, it makes little sense to blame this on the media. If the message is unattractive, we should probably not shoot the messenger.

Of course, the role played by the media is not without its own risks. The media's control over the way in which the political debate is staged gives them a genuine and crucial form of political power. As a result, there are many things that can go wrong in a mediatized democracy, even in western societies with an important democratic tradition. Here, the Italian case, where Silvio Berlusconi had an unhealthily strong grip on the media, readily comes to mind. Therefore, in view of the systemic quality of the democratic process, it is important to watch over the *quality* of the media (for example, through voluntary codes of conduct for journalists or by ensuring the diversity of news formats) and also to ensure media-plurality, avoiding concentrations of media-power in the hands of only a few commercial or other agents. Politicians should think carefully about the proper ways of regulating the media as well as about, for instance, the role that could or should be played by public broadcasting agencies. Nevertheless, in spite of all the legitimate concerns that we might have about the proper role of the media, I think it is important not to consider the media as part of the problem of our current 'crisis' of democracy. If they function properly, they play a crucial and indispensable role in staging the public debate and, therefore, in connecting the political system with the citizenry at large. If we want to recapture the attention and the commitment of this wider audience, the media are part of the solution, not part of the problem.

Thesis 5: Mini-publics have a very limited visibility; this severely constrains their potential contribution to the democratic system

The main weakness of mini-publics is their limited visibility. For the outside audience of citizens who do not participate in the actual deliberations, they remain essentially 'black boxes'. Outsiders do not have the opportunity to go through the same learning processes as insiders. They are not adequately informed about the issues, the policy alternatives or the reasons for preferring one option over another. Therefore, it should come as no surprise that these outsiders are not always prepared to take for granted that the outcomes of mini-public deliberation are indeed well reasoned attempts to give equal consideration to all citizens' concerns; nor that they are often reluctant to accept these outcomes as democratically legitimate.

In this context, it is important not to confuse a lack of visibility with a lack of transparency. Even if the actual deliberations are opened to the public or if the reports of the meetings are published online, it remains very hard and would require a lot of time and effort for the larger audience to really understand what is at stake. In the type of visibility typical of the oppositional representative politics discussed before, visibility is generated because political opponents have an (electoral) incentive to analyse their opponents' arguments in search of the weak spots they believe might be relevant to potential voters. The work of sorting through the bulk of all possibly relevant information and arguments and selecting those that really matter is done – in the context of oppositional politics – by political actors themselves. They stage the debate in an agonistic interplay that makes the policy alternatives, the key issues and the key arguments easily understandable and digestible for the larger audience. In contrast, in the case of the mini-public, no equivalent actors or mechanisms are present.

Some years ago, John Parkinson (2005) published an interesting case-study of a deliberative poll on the future of the British National Health Service, held at the Manchester Metropolitan University in July 1998. Although much effort was made to provide adequate media coverage of the poll and Channel 4 actually dedicated three one-hour television programmes to the event, Parkinson had to conclude that this coverage failed both to capture much of the actual deliberation and to convey the learning-experience of the participants to the wider audience. The case illustrates that the deliberative logic of the mini-public is deeply at odds with the logic of the media. Whereas the media want to have a narrative based on conflict between recognisable political actors, the mini-public consists of anonymous citizens trying to reach a reasonable consensus. As a result, the visible staging of the debate within the mini-public is next to impossible and the linkages that can be forged between the mini-public and the larger public on the outside are – to use Parkinson's felicitous phrase – 'rickety bridges' at best.

The same problem can be illustrated by looking at the G1000 experiment, as discussed in Jacquet *et al.* 2016, Chapter Four of this volume. Media coverage of the event was, in fact, much more focused on the event as such rather than on the content of the deliberations. Televised reports of the citizen-summit provided viewers with images of a large room of people sitting at tables, with some short interviews with participants asking them why they wanted to participate and what they expected. What usually followed was, most importantly, a longer interview with the main organiser of the event, the famous – and therefore recognisable – writer David Van Reybrouck, about the event's purpose. As Jacquet *et al.* also emphasise, the main impact of the event was that it provided new input into the public debate about the renewal of Belgian democracy. This is the main point the organisers wanted to make and it was the point that was publicly defended on many occasions by Van Reybrouck himself. The actual proposals generated by the G1000, on the other hand, which should have been the essence of the whole experiment from the point of view of the deliberative ideal, were hardly, if at all, taken up by the media or the formal political process. This illustrates, once more, that what the media wants is a recognisable face making a clear and controversial point, not a room full of unknown people trying to reach consensus on policy issues.

The limited visibility of mini-publics affects the epistemic and motivational contributions these deliberative events can make to the democratic system as a whole. If we focus, first, on the *epistemic dimension*, it is true, of course, that one of the reasons for promoting mini-publics as an interesting alternative (or complement) to more traditional political processes is the supposed epistemic superiority of their outcomes. Whereas ordinary political decision-making is marred by passions and short-term interests, deliberation in mini-publics is calm, reasoned and focused on the long-term common good. Although this argument is undoubtedly valid to a certain extent and justifies – as I will explain below – a potential complementary role for mini-publics in the democratic process,

I believe that there are also good reasons for caution even regarding the epistemic dimension. The requirement of 'epistemic completeness' on the input side of the mini-public as a deliberative event is highly demanding. As explained before, the ambition to take seriously all citizens as 'concrete others' implies that it is very hard or even impossible to find an adequate substitute for the actual participation of all citizens affected. Even if we try to make our sample of citizens as representative as possible, many relevant groups and perspectives in society will not be represented at the table and so, therefore, 'completeness' might turn out to be an elusive ideal. The problem here is very fundamental. If we take the perspective of the citizen as a concrete other seriously, his or her concerns and values are not simply exogenous pieces of processable data that can be entered into the deliberation. The deliberation is a transformative process, in which all possibly relevant perspectives should be confronted with each other and change as a result of this confrontation. If all perspectives are not present at the table, this learning process might be severely distorted.

In the case of the Icelandic Constitutional Council, this concern with epistemic completeness has been taken very seriously, as described by Eiríkur Bergmann (Bergmann 2016, Chapter Two of this volume). As he explains, the drafting of the constitution proceeded in an interactive 'crowdsourcing' manner, whereby different draft versions were presented to the larger audience and then amended through several feedback rounds, in order to come up with a document that incorporated as much as possible all of the legitimate concerns raised by the outside audience. This is undoubtedly a very laudable and interesting attempt to further improve the quality of the deliberation in terms of its 'epistemic completeness'. Nevertheless, here, too, there are significant limitations. This kind of interaction with the larger outside public requires quite an effort from this outside public. Citizens who wanted to provide feedback had to actively 'peruse' the new articles as presented on the Council's website and themselves search for any weak spots or omissions. When we compare this with traditional parliamentary proceedings, the latter have a much clearer division of labour with regard to this epistemic-feedback process. When the current majority presents a first draft of a bill, it is the task of the opposition (as well as established civil-society organisations) to search for the weaknesses that might concern voters and to present possible alternatives. As explained, this feedback-process, as part of ordinary legislative procedure, leads to a staged confrontation in the media between political opponents. This allows ordinary citizens to become informed about the most contested issues and, if necessary, to mobilise more extensive forms of protest if they feel they are needed. In other words, ordinary oppositional dynamics allow for a long-term legislative process in which the public at large is given time to make up its own mind and to point out potential weaknesses or omissions in the proposals. Whether mini-publics can be organised in ways that can similarly accomplish such an epistemic-feedback process with the larger audience is not clear at all. Although I am convinced that mini-publics have many epistemic qualities, the claim that they are obviously superior in epistemic terms compared to ordinary parliamentary politics is, in my mind, not as straightforward as most authors seem to assume.

If we turn, next, to the *motivational dimension* of the democratic system, it seems clear that this is the real Achilles' heel of the mini-public. As demonstrated by the well known earlier deliberative experiments regarding electoral reform in British Columbia in 2004 and Ontario in 2007, citizens are not at all automatically prepared to endorse proposals developed by a mini-public when these are put to a referendum. The reason for this, as I have suggested, is that the proposal appears to the wider public as an epistemic 'singularity', an all-or-nothing proposal without adequate epistemic context. In the case of a visibly staged debate with recognisable actors defending different alternatives, the citizen is presented with an 'extended' public space of reasons rather than a singularity. As a result, the citizen-voter is much more aware of what is at stake and is much more able to make an informed decision. The all-or-nothing nature of the outcome of the mini-public also implies that a voter who disagrees with the proposal can easily feel alienated from the political process. With ordinary oppositional politics, the minority position remains represented on the political stage by the minority parties, even after a lost vote. As a result, this point of view remains visibly recognised as a legitimate point of view and continues to operate as a real presence for possible future debates. In the absence of such a visible opposition, the voter whose point of view is not chosen has no recognisable person or party remaining within the political system with which he can still identify and which can provide a focal point for his hopes for a possible change of course in the future.

When we consider the identification of citizens with the democratic process, I feel that the term 'audience-democracy' for our present form of parliamentary democracy is not well chosen. It wrongly suggests that parliamentary politics reduce citizens to a merely passive role. Here, the original French expression used by Manin, '*la démocratie du public*' ('the public's democracy'), is much better. When the media stage the political debate, they do not thereby reduce the public to a mere audience. Citizens, either as individuals or through their civil-society organisations, are also given a voice in this debate: concerns can be raised, protest can be organised. Politicians who want to be re-elected will therefore have to take public opinion seriously. In this sense, citizens know and feel that they possess a genuine electoral power that allows them to steer their politicians between elections. This kind of indirect but real, and symbolically very important, political power is absent in the case of mini-publics. Although the ideal of deliberative democracy is obviously an ideal of empowerment and participation, the paradoxical result of using mini-publics in the legislative or constitutional process might be that the vast majority of citizens, precisely because they are not actually present at the table, feel reduced to a truly passive 'audience'. If citizens feel excluded from the democratic process in this way, it is likely that they will experience it as an alienating and external and, therefore, illegitimate form of rule.

Thesis 6: In order to maximise the legitimacy and impact of mini-publics, they need to be properly connected with traditional parliamentary political processes

As argued, I believe that attempts to make our democracy more deliberative should look at the deliberative quality of the democratic system as a whole. In spite of my emphasis on the limitations of mini-publics, I believe that mini-publics could be part of such a more comprehensive approach. Therefore, mini-publics probably work best when they are properly connected to and integrated with more traditional representative processes.

Interestingly, the Icelandic constitutional process discussed in Bergmann 2016 included a more traditional electoral moment, in the sense that the members of the Constitutional Assembly (Constitutional Council) were chosen in a general election. This type of electoral element does not seem to be very promising, though. As Bergmann notes, voter turnout for these elections was rather low (only 37 per cent) and, not surprisingly, citizens tended to vote for candidates who were already previously well known. Although the election was undoubtedly a well intentioned attempt to give more democratic legitimacy to the proceedings, the set-up seems to defeat the whole purpose of elections as a way for citizens to have an impact on the democratic process. When citizens are asked to vote, it does not make much sense to ask them to choose between people they do not know and who are, moreover, not supposed to have an ideological profile.

The set-up of the Irish Constitutional Convention provides a more interesting attempt to connect the deliberative mini-public with the outside 'maxi-public'. As explained by Suiter, Farrell and Harris (2016, Chapter Three of this volume) the Convention consisted of sixty-six randomly selected citizens, thirty-three elected legislators appointed by the political parties and a chair. Interestingly, the presence of politicians who were already elected members of parliament apparently did not undermine the deliberative quality of the actual meetings of the Convention. Politicians were not set on stealing the limelight and encouraged other members to fully contribute to the debate. At the same time, their presence presumably significantly reinforced the legitimacy of the proceedings for the outside public. The fact that elected representatives participated in the deliberative event and were, afterwards, enthusiastic about its functioning and its outcomes undoubtedly provided a kind of legitimacy-check on the process in the eyes of voters. The fact that politicians participated seems, moreover, to have greatly facilitated the political uptake of the outcomes afterwards. As Suiter, Farrell and Harris emphasise, the mixed set-up is able to avoid a 'disconnect' between the convention and the political class. The detrimental effect of such a disconnect is illustrated by the Icelandic case, where the process was, from its early stages, politicised from the outside by politicians and parties who questioned its legitimacy. As a result, the ratification of the new constitution in the Icelandic parliament is now stalled by the new majority parties, who never fully endorsed, or even strongly opposed, the whole deliberative process (Bergmann 2016, Chapter Two of this volume).

It is still too early to make a final assessment of the Irish process. The fact that the legalisation of same-sex marriage, proposed by the Convention, has been approved by a majority of 62 per cent of the Irish voters in a referendum held on 22 May 2015 is, of course, a promising result. At the same time, however, the – arguably less important – proposal for lowering the age of eligibility for presidential elections was rejected in the same referendum by 73 per cent of the voters. Regardless of these mixed outcomes, it seems clear that the Irish process provides an interesting attempt to combine the best elements of both worlds: the specific epistemic quality of mini-public deliberation and the large-scale (epistemic and motivational) legitimacy of traditional parliamentary politics.

Although I have argued before that, in an ideal case, parliamentary politics can lead to outcomes of a high epistemic quality, it is also true, of course, that, in the real world, the epistemic quality of traditional politics is often severely undermined by the impact of the short-term interests and passions that so often play a role in the wheelings and dealings of messy and mediatized oppositional politics. The calm and reasonable nature of mini-public deliberation, in which long-term interests and concerns can be reasonably weighed in an impartial manner, could therefore, under certain circumstances, provide an interesting epistemic complement to traditional politics. In this regard, it is probably safe to suggest that the use of mini-publics will be most beneficial with regards to topics that are more difficult to tackle for ordinary politicians. Here, topics with a long-term impact such as ecological issues, energy policies or pension schemes come to mind. Additionally, topics of a constitutional nature, which concern the foundations of our political community and which, ideally, should be based on a broader consensus amongst citizens, also seem appropriate. Although politics should not be depoliticised, politicisation often means that issues become (too) caught up in short-term calculations. If the semi-secluded and dispassionate setting of the mini-public allows us to take up a more impartial perspective and to also take long-term considerations more seriously in the decision-making process, this could be beneficial from the point of view of the macro-deliberative quality of the political process.

In spite of the proven epistemic qualities of reasonable face-to-face deliberation, I have argued above that mini-publics cannot stand on their own in the deliberative system. A close connection with the traditional parliamentary system seems advisable from both an epistemic and a motivational perspective. As explained, the notion of 'epistemic completeness' is a highly demanding one if the purpose of the deliberative system is to take into account the needs and values of all citizens as concrete others. Therefore, this requirement cannot be fully met without an actual discursive feedback loop between the mini-public and the maxi-public. Such a feedback-loop is, moreover, only possible if the whole process of deliberation is sufficiently extended over time. The Irish case is here probably not a very good example because the Convention usually only had one weekend to discuss a specific issue. It is probably much better to make sure that the same topic is discussed on several occasions, the time in between being used to get feedback from the larger audience. Here, the attempts in the Icelandic case to open up the deliberation and allow for a reiterative 'crowdsourcing' process seem a step in the right direction. Nevertheless, as I have argued, even this form of interaction remains insufficiently visible. Therefore, elected politicians participating in the deliberative process should play an additional legitimising role by going out into the public and explaining the current draft proposals as well as the underlying arguments. Whether lay members of the mini-public should also play a similar role in publicly explaining and defending some of the arguments (as apparently happened to a certain extent in the Irish case), is less clear to me.

From a motivational perspective, the legitimacy of mini-publics crucially depends, in my view, on the fact that citizens know and feel that they have a significant amount of control over the whole decision-making process, both through the public debate and by electoral means. Here, the feedback-moments mentioned above are vital and should take the form of a genuinely mediatized debate in which affected citizens and civil-society organisations get ample time and occasion to voice their concerns. Most importantly, the mini-public should never be used as an alternative form of decision-making but should operate, rather, as a moment within the process of public opinion-formation. In the mini-public, arguments are considered and weighed and proposals formulated which are, subsequently, used as input for more formal decision-making processes. In this more formal process, parliament should play a central role because this is the place where the mini-public's recommendations can be confronted with the more classical ideological positions that are represented by the different parties and that reflect citizens' preferences. Whether, after such a confrontation, the final political decision regarding the proposals should belong to parliament itself or whether they should be put up for a referendum in which the electorate as a whole expresses itself presumably ought to depend upon the specific national political culture as well as the importance of the issues at hand.

References

Benhabib, S. (1992) *Situating the Self: Gender, community and postmodernism in contemporary ethics*, Cambridge, UK: Polity Press.

Bergmann, E. (2016) 'Participatory constitutional deliberation in the wake of crisis: the case of Iceland', in Reuchamps, M., and Suiter, J. (eds) *Constitutional Deliberative Democracy in Europe*, Colchester, UK: ECPR Press.

Bohman, J. (2007) *Democracy Across Borders: From dêmos to dêmoi*, Cambridge, MA: MIT Press.

Caluwaerts, D., and Reuchamps, M. (2015) 'Strengthening democracy through bottom-up deliberation: an assessment of the internal legitimacy of the G1000 project', *Acta Politica* 50(2): 151–70.

Cohen, J., and Sabel, C. (1997) 'Directly-deliberative polyarchy', *European Law Journal* 3(4): 313–42.

— (2004) 'Sovereignty and solidarity: EU and US', in Ladeur, K.-H. (ed.) *Public Governance in the Age of Globalization*, Aldershot, UK: Ashgate, pp. 157–75.

Esser, F., and Strömbäck, J. (eds) (2014) *Mediatization of Politics: Understanding the transformation of western democracies*, Basingstoke, UK: Palgrave.

Føllesdal, A., and Hix, S. (2006) 'Why there is a democratic deficit in the EU: a response to Majone and Moravcsik', *Journal of Common Market Studies* 44(3): 533–62.

Goodin, R. E. (2005) 'Sequencing deliberative moments', *Acta Politica* 40(2): 182–96.

Goodin, R. E., and Dryzek, J. S. (2006) 'Deliberative impacts: the macro-political uptake of mini-publics', *Politics & Society* 34(2): 219–44.

Habermas, J. (1996) *Between Facts and Norms: Contributions to a discourse theory of law and democracy*, transl. Rehg, W., Cambridge, MA: MIT Press.

— (2003) 'Rightness versus truth: on the sense of normative validity in moral judgments and norms', in Habermas, J. *Truth and Justification*, Cambridge, UK: Polity Press, pp. 237–78.

Hajer, M. A. (2009) *Authoritative Governance: Policy-making in the age of mediatization*, Oxford, UK: Oxford University Press.

Jacquet, V., Moskovic, J., Calluwaerts, D., and Reuchamps, M. (2016) 'The macro political uptake of the G1000 in Belgium', in Reuchamps, M., and Suiter, J. (eds) *Constitutional Deliberative Democracy in Europe*, Colchester, UK: ECPR Press.

Mair, P. (2007) 'Political opposition and the European Union', *Government and Opposition* 42(1): 1–17.

Manin, B. (1997) *The Principles of Representative Government*, Cambridge, UK: Cambridge University Press.

Mansbridge, J., Bohman, J., Chambers, S., Estlund, D., Føllesdal, A., Fung, A., Lafont, C., Manin, B. and Martí, J. L. (2010) 'The place of self-interest and the role of power in deliberative democracy', *Journal of Political Philosophy* 18(1): 64–100.

Mansbridge, J., Bohman, J., Chambers, S., Christiano, T., Fung, A., Parkinson, J., Thompson, D. F., and Warren, M. E. (2012) 'A systemic approach to deliberative democracy', in Parkinson, J., and Mansbridge, J. (eds) *Deliberative Systems*, Cambridge, UK: Cambridge University Press, pp. 1–26.

Mouffe, C. (2005) *On the Political*, London, UK: Routledge.

Neunreither, K. (1998) 'Governance without opposition: the case of the European Union', *Government and Opposition* 33(4): 419–41.

Parkinson, J. (2005) 'Rickety bridges: using the media in deliberative democracy', *British Journal of Political Science* 36(1): 175–83.

— (2006) *Deliberating in the Real World: Problems of legitimacy in deliberative democracy*, Oxford, UK: Oxford University Press.

Parkinson, J., and Mansbridge, J. (eds) (2012) *Deliberative Systems*, Cambridge, UK: Cambridge University Press.

Rummens, S. (2006) 'Debate: the co-originality of private and public autonomy in deliberative democracy', *Journal of Political Philosophy* 14(4): 469–81.

— (2007) 'Democratic deliberation as the open-ended construction of justice', *Ratio Juris* 20(3): 335–54.

— (2012) 'Staging deliberation: the role of representative institutions in the deliberative democratic process', *Journal of Political Philosophy* 20(1): 23–44.

Schmidt, V. A. (2013) 'Democracy and legitimacy in the European Union revisited: input, output and "throughput"', *Political Studies* 61(1): 2–22.

Sottiaux, S., and Rummens, S. (2012) 'Concentric democracy. Resolving the incoherence in the European Court of Human Rights' case law on freedom of expression and freedom of association', *I.CON International Journal of Constitutional Law* 10(1): 106–26.

Suiter, J., and Reuchamps, M. (2016) 'A constitutional turn for deliberative democracy in Europe?', in Reuchamps, M., and Suiter, J. (eds) *Constitutional Deliberative Democracy in Europe*, Colchester, UK: ECPR Press

Suiter, J., Farrell, D. M., and Harris, C. (2016) 'The Irish Constitutional Convention: a case of "high legitimacy"?', in Reuchamps, M., and Suiter, J. (eds) *Constitutional Deliberative Democracy in Europe*, Colchester, UK: ECPR Press.

Chapter Nine

Ideas of Constitutions and Deliberative Democracy: A Conceptual Conclusion

John Parkinson

This volume is dedicated to the idea of specifically 'constitutional' deliberative democracy. What does that adjective add? For some of the contributors, the answer to that question is rather obvious – it is a deliberative event or series of events directed to constitution-making rather than policy-making, deliberation about the rules of collective life rather than specific decisions within it. But that 'obvious' answer relies on some prior assumptions about what constitutions are and what deliberative democracy is. If we start with different assumptions, new possibilities emerge. This concluding chapter sets out some of the implications of three understandings of constitutions, and three approaches to deliberative democracy, for constitution-making and research

The idea of constitutional deliberative democracy is not new (see Ackerman 1991), although it is certainly not yet a mainstream concern either; as presented here, it is more an application of existing ideas and processes to a less traditional domain than a radical change of approach; and the word 'turn' is perhaps overused, as Dryzek (2010: 6) ever-so-gently suggests. But it seems a logical step, given that the systems move in deliberative theory has re-opened room for thinking about how the various parts of democratic systems work together (Bohman 2012); and because there are issues to do with constitutions and constitution-making that deserve more attention, not least because of long-standing but often forgotten arguments between constitutionalists – who, traditionally, want to bracket off the principles of democracy and justice from interference by potentially tyrannical majorities – and proceduralists – who argue either that justice is best secured by democratic means or that what counts as just is, itself, a matter for democratic deliberation. If we move that disagreement to the foreground, constitutional deliberative democracy is far more than an attempt to apply innovative techniques to realms beyond local policy-making.

The chapter starts by setting out what I see as some fundamental disagreements about the meaning of deliberative democracy, resisting a tendency to equate it with particular techniques of public engagement. Instead, it argues that we should treat deliberative democracy as a label for a kind of democratic system that has deliberation as a salient feature. The chapter then picks out three different understandings of constitutions that interact with deliberative democracy in ways which reveal both the limits and the possibilities of applying particular kinds of technique to constitutional issues; and reveals what are, I think, important avenues for future research. It then briefly shows how the cases and, more particularly, the case-studies, fit into that overall scheme, complementing the analysis that Talpin

(2016, Chapter Six of this volume) and Rummens (2016, Chapter Eight of this volume) have already offered. It concludes with suggestions about future analysis of deliberative democracy and constitution-making.

Three models of deliberative democracy

I began with a remark about the meaning of the phrase 'deliberative democracy'. It has long been asserted – via lists of features derived from Cohen (1986), Elster (1986), Gutmann and Thompson (1996), Fung (2003) and many others – that deliberative democracy is about subjecting proposals for action to public reasoning rather than to majority votes or some market-based procedure. Such a definition would receive widespread academic assent and yet is misleading: it glosses over a variety of early starting-points, aims and developments. Some of the literature has been inspired by Habermas's (1984) ideal-speech situation and his theory of communicative action more broadly; others have their origins in American federalist, progressive, even Deweyan, traditions. Some has been an attempt to rescue democracy from the devastating attacks of public-choice theorists, by providing a richer description of everything that leads up to a vote; some is rooted in long-standing critiques of technocratic policy-making and planning in a variety of policy domains; some is rooted in more localist, participatory, communitarian traditions; sometimes it is anti-capitalist, anti-corporatist, anti-globalist. Some early literature was explicitly descriptive, particularly that which attacked aggregative models, while other literature was more exclusively normative. And, in the process of arguments over principles, the consensus criterion was downgraded, if not completely discarded, to the point that most theorists now agree that democracy is a system of 'talk, then vote' (Goodin 2008: 108), while numerous other challenges from different democrats about the nature and role of rationality,[1] amongst other things, have been integrated into a broader deliberative democratic story.[2]

Despite that variety of starting points and theoretical developments, the empirical literature, at least in political studies, quickly established a fairly standard set of normative principles – informed, reason-sensitive, other-regarding, equal and inclusive discussion, originally oriented to consensus – and began a search for, or even creation (Fishkin 1991) and analysis of, real-world examples (Bohman 1998). In almost every case, the search focused very quickly on deliberative mini-publics (Fung 2007), small-scale democratic innovations involving randomly selected citizens, a conventional – and therefore to be treated sceptically – list of which seems to be mandatory in half the papers published on the subject.

---

1. The introduction to this volume and other contributions advance a rather hard, Socratic account of rationality, which does not sit well with many deliberative theories. Early statements of competing accounts of rationality appear in Dryzek 1990 and Forester 1984; see also Chambers 2003.

2. An intellectual history of deliberative democracy is yet to be written, but existing accounts tend to present an implausibly linear story of phases of development from a single starting point (Elstub 2010); or capture some of the variety but not other important strands (Bächtiger et al. 2010). All history is simplified, selective; but ideas also swim in chaotic soups (Kingdon 1984), a messiness that my account here attempts to capture.

Figure 9.1: Publications on 'deliberative democracy' in Google Scholar, by year

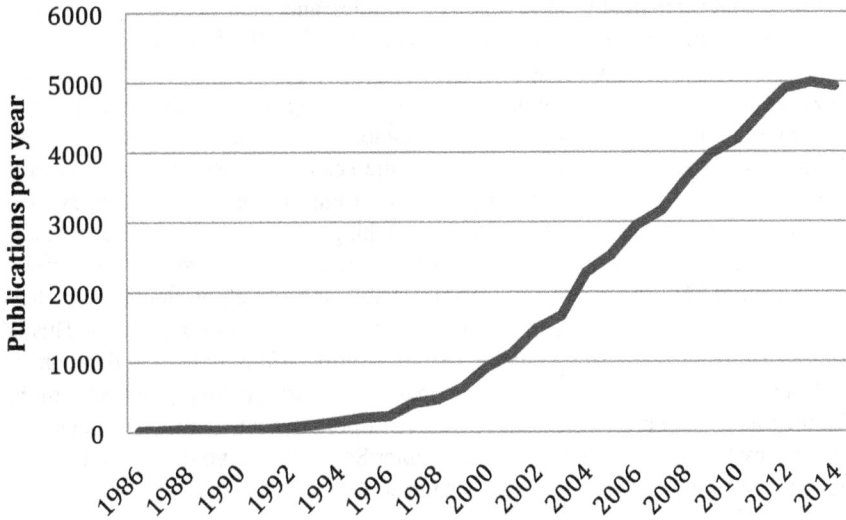

There have been exceptions, Uhr (1998) among them, but, otherwise, this rush to the small, participatory scale was near-universal and very productive, revealing examples of innovative practice; lessons about good procedure; a revival of belief in the deliberative capacities of ordinary people and the benefits of involving them directly in solving controversies; reflection on and recasting of theory; and a surge of experimentation with and, to a lesser but increasing extent, institutionalisation of participatory practices both in day-to-day governance and – as this volume attests – grander constitutional moments (Niemeyer 2011; Thompson 2008). Increasingly sophisticated empirical tools were developed and the literature has expanded steadily for fifteen years straight (*see* Figure 9.1).

However, important things were lost in the process. First, rather than challenging technocratic visions, a great deal of deliberative effort rapidly became technocratic itself, focused on institutional design and experimentation to the point that, in a great many cases, deliberative practice became more about answering academic questions, or the competitive marketing and deployment of particular technologies of engagement, than empowering citizens.[3] This was

---

3.   I have been particularly critical of the deliberative poll method in this regard (Parkinson 2006a: 48, 129–30). While it has been held up as the gold standard by some academics (Mansbridge 2010), its pre-test–post-test structure is better suited to answering academic questions than democratic ones. But similarly technocratic imperatives have been noticeable in deliberative experimentation in health policy-making in the UK (Milewa, Valentine and Calnan 1999; Mort, Harrison and Wistow 1996) and development policy more generally (Cooke and Kothari 2001; Gaventa 2006). See Olsen and Trenz 2014 and Papadopoulos and Warin 2007 for related critiques; Hendriks and Carson 2008 for an interesting discussion of the marketisation of public deliberation; and Niemeyer 2011 for a counter-argument about the emancipatory potential of mini-publics, despite their other problems.

amplified by a second problem: scholars overstated the democratic credentials of institutions based on quota samples of citizens – sometimes conflating quota samples with statistically representative samples and then conflating statistical representativeness with principal–agent representation (Parkinson 2004).[4] They took such features as *sufficient* conditions for deliberative democracy instead of *necessary* (or at least desirable) ones, overlooking many other necessary but missing conditions, such as: some act of endorsement and accountability of the decision-makers; publicity bonds between the selected deliberators and the rest of the citizenry – as Rummens (2016, Chapter Eight in this volume) emphasises; the consequent lack of legitimate decision-making power of most such processes; and the problem definition and agenda limits which further restrict legitimacy (Parkinson 2006a). In short, many scholars focused so much on deliberation they forgot the democracy, let alone wider relations of power and domination. This is seen in the usually implicit equation of deliberation and deliberative democracy that persists widely in the literature. Small-scale participatory processes might feature a lot of deliberation, and they might be important contributors to deliberative democracy (compare Grönlund 2016, Chapter Seven in this volume), but they are not deliberative democracy in, and of, themselves.

An analogy might be helpful here. If we call a car a 'diesel', we are describing it in terms of a salient feature – the fuel it uses based on the type of engine under the hood. The feature is salient because it makes an important difference in people's daily interaction with the car: there are environmental impacts, to be sure, but drivers need to know that it's a diesel when they pull up to the fuel pump, because if they get it wrong they won't be pulling terribly far away from the pump. But 'diesel' is far from a given car's only quality. It applies to the fuel and fuel systems but there is plenty else that 'diesel' fails to describe: not just obvious characteristics like steering, comfort, braking and so on, but all the identity and affective meaning that cars symbolise (Sheller 2004).

Similarly, I think the label 'deliberative democracy' best refers to a democracy which has a salient feature, 'deliberativeness'. Mini-publics are one way of injecting more of this and other qualities like participation into a democracy; but there are other means, too (Dryzek 2009), with different strengths and weaknesses. None of them are 'deliberative democracy' on their own. Equally, a deliberative democracy has many, many other features than just deliberativeness, political equality and collective popular control or decisiveness among them (cf. Beetham 1994; Dahl 1989; Dryzek 1996: 4; Smith 2009). To equate deliberative democracy with small-scale deliberation is just a conceptual mistake, like calling the fuel

---

4.   While certainly there is a democratic tradition of selecting decision-makers by lot, deliberative mini-publics do not use lot, at least not in forms that meet the conditions for just procedure set out by Broome (1984) or Goodwin (1992), assertions to the contrary notwithstanding (compare Carson and Martin 1999 and Grönlund 2016, Chapter Seven in this volume). On this point, see Gaventa (2006), who sets out the dangers of relying solely on invited spaces for public engagement and not invented spaces that citizens carve out for themselves. Democracies ought to have both: spaces in which the powerful invite people in, sometimes but not always via impersonal selection-mechanisms; and spaces in which citizens can engage without having to wait for an invitation.

system 'car' or, to take an example dear to many academic hearts, like calling an undergraduate lecture 'learning'. There is so much more to it.

I have laboured this point terribly – Warren (2012) makes it more succinctly – but it is important because it has a big impact on what scholars look for, and what they overlook, when approaching questions of constitutional (or indeed any other kind of) deliberative democracy. I will address those implications in the following sections. For now, let me turn to the next approach – or, rather, a family of approaches – to deliberative democracy. These 'macro' approaches come in two broad versions, although there are alternative categorisations; and some practices resist being put in whichever boxes we construct.

The first family of approaches is what Dryzek (1990) called 'discursive democracy' or Schlosberg (1999) called 'neopluralism', which concentrates on the reflexive, inclusive generation of discursive challenges to events and hegemonic understandings of the world. Such democracy is sometimes characterised as 'subjectless, decentred', following Habermas (1984): once discourses are generated they can take on a life of their own, being transmitted around democratic societies through everyday communicative acts that do not require much in the way of institutional architecture to get them going. They are not entirely subjectless, though: the transmission mechanisms might be relatively automatic but the discourses are generated by people jointly responding to experiences and situations and pressing claims on the wider public that result from those experiences. To use more Habermasian language, democratic discourses should be grounded in the lifeworld, not grounded in systems of institutions and procedure. This is an important point of distinction and something I will come back to in a moment.

The second family is the deliberative-systems approach (Parkinson and Mansbridge 2012), an approach which tries to model the roles that different institutions and actors play in a democratic system such that collective decisions are made both legitimate and systematically responsive to better arguments. What counts as a better argument depends on its grounding in everyday lived experience as much as Rawlsian understandings of public reason: a feature that has been used to distinguish the approach from some epistemic visions of democracy but should not be, as Rummens (2016, Chapter Eight in this volume) is right to argue. And thus, systemic analyses look at the connections between sites of law and policy-making and the wider public sphere; or, in a more normative mode, advocate institutional arrangements and linkages to transmit proposals and preferences from the 'communicative space' of the public sphere to the 'empowered spaces' of binding collective decision-making (Bohman 2012) in a way – to take on another of Rummens's criticisms – that is visible to the wider public. Some of the institutions in the system may inject more deliberation – mini-publics, legislative committees, courts, some kinds of activist networks – and many do not. The latter – voting and elections, protest, some representative processes, symbolic and performative practices, even social research (Chambers 2012) – inject other necessary qualities into a democratic system, such as equality of influence; decisive popular voice; effective grounding in lived experience and public discourse; coercive and bureaucratic structures to ensure implementation; logical, principled and evidential testing; and visibility of the entire enterprise.

Thus described, deliberative systems could be seen as quite an old approach, as Mansbridge *et al.* (2012) point out. Indeed, it is my view that some of the classic texts of deliberative democracy such as Cohen (1986), Elster (1986) and Manin (1987) are repeatedly misread as checklists or blueprints for micro-institutional design, when they could be more persuasively read as outlines of idealised deliberative systems, posited as counters to more narrowly aggregative models of democracy at the large scale.

Systemic deliberative democrats advocate institutions of inclusion and decision because they are suspicious of the structurelessness and 'ad-hockery' of the discursive approach – if the venues and language of inclusion are always changing, then only professional insiders, from full-time political advisors to well resourced activists, are able to gain access to empowered space. Casual engagers, the vast majority of citizens, look at such processes in bewilderment, wondering where the door is, let alone how to get in (Parkinson 2012b; see also Papadopoulos and Warin 2007). In turn, discursive democrats are suspicious of the degree to which people empowered in institutions come to serve their own ends and resist or formalise the perspectives of outsiders, especially when the 'division of labour' in a deliberative system is agent-based rather than site- or institution-based, sorting roles on the basis of alleged personal capacities rather than the strengths and weaknesses of different institutional designs. The result is that people in such a system become means to systemic ends rather than ends in themselves, something antithetical to the Kantian underpinnings of deliberative democratic theory (Gutmann and Thompson 1996). Clearly, the ideal is systems that balance these requirements – formal access-routes but plenty of scope for citizen-led and creative challenge; a certain amount of stability of institutions but periodic review and reform; with scrutineers or 'tribunes' in place to ensure the voices of the people are heard, often *despite* the formal channels (Thompson 2010).[5]

One element of systemic views that has not yet been adequately addressed is that they tend to draw on static analogies, rather than dynamic ones, when setting out their models. That is, the authors in Parkinson and Mansbridge (2012), and others since, have tended to depict systems in terms of network diagrams, setting out fixed relationships between venues, sites and spheres, or between actors and roles (for an example of the latter, see Christiano 2012). Such models leave out a crucial dimension, the dynamics of issues, actors and venues over time, repeating an element of the 'epistemic singularity' mistake that Rummens notes with respect to mini-publics. The sequencing of events, venues and roles can be crucial to the deliberative and democratic qualities of a system; elsewhere, I have set out my account of an ideal deliberative democratic sequence which, contrary to common

---

5.   This is very much in the same spirit as Mansbridge (1983), who did not claim that her unitary democracy was an alternative to adversarial forms but that the two were essential balances to each other. Compare Warren (1999) on the democratic need for institutions of trust and distrust; or Gaventa on invited and invented spaces once again (2006).

practice, puts relatively open, even 'wild' public agenda-setting processes at the start of the sequence, shifting small-scale deliberative processes away from that position and making them immediate precursors to empowered processes of binding collective decision-making (Parkinson 2006a; Rummens 2016, Chapter Eight in this volume; see also Goodin 2005). I will come back to that sequenced account in the next section but it is worth noting that network- and sequence-metaphors do not exhaust the possibilities. Other metaphors are available too, including Dryzek's 'soup, society and system' metaphors (Dryzek 2011); or 'bandwaggoning' and 'cascade' metaphors (Sunstein 1995). Each of these will have its biases; each will have its blind spots.

Another approach that deserves a mention is the idea of 'scaling-up' deliberation, borrowing a label from Niemeyer (2012), amongst others. Now, when Niemeyer uses the label, he is talking about improving the macro-impacts of micro-deliberative events, something that Goodin and Dryzek (2006) also discuss. Niemeyer is on the side of those like Owen and Smith (2015), MacKenzie and Warren (2012) and Grönlund (2016, Chapter Seven in this volume), who see mini-publics and similar citizen-led forums as essential elements of a deliberative democracy, not just one option among many for injecting deliberation into a democratic system. The trick is to ensure that such forums are connected effectively to the formal decision-making venues of a democratic society. So, this version of the scaling-up approach is a variant of deliberative systems, just one that is more insistent on the value of a particular set of innovations than are the authors of the systems 'manifesto' (Mansbridge *et al.* 2012). Others use the approach in a more literal sense, however. For them, scaling-up entails applying the micro-criteria of good deliberation at larger scales; but from the perspective of my definition of deliberative democracy – a democracy with deliberation as a salient feature – the idea of deliberation writ large is fraught with danger. Three dangers deserve a mention.

The first is to look for deliberation – and *only* deliberation – in every part of a given system and, not finding it, to declare the system 'non-deliberative' or the approach flawed. To repeat my car analogy, a diesel car is not a diesel-fuel sub-system 'writ large'; it is a system with many different elements, one of which is made salient. One should no more expect to find deliberation in every corner of a deliberative democracy than one should expect to find diesel oil in the gear-box, let alone the glove-box; nor then to dismiss gear-boxes and glove-boxes as pointless.

The second danger is more subtle: that the analyst is blinded to the features of a democratic system that are the products of scale and complexity themselves, something that is usefully highlighted in Geissel and Gherghina's contribution (2016, Chapter Five of this volume). This has three aspects: one, that the items on an ideal small-scale deliberative checklist change as one moves up in scale; two, that scale introduces new features entirely; and three, that features have interaction effects that depend on scale. For example, a clear agenda is often seen as a necessary condition in small-scale deliberation but, as one moves out of the confines of a mini-public, agendas become harder to control and competing problem definitions are more the stuff of political argument. At the small scale, there is a tendency to think of people's perspectives or preferences on a policy issue as givens, materials that are brought to the forum by participants in a more-or-less raw state, and which are then transformed by the deliberative process. In large-scale democracy, perspectives are both a 'product' and a contextual constraint on deliberation and decision-making, things that have material, social and discursive foundations and which are thus not so amenable to transformation in the face of facts and arguments.

The third danger of the 'deliberation writ large' approach is of encouraging analysts to think that deliberation is only ever about the topic at hand, even when there is agreement about the topic and agenda. Deliberative moments are themselves performances and symbols, communicating something important about the status of citizens, about proper procedure, about 'the way we do things'. Whether they are inclusive and deliberative, and make good or bad or indifferent decisions, are only some of the reasons to support or vilify them – important reasons, to be sure, but not the only ones.

For these reasons, the scaling-up label is not terribly useful – when used figuratively it is perhaps a poor choice of words to describe a sensible variant of the systemic approach; when used literally it blinds analysts to much that could be going on in large-scale deliberative systems.

Those, then, are my three main models of deliberative democracy, one micro and two macro, with an emerging but somewhat problematic 'scaling' approach that, in its sensible guise, is a variant of one of the latter two. Next, let's unpack the term 'constitutional' and see what that adds to the picture.

Constitutional deliberative democracy

Just as deliberative democracy means several different things, so does 'constitutional'. In the introduction, Suiter and Reuchamps (2016, Chapter One of this volume) cite Dworkin (1995) and Elster (1995) who, with varying emphases and insights, frame constitutionalism as standing in tension with democratic norms. Constitutions are meant to act as restraints on a majority's, or the state's, ability to act tyrannically with respect to individuals and minorities; and, while democracy itself is one means by which the people exercise such restraint, it is just one such means, a necessary but not sufficient condition. Other means include specification of the relative powers of different branches and agencies of the state; 'entrenchment' rules; statements of individual rights against the state; and so forth.

Now, what this framing of constitutions assumes is a liberal order featuring democracy of the usual liberal kind – aggregative, preference-respecting and so on. I will come back to what a more deliberative framing might assume in a moment but first it is important to highlight a point that Elster makes about this understanding of constitutions: that it is highly normative and idealised. Real constitutions, Elster insists, are the products of political processes at times of crisis; such times produce documents and amendments that are varying mixtures of liberal and illiberal principle; nationalist mythology; populism; symbolism; procedural rules; and specific, substantive law. When using the label 'constitutional deliberative democracy', one needs to be clear about which of these two options one means: is it idealised deliberation about rights and procedures? Or is it something more pragmatic, deliberation about whatever happens to be in the documents labelled 'the constitution' and thus entrenched in some way? If the former, then what is at stake in constitutional deliberative democracy is something approaching democratic deliberation about the procedures and substantive underpinnings of a properly deliberative democracy – second-order or 'meta-deliberation' (Landwehr 2015). If it is the latter, then the issue is more about the *means* of entrenching measures or changing entrenched provisions, which requires the building of larger and more diverse coalitions over time to amend or redraft.

From a more deliberative standpoint, we find something like the first view most clearly supported by Gutmann and Thompson (1996: 33), who distinguished some years ago between what they saw as the relatively unobjectionable constitutional entrenchment of things that are integral to democracy and its underpinnings – freedoms of speech and assembly on the one hand, or subsistence rights on the other – and the more questionable entrenchment of things that neither underpin nor specify democratic procedures. In other words, they are, like Pettit (2012: 25), democratic proceduralists 'with a democratic proviso', for whom constitutionalist claims of justice and rights do not trump democratic procedures, except when it comes to protecting those procedures (see also Waldron 1999). However, Gutmann and Thompson are ambiguous about the scope of deliberative democracy – the formulation above might be taken to imply that deliberative democracy ought not to be allowed to meddle with its own procedures but elsewhere (1996: 358) they argue that the 'best forum for considering the design of deliberative institutions is likely to be one in which deliberation, however nascent, has a prominent place'.

A third, more critical standpoint is possible, one that has something in common with Elster's real-world concerns. Let's take the 'constitutional' adjective in another sense, as a qualifier that specifies that people ought to deliberate in a constitutional way rather than an 'unconstitutional' way. For discursive democrats like Dryzek (2000: 18–19) this is anathema, because constitutions 'are not ... the only forces that order deliberation in the liberal polity'. Constitutions focus on relationships between people and the state, and between parts of the state, but they never completely describe those relationships; and therefore they overlook – and thus fail to give citizens purchase on – other structuring forces, such as the political economy; discourses; administrative cultures and governance-networks (Bevir and Rhodes 2010); or the international system. A constitutional deliberative democracy in *this* sense would be an attenuated one, a coercive structure wearing the clothes of free debate, one which forces most citizens to play one game in public while the powerful play an entirely different game behind closed doors, pretending that there is no other game in town. This, critical theorists and Marxists generally would say, has always been the case with democracy under capitalism.

So, we have two normative understandings of constitutions that imply that they codify the 'rules of the game', one of which brackets those rules off from majority interference and the other which encourages their meta-deliberative creation; and a third, more pragmatic understanding that sees constitutions as a hotchpotch of elements, for which the main consideration is not whether or not demoi *should* get involved but the degree to which they *can*.

These different understandings of what it means to be constitutional interact with the three approaches to deliberative democracy in interesting ways and I pick out a few salient features in Figure 9.2. If we take the first of our two normative approaches and think of constitutions as procedures and principles bracketed off from democratic interference in order to protect liberty and democracy themselves, then deliberative *democracy* has no role whatsoever to play in constitutions. Deliberation, on its own, might have a role in the form of elite deliberation among philosophers and jurists, say, perhaps applying a kind of mini-public design without necessarily having lay participants; and it might be that the principles have to be able to pass a Rawlsian 'public reason' test (although how they do that without actual testing against real publics is a mystery); but that is about it.

If we take that need to test the acceptability of reasons with real publics seriously, then the second understanding of constitutions makes more sense and a wider range of understandings of deliberative democracy and its tools become relevant. One approach might be to take the standard micro position and deploy small-scale democratic innovations to answer questions about the polity's procedures and principles. I have already discussed some general strengths and weaknesses of micro-deliberation, but two more objections become relevant in this particular context. The first concerns sceptical views of citizens' capacities to handle complex, abstract questions and is easily dismissed. From such a viewpoint, it might be all right for citizens to deliberate about local, well defined policy issues but do not let them loose on the rules of the game. That view has been rebutted by repeated cases in which randomly selected citizens have shown exactly the required abilities to handle complexity, abstraction and technical detail, given the right institutional

Figure 9.2: Interaction of constitutional understandings and deliberative approaches

		Deliberative democracy approach		
		Micro-	*Systemic*	*Discursive*
	Normative, non-interference	No public role; perhaps elite deliberation?	Limited elite deliberation	No role
Constitutional understanding	*Normative, deliberative design*	One tool; limited legitimation power	Broad sites of co-production channelled into empowered site	Restricted domain; delegitimised
	Pragmatic, coalition-building	No role on their own; strategic and symbolic use in wider system	Various sites; engagement on amendments; access to empowered sites; limited critical power	Counter-hegemonic discourse; coalition building

context (see, for example, Farrell, O'Malley, and Suiter 2013; Niemeyer 2004, again). As a result, questions of deliberative capacity are not generally ones of individual psychology – although see Jennstål (2011) – but one of the likelihood that institutional arrangements will activate deliberation (Dryzek 2009). Questions about such institutional arrangements might be the very sorts of things that could be settled well by deliberative encounters between institutional designers and the citizens who have to use such institutions, so long as the particular question was *salient* at the time. If it was not salient, then it is hard to motivate participation let alone activate deliberation (Elster 1995; Parkinson 2006a).

Perhaps a more significant challenge is this: constitutions, by the fact that they set the rules of the game for everyone subject to a regime, require broadly inclusive processes of legitimation, well beyond what a single mini-public can deliver. If the standard of constitutional legitimacy is that those subject to the regime have consented to its terms then, clearly, a mini-public can only ever be advisory.[6] No matter how statistically representative its participants are, or what our judgements of the event's epistemic quality (MacKenzie and Warren 2012), those features are not enough on their own to confer legitimate authority to decide on the rules of the game that all must follow. The question that then arises is what or whom should mini-publics advise? Where is the decision being taken and how is that informed by the micro-event or -events? In short, a constitutional focus drives beyond purely micro-conceptions of deliberation towards something more systemic.

It is at this point that I become a little more prescriptive. As already noted, I have set out a model of an ideal deliberative system that places five different and broad process and venue combinations in a sequence that depends on those processes' strengths and weaknesses relative to the stages of a decision-making process (Parkinson 2006a; cf. Rummens 2016, Chapter Eight of this volume). Compressing that account somewhat, the sequence includes: a very broad and open agenda-setting stage that is anchored in the informal public sphere; a more small-scale, but public, deliberative option-generation stage, which combines experts, lay-citizen representatives and other stakeholders; an option selected by direct, mass selection or indirect selection via representatives, elected and otherwise endorsed;[7] and then more narrow implementation and scrutiny

---

6. I do not have space for a detailed discussion of the legitimacy framework deployed in this volume, one based on Schmidt (2013): Rummens (2016, Chapter Eight of this volume) provides an excellent analysis. However, in the context of the EU, an obvious alternative approach is being missed, namely, the egalitarian, democratic social theory of Beetham (1991). His approach captures a broader range of features of cases, including ideas about justice, publicity, rationality and the sources of legitimacy-claims; and it has been applied to the EU context (Beetham and Lord 1998). My own account of legitimacy is likewise based on Beetham and not the competitive elitism of Scharpf (1970), the originator of the input/output legitimacy distinction on which Schmidt ultimately relies. See Parkinson 2003, 2006a.

7. The otherwise-endorsed category is a nod to Saward (2010), who shows how non-elected representatives can, nonetheless, exercise considerable, legitimate authority to speak for certain groups or experiences, if their claims are endorsed by those they claim to represent. Talpin alludes to related ideas (2016, Chapter Six of this volume).

processes. Such a sequence is diffuse and creative at the start, to capture narratives of experience, ideas and claims against the public; it then focuses its energies into some deliberative venues, to sort out what is at stake; then goes big again, for mass choice and legitimacy; then focuses once more for implementation and scrutiny. It is inclusive where it needs to be; focused and deliberative where it needs to be; and also empowered, creative, legitimate, representative, and all the other values we want to maximise in a deliberative democracy where it needs to be. It leaves a great deal of room for the demands of a particular moment: the nature of the issues being considered; local practice and the meanings those practices have; scale; and whether the occasion of debate is a grand constitution-making moment or there is a more specific issue to decide.

Mini-publics and other democratic innovations can play important roles in such a system but they should play roles that they are good at – sorting through options; connecting ideas with evidence and values; providing publicity focal points – and not ones at which they are weak. These weaknesses are particularly evident when we shift to the third understanding of constitutions, which is the more pragmatic 'confection' model, in which what really matters is building broad coalitions of support to overturn entrenched provisions when it comes to amendments, or mobilising pre-existing coalitions when it comes to moments of crisis. This a familiar kind of democratic politics, celebrated by discursive democrats and scholars of social movements alike – grassroots mobilisation-activity, collaborative online spaces, large-scale performative action – all of which can have deliberative elements, certainly, but which are at least as much about building symbols with rich layers of meaning, and with which people come to identify, as anything else (Hajer 2009; Parkinson 2012a; Tilly and Tarrow 2007). That is not to say that mini-publics cannot themselves become such symbols. They can, as some of the cases in this volume illustrate.

The cases revisited

In the context of those three understandings of constitutions, and the three approaches to deliberative democracy, what do the case-studies in this volume provide? Grönlund's experiments and Geissel and Gherghina's examples are used to make more general points about the applicability of mini-publics and other innovations to constitution-making and since I have already discussed the relevant issues in preceding sections I will not spend more time on them here. The remaining cases offer more meat. Bergmann (2016, Chapter Two of this volume), while largely using micro-level language and assumptions when talking about deliberative democracy, nonetheless provides something rather more systemic in his discussion of the Icelandic case, showing how different institutions were sequenced, consciously or unconsciously, to produce what was hoped to be a broadly legitimate and well deliberated outcome, although clearly much of that hope was frustrated by eventual elite inaction following a change of government. The sense of focusing crisis is well described too, but what is missing is more of the discursive context in which it took place. For example, Icelandic politicians and activists from the Citizens' Movement and its offshoots tell a story about digital citizenship in a context of surveillance, commercialisation and globalisation which, while hardly the whole story and often romanticised, nonetheless formed an important part of the context in which the constitutional challenges took place. The online engagement emerged from that context. But Iceland was also another case in which the various steps of the process were not hard-wired into the formal, binding, collective decision-making processes, the empowered spaces of the Icelandic polity. This meant that when a new government was elected, with a different constellation of interests and allegiances, the whole process could be parked.

Suiter, Farrell and Harris (2016, Chapter Three of this volume) similarly present a systemic story, despite often using more micro-level language and assumptions. From the perspective of this discussion, the Irish case is distinct from the Icelandic in two main ways. First, it was not originally set up to be a grand constitution-making moment like in Iceland, but nor was it an effort to amend a specific article; it was something in between that then took on a life of its own, developing new agenda-items as the members of the Convention felt the surge of wider legitimacy building beneath them. Second, the process was better connected to empowered space: grounded not only in wider public debate, with a focusing sense of crisis, but also in public commitments from three major political parties and a clear pathway to, and pressure for, implementation afterwards. Once again, though, that pathway to implementation was not as solid as is sometimes presented – only two referendums have been held, on equal marriage and an age limit for the president, and while the equal marriage referendum was a stunning success, provoking change even beyond Ireland itself, the other failed, while still other proposals have been kicked into the long grass, some getting no further than committee discussions.

Just as is already evident with the Iceland case, and as happened with the case of the British Columbia Citizens' Assembly many years before, there is a risk that the Irish story will be romanticised, with deliberative democratic attention so focused on the conventions themselves that their contexts, successes and failures in other regards are glossed over. This is perhaps more of a risk in the Irish case, ironically, because of its single, extremely high-profile success, *contra* the BC and Icelandic cases which, at least in terms of the constitutional changes with which they were connected, were signal failures. A consequence of such glossing over is to make it harder to ask certain kinds of question about the roles that different institutions played in the overall process. For example, it is not possible to assert that the Irish would have voted for equal marriage with or without the Convention: as well as the usual difficulties of addressing counter-factuals, we simply are not told enough about the broader political forces to make an educated judgement, which makes it hard to recommend one process or another for other issues or in other contexts.

But then, perhaps this is to limit too narrowly the idea of impact. As has been shown by Goodin and Dryzek (2006), Niemeyer (2012) – and Parkinson (2001) incidentally, anticipating Talpin's call (2016, Chapter Six of this

volume) – democratic processes can fail in a narrow sense of failing to change
the law, but succeed in a broader sense of setting the agenda or even establishing
a new norm about whom ought to be consulted and how. There are many other
possible impacts, and Geissel and Gherghina (2016, Chapter Five of this volume)
usefully stress this point. Unfortunately, we are not given much on these issues in
the first two cases but it is something that Jacquet et al. (2016, Chapter Four of
this volume) can address, given that their case was deliberately insulated from the
usual political processes at a time of increasing polarisation and the near-failure of
formal politics in Belgium. The authors call the G1000 'large-scale' but that is not
quite right. It might have been large relative to a citizens' jury but it was not large
in the sense that systemic analysts generally mean it[8] and most of the analysis is
of a familiar micro kind. When discussing impacts, what they focus on is media-
coverage; general public awareness of the event via a conventional opinion-survey
and public support for the recommendations that came out the event (which ought
not to be linked, necessarily); and mentions of the event in parliament. While it
is easy to be critical of the impact achieved and the methods used to measure it,[9]
a topic that Talpin (2016, Chapter Six of this volume) usefully takes up, what is
important here is the thought that a properly macro analysis ought to look at these
wider contexts both before and after a set of interventions. What is more enticing
is the discussion of the wider social impact of the events themselves – that the
G1000 became a symbol for some people (not many, but some), to the extent that
they ran events inspired by it in other towns and communities, and not just in
Belgium. This is precisely the sort of thing that one might hope that a more macro
analysis would identify and develop.

Conclusion

Attention to connections between deliberative democracy and constitutions could
be fruitful in several ways, both intellectual and pragmatic. Intellectually, the
move to examine constitutional moments makes salient once more a long-standing
dispute between proceduralists and constitutionalists about the limits of democracy,
a dispute to which deliberative democrats can now bring new arguments and new
evidence after decades of theoretical and empirical development. But, as I hinted
when discussing the differences between normative understandings of constitutions
and the more pragmatic approach of Elster, there is also a lot of room for thinking
about how deliberative democrats should approach constitutional questions. I, for
one, am all for creative engagement between normative statements, descriptive

---

8. The three-step process involved around 6000 people in the initial agenda survey, 1000 people
in the citizen-summit and another thirty-two in the panel afterwards: just over 7000 people in a
country of just over eleven million, assuming there was no overlap between the three groups.

9. For instance, I have remarked elsewhere (Parkinson 2006b) on the tendency of deliberative event-
organisers to overstate the impact of their events in media terms because they count the number
of articles without thinking about whether a lot of articles at one time makes more impact (on
whom, precisely?) than a small number of articles in the right places, sustained over time (see
Lindenmann 1997).

theory and rigorous empirical work – by which I do not just mean Elster's positivism but something that is sensitive to the political fact that constitutions are constructed by people in a specific time and place, in the shadow of power, norms, values and interests. I am therefore also all for the study of constitution-*making*, in the light of suitably expansive theoretical expectations and norms.

It is also interesting, at a micro-level, to see deliberative processes gradually changing from 'quaint academic experiments', as a former UK government advisor once acidly remarked to me, to tools that are being integrated into collective decision-making processes at times of constitutional crisis. While I have questioned at length the wisdom of thinking that a mini-public *alone* can address such issues, they certainly can have a role in a wider deliberative system; and I have sympathy with the view that they can inject a unique mixture of goods into deliberative systems that no other devices can (Smith 2009). That is not to say that all mini-publics feature the same strengths and weaknesses, or even that they are all equally deliberative; and there are certainly goods that mini-publics are poor at delivering, especially legitimate 'consequentiality', to use Dryzek's (2010) term. That requirement for 'horses for courses' is what the systems approach is meant to capture – it is a caricature of the approach to suggest that it is hostile to mini-publics, full stop. That said, the systems approach faces challenges of its own, particularly a tendency to rely on static models rather than capturing the dynamics of collective decision-making and the performativity of governance; and there is still a long way to go in integrating systemic and discursive perspectives to their mutual benefit.

I have suggested that there are links between how such deliberative democratic disputes play out and how we conceptualise constitutions; but, no matter how we do that, two difficulties remain, to do with how well democratic processes are 'plugged in'. The cases in this volume raise, more or less explicitly, the issue of connecting small-scale deliberative events to decision-making sites; that is, connecting communicative spaces to empowered spaces in binding, responsive ways. That is only one aspect of the problem. The other arises when mini-publics are not connected to the wider public sphere; when deliberative democrats continue to tinker with domestic institutions that address ends set by the state and wider regimes of governance but fail to establish any grounding in the lived experience of the people subject to those regimes. I criticised the technocratic approach to mini-publics in these terms but the systems-approach could easily be deployed for the same anti-democratic ends, if systems are not grounded in the narratives of the people. These narratives need to be those of actual people who have been able to make active, effective choices to engage and not only narratives generated by randomly sampled citizens in invitation-only experiments.

The spirit of this is, perhaps, captured best by someone closely involved in a case that is not discussed in this volume, the Scottish independence referendum of 2014. Most official and media discussion of the event outside of Scotland refers to the 'indyref' as being about independence – a logical enough thing to think, perhaps, but a framing that misses more than seven years' of official and activist efforts to generate a wide-ranging 'national conversation' about what sort of democracy Scots wanted (Scottish Executive 2007). Independence was a catalyst to debate, given that a binding referendum would be held, and a possible means to some of the wider ends being sought; but most of the public debate in formal and informal settings over the final eighteen months of the campaign was about the ends, not about the means *per se*.

One of the crucial factors in generating that widespread debate, according to participants at a workshop I ran at the Academy of Government at the University of Edinburgh in April 2015, was not active engagement in institutional design by the Scottish government but its conscious decision to step back and let activists in NGOs with pre-existing networks take over. The government felt that to be too 'institutional' would be to kill off any chance of engaging people and so they claimed to have created a vacuum into which more-or-less critical organisations stepped. A representative from the Scottish cabinet office put it this way: that the job of government was to be 'hosts, not heroes', to create a space for the public sphere rather than to organise it, institutionalise it, and dominate it.

While it clearly helped that there were techniques, and experience with those techniques, to draw on, the lessons of the example are these: first, there are limits to what can be achieved in constitution-making using mainstream, institutionally focused approaches to deliberative democracy; and, second, the absolute necessity that the more-or-less diffuse processes that are used are connected *both* to formal, empowered decision-making sites *and* to the debates of ordinary people around kitchen tables and on street corners. Without plugging into both empowered spaces and the informal public sphere, we might have deliberation but we do not have deliberative democracy.

References

Ackerman, B. (1991) *We the People*, vol. 1, *Foundations*, Cambridge, MA: Harvard University Press.

Bächtiger, A., Niemeyer, S., Neblo, M., Steenbergen, M. R., and Steiner, S. (2010) 'Disentangling diversity in deliberative democracy: competing theories, their blind spots and complementarities', *Journal of Political Philosophy* 18(1): 32–63.

Beetham, D. (1991) *The Legitimation of Power*, Basingstoke, UK: Macmillan.

—   (ed.) (1994) *Defining and Measuring Democracy*, London, UK: Sage.

Beetham, D., and Lord, C. (1998) *Legitimacy and the European Union*, Harlow, UK: Addison Wesley Longman.

Bergmann, E. (2016) 'Participatory constitutional deliberation in the wake of crisis: the case of Iceland', in Reuchamps, M. and Suiter, J. (eds) *Constitutional Deliberative Democracy in Europe*, Colchester, UK: ECPR Press.

Bevir, M., and Rhodes, R. (2010) *The State as Cultural Practice*, Oxford, UK: Oxford University Press.

Bohman, J. (1998) 'Survey article: the coming of age of deliberative democracy', *Journal of Political Philosophy* 6(4):400–25.

—   (2012) 'Representation in the deliberative system', in Parkinson, J., and Mansbridge, J. (eds) *Deliberative Systems: Deliberative democracy at the large scale*, Cambridge, UK: Cambridge University Press, pp. 72–94.

Broome, J. (1984) 'Selecting people randomly', *Ethics* 95(1): 38–55.

Carson, L., and Martin, B. (1999) *Random Selection in Politics*, Westport, CT: Praeger.

Chambers, S. (2003) 'Deliberative democratic theory', *Annual Review of Political Science* 6: 307–26.

—   (2012) 'Deliberation and mass democracy', in Parkinson, J. and Mansbridge, J. (eds) *Deliberative Systems: Deliberative democracy at the large scale*, Cambridge, UK: Cambridge University Press, pp. 52–71.

Christiano, T. (2012) 'Rational deliberation between experts and citizens', in Parkinson, J. and Mansbridge, J. (eds) *Deliberative Systems: Deliberative democracy at the large scale*, Cambridge, UK: Cambridge University Press, pp. 27–51.

Cohen, J. (1986) 'An epistemic conception of democracy', *Ethics* 97(1): 26–38.

Cooke, B., and Kothari, U. (eds) (2001) *Participation: The new tyranny?* London, UK: Zed Books.

Dahl, R. (1989) *Democracy and Its Critics*, New Haven, CT: Yale University Press.

Dryzek, J. (1990) *Discursive Democracy*, New York, NY: Cambridge University Press.

—   (1996) *Democracy in Capitalist Times: Ideals, limits, struggles*, New York, NY and Oxford, UK: Oxford University Press.

—   (2000) *Deliberative Democracy and Beyond: Liberals, critics, contestations*, Oxford, UK: Oxford University Press.

—   (2009) 'Democratization and deliberative capacity building', *Comparative Political Studies* 42(11): 1379–1402.

—   (2010) *Foundations and Frontiers of Deliberative Governance*, Oxford, UK: Oxford University Press.

—   (2011) 'Global democratization: soup, society, or system?', *Ethics & International Affairs* 25(2): 211–34.

Dworkin, R. (1995) 'Constitutionalism and democracy', *European Journal of Philosophy* 3(1): 2–11.

Elster, J. (1986) 'The market and the forum: three varieties of political theory', in Elster, J., and Hylland, A. (eds) *Foundations of Social Choice Theory*, Cambridge, UK: Cambridge University Press, pp. 103–32.

—   (1995) 'Forces and mechanisms in the constitution-making process', *Duke Law Journal* 45(2): 364–96.

Elstub, S. (2010) 'The third generation of deliberative democracy', *Political Studies Review* 8(3): 291–307.

Farrell, D., O'Malley, E., and Suiter, J. (2013) 'Deliberative democracy in action Irish-style: the 2011 We the Citizens pilot citizens' assembly', *Irish Political Studies* 28(1): 99–113.

Fishkin, J. S. (1991) *Democracy and Deliberation*, New Haven, CT: Yale University Press.

Forester, J. (1984) 'Bounded rationality and the politics of muddling through', *Public Administration Review* 44(1): 23–30.

Fung, A. (2003) 'Survey article: recipes for public spheres: eight institutional design choices and their consequences', *Journal of Political Philosophy* 11(3): 338–67.

—   (2007) 'Minipublics: deliberative designs and their consequences', in Rosenberg, S. W. (ed.) *Deliberation, Participation, and Democracy: Can the people govern?*, New York, NY: Palgrave Macmillan, pp. 159–183.

Gaventa, J. (2006) 'Finding the spaces for change: a power analysis', *IDS Bulletin* 37(6): 23–33.

Geissel, B., and Gherghina, S. (2016) 'Constitutional deliberative democracy and democratic innovations', in Reuchamps, M. and Suiter, J. (eds) *Constitutional Deliberative Democracy in Europe*, Colchester, UK: ECPR Press.

Goodin, R. (2005) 'Sequencing deliberative moments', *Acta Politica* 40(2):182–96.

—   (2008) *Innovating Democracy: Democratic theory and practice after the deliberative turn*, Oxford, UK: Oxford University Press.

Goodin, R., and Dryzek, J. (2006) 'Deliberative impacts: the macro-political uptake of mini-publics', *Politics & Society* 34(2): 219–44.

Goodwin, B. (1992) *Justice by Lottery*, Hemel Hempstead, UK: Harvester Wheatsheaf.

Grönlund, K. (2016) 'Designing mini-publics for constitutional deliberative democracy', in Reuchamps, M. and Suiter, J. (eds) *Constitutional Deliberative Democracy in Europe*, Colchester, UK: ECPR Press.

Gutmann, A., and Thompson, D. (1996) *Democracy and Disagreement*, Cambridge, MA: Belknap Press of Harvard University Press.

Habermas, J. (1984) *The Theory of Communicative Action*, transl. T. McCarthy, Boston, MA: Beacon Press.

Hajer, M. (2009) *Authoritative Governance: Policy-making in the age of mediatization*, Oxford, UK: Oxford University Press.

Hatton, L. (2014) 'The European citizens' initiative and the activation of EU demoi: the role of knowledge and expertise', in Holst, C. (ed.) *Expertise and Democracy, ARENA Report 1/14*, Oslo, NO: ARENA Centre for European Studies, University of Oslo, pp. 239–62.

Hendriks, C., and Carson, L. (2008) 'Can the market help the forum? Negotiating the commercialization of deliberative democracy', *Policy Sciences* 41(4): 293–313.

Jacquet, V., Moskovic, J., Calluwaerts, D., and Reuchamps, M. (2016) 'The macro-political uptake of the G1000 in Belgium', in Reuchamps, M. and Suiter, J. (eds) *Constitutional Deliberative Democracy in Europe*, Colchester, UK: ECPR Press.

Jennstål, J. (2011) 'Is there a deliberative personality? Explaining deliberative behavior in trait terms', paper given at the International Society of Political Psychology Annual Meeting, Bilgi University, Istanbul, 12 July.

Kingdon, J. W. (1984) *Agendas, Alternatives, and Public Policies*, Boston, MA: Little, Brown.

Landwehr, C. (2015) 'Democratic meta-deliberation: towards reflective institutional design', *Political Studies* 63(S1): 38–54.

Lindenmann, W. (1997) 'Setting minimum standards for public relations effectiveness', *Public Relations Review* 23(4): 391–408.

MacKenzie, M. K., and Warren, M. (2012) 'Two trust-based uses of mini-publics in deliberative systems', in Parkinson, J. and Mansbridge, J. (eds) *Deliberative Systems: Deliberative democracy at the large scale*, Cambridge, UK: Cambridge University Press, pp. 95–124.

Manin, B. (1987) 'On legitimacy and political deliberation', *Political Theory* 15(3): 338–68.

Mansbridge, J. (1983) *Beyond Adversary Democracy*, 2nd edn, Chicago, IL: University of Chicago Press.

— (2010) 'Deliberative polling as the gold standard', *The Good Society* 19(1): 55–62.

Mansbridge, J., Bohman, J., Chambers, S., Christiano, T., Fung, A., Parkinson, J., Thompson, D., and Warren, M. (2012) 'A systemic approach to deliberative democracy', in Parkinson, J. and Mansbridge, J. (eds) *Deliberative Systems: Deliberative democracy at the large scale*, Cambridge, UK: Cambridge University Press, pp. 1–26.

Milewa, T., Valentine, J., and Calnan, M. (1999) 'Community participation and citizenship in British health care planning: narratives of power and involvement in the changing welfare state', *Sociology of Health & Illness* 21(4): 445–65.

Mort, M., Harrison, S., and Wistow, G. (1996) 'The user card: picking through the organisational undergrowth in health and social care', *Contemporary Political Studies* 2: 1133–40.

Niemeyer, S. (2004) 'Deliberation in the wilderness: displacing symbolic politics', *Environmental Politics* 13(2): 347–72.

—— (2011) 'The emancipatory effect of deliberation: empirical lessons from mini-publics', *Politics & Society* 39(1): 103–40.

—— (2012) 'From a minipublic to a deliberative system: is scaling up deliberation possible?', paper given at the conference Deliberative Democracy in Action, 7–8 June, Åbo Akademi, Åbo/Turku, Finland; also available online, http://www.abo.fi/fakultet/media/23741/simonniemeyer.pdf (accessed 4 March 2016).

Olsen, E. D. H., and Trenz, H.-J. (2014) 'From citizens' deliberation to popular will formation? Generating democratic legitimacy in transnational deliberative polling', *Political Studies* 62 (S1):117–33.

Owen, D., and Smith, G. (2015) 'Survey article: deliberation, democracy, and the systemic turn', *Journal of Political Philosophy* 23(2): 213–34.

Papadopoulos, Y., and Warin, P. (eds) (2007) 'Are innovative, participatory, and deliberative procedures in policy-making democratic and effective?', *European Journal of Political Research* 46(4): 445–72.

Parkinson, J. (2001) 'Deliberative democracy and referendums', in Dowding, K. M., Hughes J. and Margetts, H. (eds) *Challenges to Democracy: Ideas, involvement and institutions*, London, UK: Palgrave, pp. 131–52.

—— (2003) 'Legitimacy problems in deliberative democracy', *Political Studies* 51(1): 180–96.

—— (2004) 'Why deliberate? The encounter between deliberation and new public managers', *Public Administration* 82(2): 377–95.

—— (2006a) *Deliberating in the Real World: Problems of legitimacy in deliberative democracy*, Oxford, UK: Oxford University Press.

—— (2006b) 'Rickety bridges: using the media in deliberative democracy', *British Journal of Political Science* 36(1): 175–83.

—— (2012a) *Democracy and Public Space: The physical sites of democratic performance*, Oxford, UK: Oxford University Press.

—— (2012b) 'Democratizing deliberative systems', in Parkinson, J. and Mansbridge, J. (eds) *Deliberative Systems: Deliberative democracy at the large scale*, Cambridge, UK: Cambridge University Press, pp. 151–72.

Parkinson, J., and Mansbridge, J. (eds) (2012) *Deliberative Systems: Deliberative democracy at the large scale*, Cambridge, UK: Cambridge University Press.

Pettit, P. (2012) *On the People's Terms: A republican theory and model of democracy*, Cambridge, UK: Cambridge University Press.

Rummens, S. (2016) 'Legitimacy without visibility? On the role of mini-publics in the democratic system', in Reuchamps, M. and Suiter, J. (eds) *Constitutional Deliberative Democracy in Europe*, Colchester, UK: ECPR Press.

Saward, M. (2010) *The Representative Claim*, Oxford, UK: Oxford University Press.

Scharpf, F. W. (1970) *Demokratietheorie zwischen Utopie und Anpassung*, Konstanz, DE: Universitätsverlag.

Schlosberg, D. (1999) *Environmental Justice and the New Pluralism: The challenge of difference for environmentalism*, New York, NY: Oxford University Press.

Schmidt, V. (2013) 'Democracy and legitimacy in the European Union revisited: output, input, throughput', *Political Studies* 61(1): 2–22.

Scottish Executive (2007) *Choosing Scotland's Future: A national conversation: independence and responsibility in the modern world*, Edinburgh, UK: Scottish Executive, available online: http://www.gov.scot/resource/doc/194791/0052321.pdf (accessed 4 March 2016).

Sheller, M. (2004) 'Automotive emotions: feeling the car', *Theory, Culture & Society* 21(4–5): 221–42.

Smith, G. (2009) *Democratic Innovations*, Cambridge, UK: Cambridge University Press.

Suiter, J., Farrell, D. M., and Harris, C. (2016) 'The Irish Constitutional Convention: a case of "high legitimacy"?', in Reuchamps, M. and Suiter, J. (eds) *Constitutional Deliberative Democracy in Europe*, Colchester, UK: ECPR Press.

Sunstein, C. (1995) 'Social norms and social rules', John M. Olin Law & Economics Working Paper No 36 (The Coase Lecture, Law School, University of Chicago), available online: http://www.law.uchicago.edu/files/files/36.Sunstein.Social.pdf (accessed 4 March 2016).

Talpin, J. (2016) 'How can constitutional reforms be deliberative? The hybrid legitimacies of constitutional deliberative democracy', in Reuchamps, M. and Suiter, J. (eds) *Constitutional Deliberative Democracy in Europe*, Colchester, UK: ECPR Press.

Thompson, D. F. (2008) 'Deliberative democratic theory and empirical political science', *Annual Review of Political Science* 11: 497–520.

— (2010) 'Representing future generations: political presentism and democratic trusteeship', *Critical Review of International Social and Political Philosophy* 13(1): 17–37.

Tilly, C., and Tarrow, S. (2007) *Contentious Politics*, Boulder, CO: Paradigm.

Uhr, J. (1998) *Deliberative Democracy in Australia: The changing place of parliament*, Cambridge, UK: Cambridge University Press.

Waldron, J. (1999) *Law and Disagreement*, New York, NY: Oxford University Press.

Warren, M. (1999) 'Democratic theory and trust', in Warren, M. (ed.) *Democracy and Trust*, Cambridge, UK: Cambridge University Press, pp. 310–45.

— (2012) 'When, where and why do we need deliberation, voting, and other means of organizing democracy? A problem-based approach to democratic systems', paper given at the American Political Science Association Annual Meeting, 30 August–2 September, available online: http://papers.ssrn.com/sol3/papers.cfm?abstract_id=2104566, (accessed 4 March 2016).

Index

Arnold, T. 34
Ásgrímsson, H. 26
Australia
  Citizens Assembly 21, 93
  Constitutional Convention (1998)
    19

Belgian G1000 xiii, 1, 4–5, 19, 20,
  53–71, 80ff., 98–9, 139, 160
  agenda-setting in 53, 54–5, 59, 81,
    82, 96, 97
    public consultation in 54–5, 81,
      82, 96, 97
  aim of 53, 59, 69, 71, 80, 82
    political context in 59–60, 63,
      93
  deliberation in 53, 54–8, 83, 97,
    98–9
    citizen-panel (G32) in 54, 55–6,
      57, 61, 62, 70, 80, 81, 97, 99,
      101
    citizen-summit in 54, 55, 57, 61,
      62, 80, 81, 95, 96
    epistemic quality of 98–9
    experts, role in 57, 98, 99
    G'Home 55, 69
    G'Offs 55, 69
    issue selection in 57
  impact of 54, 59, 63–8, 69–71, 82,
    83, 84, 86, 95, 100, 101, 103,
    160
    on democratic renewal 59, *64*,
      66–8, 70, 71, 86, 139
    on public awareness 63–4, 83,
      86, 160
    survey data results 65–6, 160
  interactive technology, use in 36,
    69, 96

legitimacy in 24, 54, 56–8, 81, 82,
  83, 84
  input 54, 56–7, 59, 70, 84, 95,
    96, 97
  output 54, 58–9, 70, 82, 83, 84,
    86, 97, 100
  throughput 54, 57, 58, 70, 82, 84
maxi-public uptake 59, 62–4, 103,
  139
  socio-demographic survey 63–4,
    103
media uptake of 59–62, 63, 64, 83,
  101, 103, 139, 160
participant selection in 53, 55,
  56–7, 80, 81, 85, 95
  Random Digit Dialling in 81
political uptake of 53, 58–9, 66–8,
  69, 71, 82, 100, 101, 139
  parliamentary attention to 69,
    100, 139
  party manifestos analysis 66–8
representativeness in 53, 56–7, 80,
  81
social uptake of 59, 69–71
three phases of 54–8, 61
Belgium xiii, 53–71
  deliberative democracy in 4–5, 10,
    16, 53
  G100 70
  2010 election 53
    and government crisis period 53,
      160
  see also Belgian G1000
Berlusconi, S. 138
Brazil
  National Public Policy Conferences
    85
  participatory budgeting in 1–2, 19

www.ingramcontent.com/pod-product-compliance
Lightning Source LLC
Chambersburg PA
CBHW050228270326
41914CB00003BA/616